Joey Green's

INCREDIBLE

Country Store

Also by Joey Green

Hellbent on Insanity
The Unofficial Gilligan's Island Handbook
The Get Smart Handbook
The Partridge Family Album
Polish Your Furniture with Panty Hose
Hi Bob!
Selling Out
Paint Your House with Powdered Milk
Wash Your Hair with Whipped Cream
The Bubble Wrap Book
Joey Green's Encyclopedia
The Zen of Oz
The Warning Label Book
Monica Speaks
You Know You've Reached Middle Age If . . .
The Official Slinky Book
The Mad Scientist Handbook
Clean Your Clothes with Cheez Whiz
The Road to Success Is Paved with Failure
Clean It! Fix It! Eat It!
Joey Green's Magic Brands
Jesus and Moses: The Parallel Sayings
The Mad Scientist Handbook 2
Senior Moments
Joey Green's Amazing Kitchen Cures
Jesus and Muhammad: The Parallel Sayings
Joey Green's Gardening Magic
How They Met

Joey Green's
INCREDIBLE
Country Store

POTIONS, NOTIONS, AND
ELIXIRS OF THE PAST
and How To Make Them Today

BY JOEY GREEN

author of

AMAZING KITCHEN CURES AND
GARDENING MAGIC

RODALE

The information in this book has been carefully researched, and all efforts have been made to ensure accuracy. Neither the author, publisher, manufacturers, nor distributors can assume responsibility for the effectiveness of the suggestions. Caution is urged in the use of the cleaning solutions, folk medicine remedies, and pest control substances.

The brand-name products mentioned in this book are registered trademarks. The companies that own these trademarks and make these products do not endorse, recommend, or accept liability for any use of their products other than those uses indicated on the package label or in current company brochures. This book should not be regarded as a substitute for professional medical treatment, and neither the author, publisher, manufacturers, nor distributors can accept legal responsibility for any problem arising out of the use of or experimentation with the methods described. For a full listing of trademarks, see page 336. All photographs and historic advertisements herein are printed by permission of the trademark holders.

© 2004 by Joey Green

"Words of Wisdom" on pages 273–275 © 2004 by Joey Green and Alan Corcoran. Used with permission.

Photographs © 2004 by Joey Green, except the photograph of Tiger Balm on page 46, © Haw Par Corporation Limited, used with permission; the photograph of a Baby Ruth bar on page 56, © 2004 by Nestlé; the photograph of Goetze's Caramel Cream on pages 74 and 75, © 2004 by Goetze's Candy Company, Inc., used with permission; and the photographs of Crayola crayons on pages 98, 99, and 100, © 2004 by Binney & Smith, used with permission.

All rights reserved. No part of this publication may be reproduced or transmitted in any form or by any means, electronic or mechanical, including photocopying, recording, or any other information storage and retrieval system, without the written permission of the publisher.

Printed in the United States of America

Rodale Inc. makes every effort to use acid-free (∞), recycled paper (♻).

Choo Choo Charlie Good & Plenty lyrics on page 67 are reprinted with permission of Hershey Food Corporation.

Book design by Joey Green
Research by Debbie Green

Library of Congress Cataloging-in-Publication Data

Green, Joey.
  Joey Green's incredible country store : potions, notions, and elixirs
of the past—and how to make them today / by Joey Green.
      p.   cm.
  Includes bibliographical references and index.
  ISBN 1–57954–849–0 paperback
  1. Handicraft.   2. General stores.   I. Title: Incredible country
store. II. Title.
TT157.G638   2004
745.5—dc22   2003025711

Distributed to the book trade by St. Martin's Press

2 4 6 8 10 9 7 5 3 1 paperback

WE **INSPIRE** AND **ENABLE** PEOPLE TO IMPROVE
THEIR LIVES AND THE WORLD AROUND THEM

FOR MORE OF OUR PRODUCTS
WWW.RODALESTORE.COM
(800) 848-4735

FOR DEBBIE,
my angel

The CONTENTS

INTRODUCTION

In 1986, my wife and I drove along the backroads of Vermont, exploring the countryside. At dusk we came to the village of Weston, a single street lined with quaint New England houses. A white gazebo sat in the center of the serene village green, across the street from the small Weston Theater. We spent the night in a cozy bed-and-breakfast just off the green. The next morning, we walked around the tiny hamlet and stumbled upon The Vermont Country Store. From the outside, it looked like a modest, rustic store.

A small brass bell tinkled as we opened the front door. Inside, our senses were overwhelmed by a blend of homey aromas—cheeses, candies, coffees, teas, and jams. We saw long wooden counters jam-packed with jars of penny candies, a multitude of drawers and cubbyholes crammed full of tins of spices and sugar, endless shelves towering from floor to ceiling—all overstuffed with bottles, jars, tins, pots, and pans. A checkerboard sat on top of a barrel next to a cast-iron stove surrounded by cracker barrels and rocking chairs. Gas lanterns hung from the rafters. Glass cases overflowed with toasters, perfume bottles, and egg beaters. We felt curiously cozy and comfortable, strangely at home, warmly embraced by this oddly familiar environment that captured the innocence of a bygone era. We had stepped into a painting by Norman Rockwell.

Ever since then, I've yearned to unlock the secret formulas for all those liniments and elixirs, homemade candles, perfumes, potpourri, household cleansers, and candies—like how to make maple syrup, those wonderful soda crackers your grandma served with chowder, homemade cough syrup, and old-fashioned peppermint candy you thought you'd never taste again.

And so, seventeen years later, I returned to The Vermont Country Store, visited Cracker Barrel Old Country Store Restaurants in Ohio and Florida, journeyed to Home and Garden shows across the country, rummaged through antique stores, made pilgrimages to ghost towns in California, and locked myself in museums and libraries to unearth a treasury of bizarre tips, unique recipes, and make-it-yourself concoctions.

But I had to know more. Who created the Raggedy Ann doll? How do you play marbles? Who invented the Tootsie Roll? How did F. W. Woolworth's get its start? Who invented the can opener? Who were the Smith Brothers, and what possessed them to make cough drops? Who concocted Dr Pepper, and where did he go to medical school?

This book is a result of my obsessive stroll down the aisles of an old country store. Inside you'll discover a practical yet quirky hodgepodge of unusual tips, formulas, and fun facts—so you, too, will feel like you've stepped into a Norman Rockwell painting. Because frankly, I really don't want to be stuck in here all alone.

The Vermont Country Store

In October 1945, Vrest Orton and his wife Ellen founded The Vermont Country Store from their garage in the village of Weston, Vermont, by starting with a twelve-page mail-order catalog featuring thirty-six items. The catalog, entitled *The Voice of the Mountains*, printed in black and white and illustrated with woodcuts, looked like a nineteenth century New England Almanac, advertised soaps, toothpastes, candies, and liniments, and included poetry and an editorial by Orton on such topics as the evils of the telephone. The Ortons mailed the catalog to some one thousand friends and relatives on their Christmas card list. They filled the resulting orders in their garage and then carted the packages across the street to the Weston post office.

Vrest Orton's father and maternal grandfather had run a general store in North Calais, Vermont, thirteen miles outside of Montpelier. When Vrest was about twelve, his father moved his family to western Massachusetts to open his own department store. Vrest became editor of his high school newspaper, went to college, served in the Army during World War I, and moved to New York to work on the *American Mercury*, the renowned magazine edited by H. L. Mencken and George Jean Nathan. Vrest also contributed to the *Saturday Review of Literature*, wrote articles on bibliography, and founded the bookman's magazine, *The Colophon*. After the stock market crash of 1929, Vrest saw his friends lose their jobs, homes, cars, and wives. Although he still had his job, he decided to leave the heartless city and return to the comfort and solace of the country. In 1934, while driving through Vermont during a vacation, he explored the area surrounding Manchester and happened upon the village green at Weston. The next day, feeling curiously at home in this quaint, tranquil village, Vrest bought a house on the village green. He returned to New York, quit his job a few months later, and moved to Weston.

The Ortons opened their store in the spring of 1946. Determined to create a warm, cozy store that captured the authentic flavor of rural America, Orton stocked the two-and-a-half-story building with cracker barrels, hand-cranked coffee mills, coleslaw slicers, Vermont cheeses, long-handled wooden spoons, spice mills, glass jars filled with licorice root and gum drops, sachets of potpourri, tubs of scented soaps, and tins of freshly ground coffee. A checkerboard sat—and still sits—atop a barrel in front of a huge cast-iron stove.

Vrest decided to specialize in hard-to-find products, reviving the manufacture of many obsolete items. He located a tinsmith who made nutmeg graters, and soon Vrest sold thousands of them. The catalog slowly tripled in size, featured five hundred items, and was sent to 35,000 customers. People who received the catalog came to visit the store.

Over the years the Ortons expanded the building, adding on bit by bit in the New England fashion, until it grew ten times larger than the original store. In 1952, a feature story in *The Saturday Evening Post* popularized The Vermont Country Store and its mail-order catalog.

Vrest Orton began The Vermont Country Store by stocking quality merchandise produced by craftspeople and factories in Vermont and elsewhere in New England and the United States, offering his customers quality products at a fair price.

In the early 1970s, Vrest Orton's son Lyman, a graduate of Middlebury College who had been involved in the family business his entire life, took over the store and catalog, expanding on his father's vision. In 1984, the Vermont Country Store's continual growth prompted Lyman to move the mail-order portion of the business from the back of the store in Weston to a new warehouse and office space specially built for the company twenty miles west in Manchester, Vermont. Today, The Vermont Country Store is owned by Lyman Orton and his sons, Cabot, Gardner, and Eliot.

STRANGE FACTS

• The building that housed the *Weston Post Office* in 1945 now houses The Vermont Country Store Catalog Outlet. A second retail store in Rockingham, Vermont, opened in 1967.

• The Vermont Country Store sells reproductions of the antique chairs that originally furnished the store and the oil lamps originally used to light the store.

• Ellen Orton wrote a best-selling cookbook, filled with recipes for wholegrain breads, biscuits, hush puppies, johnnycakes, apple crunch, suet pudding, and corn dodgers.

• In 1982, Lyman hired Bob Allen as his assistant, and two years later, promoted him to president, making him the first non-family member to run the business.

• The Vermont Country Store employs 600 people.

• Every April, The Vermont Country Store holds its Annual Town Meeting, based on the long-standing tradition of Vermont Town Meetings, inviting all of its employees to attend and voice their opinions about how the company does business.

• Every June, The Vermont Country Store hosts an annual summer party, and every employee may bring a guest.

• Approximately 15 percent of The Vermont Country Store employees have been with the company for ten years or more.

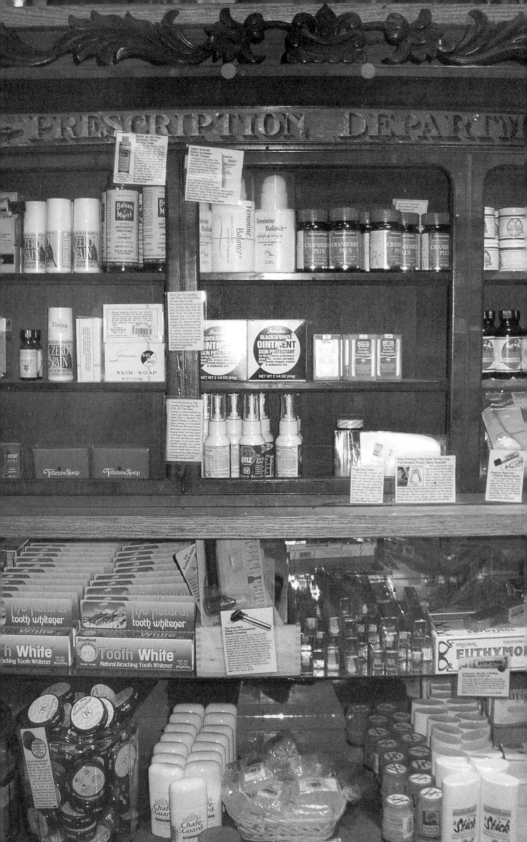

1

The APOTHECARY

Elixirs, Remedies, and Tonics

Most bottled elixirs, liniments, and tonics—better known as "patent medicines"—revitalized the ailing sufferer because they just happened to contain a healthy slug of whiskey or a strong dose of morphine. The patent medicines—with fanciful names like Hostetler's Celebrated Stomach Bitters, Dr. Bennett's Golden Liniment, and Stoughton's Elixir—were never actually patented. Self-proclaimed doctors and professors, whose stoic images graced the bottles, merely concocted the mixtures, trademarked the brand name, and used the word patent to imply that the United States Patent Office had blessed the secret formula. The 1907 Food and Drug Act forced many quack medicines out of business, leaving only proven remedies—and new ones—to feature stoic pictures of the inventors.

ALKA-SELTZER

The editor of the *Elkhart Truth*, the daily newspaper in Elkhart, Indiana, made his staff take a mixture of aspirin and bicarbonate of soda to ward off colds. When Andrew Hubble Beardsley, president of Miles Laboratories, discovered that no one at the *Truth* caught the flu during the epidemics of 1918 and 1927, he ordered his chief chemist, Maurice Treneer, to formulate a tablet of aspirin, bicarbonate of soda, and citric acid. Beardsley called the tablet Alka-Seltzer—invented a name that suggests *alka*linity and the carbonation of *seltzer*—and began promoting it in 1931. When Prohibition ended two years later, Alka-Seltzer took off as the antidote for hangovers—even though the secret formula for Alka-Seltzer is hardly a secret at all.

Secret Formula

LEMON-FLAVORED ANTACID

WHAT YOU NEED

From the supermarket:
- 1/2 teaspoon baking soda
- 1/2 teaspoon lemon juice

From the drugstore:
- 1 aspirin tablet

From the tap:
- 4 ounces water

WHAT TO DO

Measure a level 1/2 teaspoon of baking soda and add it to a glass containing four fluid ounces of water. Using a mortar and pestle, grind up the aspirin tablet and add the powder to the water. Dissolve the baking soda and aspirin powder completely. Add 1/2 teaspoon lemon juice and stir. Makes one dose.

HOW YOU USE IT

Using baking soda, also known as bicarbonate of soda, to relieve indigestion is a remedy that works wonders.

Simply drink one dose of the mixture (unless you are on a sodium restricted diet, allergic to aspirin, or overly full from food or drink). One dose should do the trick.

If necessary, repeat every two hours up to a maximum of eight doses per person if under sixty years old, or up to a maximum of four doses if over sixty years old, or as directed by a physician.

Do not exceed recommended dose. Do not administer to children under five years of age.

Do not use the maximum dose for more than two weeks. Should severe stomach pain occur after taking this mixture, consult a doctor.

BADGER BALM

In 1993, William Whyte, a carpenter living in Gilsum, New Hampshire, suffered from dry, chapped hands. Working with natural beeswax, herbal extracts, and natural oils, he concocted his own homemade healing balm. With help from his wife, daughter, brother, and friends, Whyte named his balm Bear Paw, but before producing the first tins, Whyte discovered that the name Bear Paw was already trademarked. He renamed his product Badger Balm and used storybook type art to depict tough and snarly badgers as friendly animals. Rather than spending money on advertising, Whyte relied solely on word of  mouth and magazine product reviews. Soon Badger Healing Balm was being sold in The Vermont Country Store, Cracker Barrel Old Country Stores across the country, and in the Harrods department store in London. Whyte extended the product line to some twenty balms made from olive oils, beeswax, castor oils, ginger, rose hip extracts, and other organic ingredients.

STRANGE FACTS
• William "Badger Bill" Whyte calls his employees "busy badgers" and his small factory "Badger Mines."
• The Badger Company sells its line of products in more than five thousand shops around the world, with annual sales of more than two million dollars.
• Before founding Badger, Bill Whyte worked as a carpenter, cab driver, conference center coordinator, photographer, massage therapist, and cook.
• The company's website features testimonials for Badger Balm from fly fishermen in Scotland, scientific workers in the polar regions, backpackers in California, and safari travelers in Africa.
• Badger makes Sore Muscle Rub, Foot Balm, Healing Balm, Anti-Bug Balm, Baby Balm, Bali Balm, Evolving Body Balm, Sleep Balm, Lip Balms, and Winter Wonder Balm.

BAG BALM

Invented in 1899, Bag Balm is named for the fact that this balm is intended to be used as a salve on a cow's udder, also known as a bag. Vermont farmers use Bag Balm on cows' udders made sore from milking. Available in dilators, Bag Balm speeds the healing of bruised, sore, or injured teats. Flexible dilators packed in Bag Balm ointment help keep the teat canal open for easier milking. Farmers discovered that Bag Balm could also be used to soothe chapped lips and hands, soothe nipples made sore from breastfeeding, and speed the healing of eczema and abrasions—popularizing Bag Balm among people.

Secret Formula

NATURAL MOISTURIZER

WHAT YOU NEED

From the supermarket:
- 3 ounces olive oil
- 3 ounces coconut oil
- 3 ounces sunflower oil

From the drugstore:
- 1 teaspoon anhydrous lanolin

From the health food store:
- 10 drops vitamin E oil
- 4 drops essential oil of bergamot

WHAT TO DO

Mix the ingredients in a medium-size bowl. Blend well. Store in a clean pump bottle. Makes ten ounces.

HOW YOU USE IT

Now you can soothe and soften cracked fingertips and painful skin fissures by simply applying this healing moisturizer—blended from three natural oils—to the afflicted area and rubbing in well. You'll instantly feel precious moisture infusing and revitalizing your chapped, dry skin.

This soothing lotion locks in moisture, speeds healing, and rejuvenates skin with a healthy dose of lanolin, vitamin E, and sweet bergamot. Generations of families swear by its healing powers. Shouldn't you?

STRANGE FACTS

• Dairy cows typically give milk for five to six years, producing an average of 12,147 pounds of milk.

• Holstein cows produce more milk than any other breed of cow, but their milk contains less butterfat than other breeds. (Butterfat is used to make butter.)

• Wisconsin has the largest population of dairy cattle (with over 2.5 million cows), followed by New York, Minnesota, and California.

BURT'S BEES

In 1975, Roxanne Quimby and her husband moved to Maine from San Francisco with their twin babies and bought a thirty-acre parcel of land for three thousand dollars. Soon afterwards, Roxanne found herself divorced and supporting her children by buying low and selling high at yard sales and flea markets, earning roughly 150 dollars a week. She met Burt Shavitz, a former photographer for *Time* and *Life* magazines, who lived in a small, remodeled chicken coop and earned a living selling jars of honey off the back of his Datsun pickup on weekends in Dexter, Maine.

To get to know Burt better, Roxanne volunteered to help out with his thirty hives of bees. She discovered that Burt had been storing beeswax in his honey house for years, hoping to one day find a use for it. Roxanne asked if she could try making candles. When she brought her candles to a craft fair at Dover-Foxcroft and made two hundred dollars in one day, she and Burt decided to go into business together.

Burt and Roxanne rented an old one-room schoolhouse for 150 dollars a year. The building had no heat, lights, running water, or windows—until

Secret Formula

BEESWAX SALVE

WHAT YOU NEED

From the supermarket:
- 1 quart almond oil
- Cooking thermometer

From the health food store:
- 3 ounces fresh calendula herb flowers
- 5 to 6 ounces beeswax

WHAT TO DO

Mix the calendula and almond oil and heat to 175 degrees Fahrenheit in a Crock-Pot overnight.

Strain the oil, removing and dis- carding the calendula flowers, and place in a saucepan over medium heat. Add the beeswax and stir.

When the mixture melts to the consistency of paste, pour into jars. Let cool, then secure lids tightly.

HOW YOU USE IT

Apply this soothing, healing salve to cold sores, rashes, and burns for instant relief. Why, it's as easy as $6x^2 + y^5$. Hubby should be overjoyed, and won't that snooty Mrs. Jones next door be surprised!

---

friends helped fix up the place, adding a gas kitchen range so Roxanne could make candles and beeswax lip balm.

Roxanne made the products, designed containers using Burt's bearded face as the company's trademark, and owned 70 percent of the business. Burt did the bill collecting. The team sold their beeswax products at craft fairs and wholesale gift shows—until a New York buyer ordered hundreds of Roxanne's teddy bear candles. Burt's Bees expanded beyond candles to balms, bath salts, lotions, deodorants, cremes, and fragrances—all made with natural herbs, flowers, beeswax, and essential oils. Suddenly, Burt's Bees natural products became available in Macy's, Bergdorf Goodman, and through the L. L. Bean catalog.

By 1993, sales exceeded three million dollars, and the company needed larger production facilities. When the state of Maine dragged its heels to provide assistance, the state of North Carolina's tax incentives lured Burt's Bees to Raleigh-Durham. Burt returned to Maine after three months. Roxanne returned three years later, leaving a management team to run the operation. Burt retired to Parkman, Maine, where he lives in a modest cabin with no electricity and an outhouse. He works a few days a month doing public relations work for the company.

STRANGE FACTS

• Roxanne bought out Burt's interest and now owns the entire company.

• Burt's Bees products are sold in thousands of stores across the United States.

• With the profits she earned from Burt's Bees, Roxanne acquired sixteen thousand acres of land in Maine that she hopes to give away to help the state establish a new national park. The Maine Woods, a region in northern and eastern Maine, contains lakes, trout streams, mountains, bears, moose, lynx, and more than one thousand miles of hiking trails. The proposed 3.2 million-acre park would be larger than Yellowstone and Yosemite combined.

Secret Formula

EUCALYPTUS LIP BALM

WHAT YOU NEED

From the supermarket:
• 1 tablespoon sesame seed oil
• 1 drop red food coloring
• 3 drops yellow food coloring

From the drugstore:
• $1/8$ cup cocoa butter
• $1/4$ teaspoon camphor
• 1 tablespoon petroleum jelly
• 1 tablespoon lanolin

From the health food store:
• 4 drops essential oil of eucalyptus

From the hobby center or candle supply store:
• $1/4$ cup beeswax

WHAT TO DO

Melt the sesame seed oil, beeswax, cocoa butter, petroleum jelly, and lanolin together in the top of a double boiler over simmering water. Stir to blend well, then add the camphor, essential oil of eucalyptus, and food coloring. Stir the mixture until it blends together well. Using a funnel, pour into candle molds. Let cool. Cut into two-inch lengths and wrap each stick in aluminum foil.

HOW YOU USE IT

Chapped lips have finally met their match when you liberally apply this moisturizing balm to those cracked smackers. This dynamic lip balm concentrates its medicinal muscle precisely where it's needed—on your lips. Carry this lipsaver in an outer jacket pocket wherever you go so your body heat doesn't melt the lip balm stick, and you're always ready to give those lips a healthy dose of tender, loving care.

Secret Formula

CHERRY LIP BALM

WHAT YOU NEED

From the supermarket:
- 3 tablespoons Crisco All-Vegetable Shortening
- One packet cherry Kool-Aid
- One clean, empty 35mm Kodak film canister

WHAT TO DO

Place three tablespoons of Crisco All-Vegetable Shortening in a ceramic coffee cup and heat in a microwave oven for one minute (or until the shortening liquefies). Empty the packet of cherry Kool-Aid into the cup of melted shortening and stir well until dissolved. Carefully pour the colored liquid into a clean, empty 35mm Kodak film canister, cap tightly, and refrigerate overnight. In the morning, you've got tasty homemade lip gloss that moisturizes chapped lips.

HOW YOU USE IT

A dab of this cherry-flavored lip balm heals and soothes chapped lips, giving you quick relief so you and your snuggle bunny will be puckering up on the sofa in no time.

Secret Formula

LIP GLOSS

WHAT YOU NEED

From the supermarket:
- 1/4 cup sesame oil

From the hobby center or candle supply store:
- 2 teaspoons beeswax

From the health food store:
- 1/2 teaspoon menthol
- Alkanet root (optional)

WHAT TO DO

Melt the beeswax in a small saucepan over low heat. Add the sesame oil and menthol and stir until blended. Remove from heat and continue stirring until the mixture cools to prevent the ingredients from separating. Pour into a small, air-tight container, and continue whipping until the mixture sets. Makes about 1/4 cup.

(To make colored gloss, soak alkanet root in the sesame oil for two weeks to color the oil dark red, strain, and follow the directions above.)

HOW YOU USE IT

Dab some of this glamorous gloss onto your lips to give those smackers a protective shimmer. The mighty menthol provides a just-kiss-me minty taste that will have every boy in school just begging to carry your books home.

CHAPSTICK

In the early 1880s in Lynchburg, Virginia, physician and pharmacological tinkerer Dr. C. D. Fleet invented a lip balm in the shape of a wickless candle wrapped in tin foil. He called his invention ChapStick and sold it locally. In 1912, another Lynchburg resident, John Morton, bought the rights to ChapStick for five dollars. In the family kitchen, his wife melted the pink ChapStick mixture on her kitchen stove, poured the liquid through a small funnel into brass tubes held in a rack, and then set the rack on the porch to cool. The Mortons cut the molded ChapStick into sticks and placed them into containers for shipping. If the Mortons could make ChapStick in their turn-of-the-century kitchen, there's no reason why we can't do the same in a modern-day kitchen.

COCA-COLA

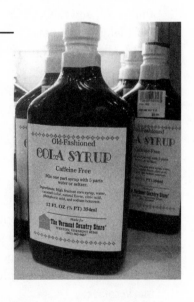

Dr. John Styth Pemberton, inventor of Globe of Flower Cough Syrup, Indian Queen Hair Dye, Triplex Liver Pills, and Extract of Styllinger, was eager to duplicate Vin Mariani, a popular wine elixir made with coca. On May 8, 1886, in his backyard at 107 Marietta Street in Atlanta, Georgia, Pemberton developed a thick syrup drink from sugar water, a kola nut extract, and coca. Pemberton brought his new syrup elixir to Jacob's Drugstore where druggist Willis Venable added carbonated water.

Bookkeeper Frank M. Robinson, one of Pemberton's four partners, suggested naming the elixir after two of the main ingredients: the coca leaf and the kola nut. He suggested spelling *kola* with a *c* for the sake of alliteration. Robinson wrote the name in his bookkeeper's Spencerian script, much the way it appears today.

In 1888, Asa G. Candler acquired the rights to the name and formula. He kept the formula a well-guarded secret, and on January 31, 1893, trademarked the name. The distinctively shaped Coke bottle was designed by Alexander Samuelson at Root Glass in Terre Haute, Indiana.

STRANGE FACTS

• Coca-Cola stock went public in 1919 at forty dollars per share. In 1994, one of those shares was worth $118,192.76, including dividends.

• Rumor contends that a piece of meat left in a glass of Coca-Cola overnight will be completely dissolved by the following morning. It won't. A piece of meat soaked in Coca-Cola overnight will, however, be marinated and tender.

• During the 1960s, the Coca-Cola jingle was sung by Roy Orbison, the Supremes, the Moody Blues, Ray Charles (who sang the Diet Pepsi jingle in the 1990s), The Fifth Dimension, Aretha Franklin, and Gladys Knight and the Pips.

• The World of Coca-Cola, a three-story pavilion in Atlanta, Georgia, features exhibits (including a one-thousand-piece memorabilia collection and John Pemberton's original handwritten formula book), soda fountains of the past and future, bottling exhibits, samples of Coca-Cola products from around the world, and films of Coca-Cola commercials.

• If all the Coca-Cola ever produced were in regular-size sixteen-ounce bottles and laid end-to-end, they would reach to the moon and back 1,045 times. That is one trip per day for two years, ten months, and eleven days.

• "Good to the Last Drop," a slogan used by Maxwell House coffee, was first used by Coca-Cola in 1908.

• The Coca-Cola Catalog, a mail order catalog filled with Coca-Cola memorabilia from boxer shorts to "O" gauge boxcars emblazoned with the Coca-Cola logo, is available for free by calling (800) 746-7265.

• Since 1893, the recipe for Coca-Cola has been changed only once. In 1985, when Pepsi-Cola outsold Coca-Cola in the United States for the first time in history, the Coca-Cola Company sweetened its product and renamed it New Coke. Within three months, consumers forced the company to bring back the old formula. It became known as Coca-Cola Classic, and New Coke, considered the marketing fiasco of the decade, soon disappeared from the marketplace.

• On an average day in 1993, consumers drank 705 million servings of Coca-Cola and other Coca-Cola soft drinks worldwide.

• 2,386.7 million gallons of Coca-Cola Classic were sold in 1992.

• Coca-Cola outsells Pepsi worldwide by a more than a two-to-one margin.

• Coca-Cola is available in Coca-Cola Classic, Caffeine Free Coca-Cola Classic, Diet Coke, Caffeine Free Diet Coke, Cherry Coke, Diet Cherry Coke, Diet Coke with Lemon, Diet Vanilla Coke, Vanilla Coke, and Coke II (previously known as New Coke).

That Crazy Calendar

January and February are actually the eleventh and twelfth months of the year, not the first and second.

When the Roman calendar was first introduced in the eighth century B.C.E., it inaccurately contained only 304 days for a total of ten months: Martius, Aprilis, Maius, Junius, Quintilis, Sextilis, September, October, November, and December. The names of the last six months were taken from the Roman words for five, six, seven, eight, nine, and ten.

In 452 B.C.E., when the months started to slide out of sync with the seasons, Roman ruler Numa added the month of January at the end of the year and the month of February at the beginning of the year. To make the calendar match the solar year, he decreed that the month of Mercedinus (with 23 days) be inserted between February 23 and 24 every other year. Four hundred years later, the calendar had slid so far out of sync that winter began in September. In 46 B.C.E., Roman emperor Julius Caesar, advised by astronomer Sosigenes, dropped the month of Mercedina and gave each of the remaining twelve months 30 or 31 days, except for February, which he gave 29 (adding a thirtieth day to February every fourth year). Caesar realigned the new Julian calendar with the seasons by adding an extra eighty days to the year as 46 B.C.E., which the Romans dubbed "the year of confusion."

Unfortunately, the Julian calendar, while nearly accurate, was off by twelve minutes. The Romans figured a year had 365.25 days, but in reality, a year has 365 days, 5 hours, 48 minutes, and 46 seconds. By 730 C.E., a monk realized that this slight inaccuracy (eleven minutes, fourteen seconds) had caused the calendar to fall 5.5 days behind the change in season. He tried to make adjustments, but nobody listened until 800 years later. In 1582, Pope Gregory XIII corrected the mistake by shortening October 1582 by ten days and decreed that February would have an extra day each fourth year except in century years that could not be divided by 400 (such as 1700). England and its colonies (including America) did not adopt the Gregorian calendar until 1752, by which time the calendar was off by eleven days. Russia did not change to the Gregorian calendar until 1918.

COLGATE TOOTHPASTE

The Egyptians used toothpaste as early as 2000 B.C.E. made from powdered pumice stone and wax. The Romans used toothpaste made from human urine, which Roman physicians insisted whitened teeth. (Oddly, the ammonia in urine does work as a whitener.)

In 1806, twenty-three-year-old William Colgate opened a "Soap, Mould & Dipt Candles" factory in a rented two-story brick building at #6 Dutch Street in downtown Manhattan. In 1877, the Colgate Company, run by Colgate's son, Samuel Colgate, began selling toothpaste in jars. The business prospered, and Samuel and his brother James made generous donations to Madison University in Hamilton, New York—so much so that the University renamed itself Colgate University in 1890. Six years later, Colgate introduced the first toothpaste in a tube. In 1968, Colgate toothpaste was reformulated with MFP (monofluorophosphate) fluoride.

Secret Formula

PEPPERMINT TOOTHPASTE

WHAT YOU NEED
From the supermarket:
- 8 tablespoons baking soda
- 2 teaspoons peppermint flavoring

From the drugstore:
- 3 tablespoons glycerin

WHAT TO DO
Blend all the ingredients thoroughly and store the finished mixture in a small, sanitized glass jar, tightly sealed. Makes roughly 1/3 cup.

HOW YOU USE IT
To use, dip your moistened toothbrush into the paste, place it in your mouth, and brush those pearly whites like they've never been brushed before for a glamorous shine that will sparkle like your best china.

Secret Formula

WINTERGREEN TOOTHPASTE

WHAT YOU NEED
From the drugstore:
- 1/2 cup precipitated chalk (calcium carbonate)
- 1/4 cup glycerin

From the health food store:
- 1/4 teaspoon essential oil of wintergreen

From the liquor store:
- 1/4 teaspoon 100-proof vodka

From a perfume and cosmetic supply house:
- 2 tablespoons orrisroot powder

WHAT TO DO
Mix the chalk and orrisroot powder together in a small bowl. Add the glycerin and blend well to form a thick paste. Dissolve the essential oil of wintergreen in the vodka, then mix into the paste. If paste is too thick, add more vodka until the desired consistency is obtained. If paste is too loose, add more glycerin. Store at room temperature in a tightly covered jar or airtight container.

HOW YOU USE IT
Dip your toothbrush into this luxurious toothpaste and brush away tartar and plaque with ease.

The mild abrasive in this ingenious formula brightens and whitens your teeth while the zesty blend of wintergreen and orrisroot leaves your mouth feeling fresh and clean. Preferred by dentists who prefer this preferable toothpaste.

Secret Formula

DENTURE CLEANSER

WHAT YOU NEED
From a drugstore or health food store:
- 1 1/2 tablespoons sodium perborate

From the health food store:
- 2 drops essential oil of peppermint

From the tap:
- 1 cup warm water

WHAT TO DO
Spoon the sodium perborate into a glass, and add the warm water. Immediately place the dentures into the mixture, then add the essential oil of peppermint.

HOW YOU USE IT
Wait just five simple minutes, then remove the dentures, and rinse thoroughly with warm water. It's that easy!

Making a daily habit of cleaning your dentures with this marvelous concoction means stained dentures can't spoil your charm!

The Old Brush-Off

Throughout history, denture wearers brushed their dentures—until 1967 when Warner-Lambert introduced Efferdent, the world's first denture

effervescent cleansing tablet. An Efferdent tablet in a glass of water seems like a modern miracle—foaming and fizzing to remove stains and tartar. For a simpler way to clean dentures, soak them overnight in a glass filled with Heinz White Vinegar. The acetic acids eats away all the gunk and tartar. Then rinse the dentures clean.

DR. HUNTER'S

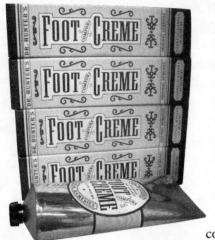

In 1752, Dr. William Hunter opened an apothecary in Newport, Rhode Island, offering his customers his proven remedies formulated from high quality natural ingredients. In his day, feet took a real beating due to ill-fitting shoes, fierce winters, poor transportation, and harsh working conditions. Dr. Hunter combined natural essential oils and cooling extracts to concoct a crème to rejuvenate tired, aching feet with just one application.

Today, Caswell-Massey celebrates the company's founder, Dr. Hunter, with an array of Dr. Hunter's Original Remedies. These include Pure Vegetable Castile Soap (purveyed for the first time just before Abraham Lincoln's inauguration as President in 1861), Rosewater & Glycerine Hand Crème (an enriched version of Dr. Hunter's classic formula), Cuticle Cream, Lip Salve, and Lip Balm.

Secret Formula

CUTICLE CREAM

WHAT YOU NEED
From the drugstore:
- 1 tablespoon glycerin
- 1/2 cup mineral oil

From the health food store:
- 3 tablespoons paraffin
- 1 tablespoon coconut oil

WHAT TO DO
In a double boiler, slowly heat the paraffin, mineral oil, and coconut oil until blended. Stir in the glycerin, remove from the heat, pour into a tin or tiny jar, and store in the refrigerator until the mixture thickens. Let cool before sealing the lid. Makes 3/4 cup.

HOW YOU USE IT
This potent cuticle cream packs a lot of wallop. Use cotton swabs or cotton balls to rub this soothing cuticle cream directly on the cuticles to maintain healthy cuticles and nails that look manicured to perfection. Now you can say good-bye forever to those ragged edges and futile cuticles!

DR. SCHOLL'S FOOT PADS

While working as a shoemaker in Chicago, Illinois, William Scholl first noticed that bunions, corns, and fallen arches plagued most of his customers. Determined to help people take better care of their feet, Scholl sold shoes by day and attended Chicago Medical School at night, receiving his medical degree in 1904. That same year, at age twenty-two, Scholl patented and launched his first arch support, a shoe insert he called "Foot-Eazer." The popularity of the Foot-Eazer helped Scholl launch an entire line of foot care products.

To help sell his foot pads, Scholl set up a correspondence course on podiatry for shoe store clerks and hired consultants to travel around the country delivering lectures to doctors and the general public on proper foot care.

In 1916, Scholl sponsored the Cinderella Foot Contest to find the most perfect female feet in America. Tens of thousands of women went to their local shoe stores to have their feet measured and their footprints taken. Scholl published the winning footprint in newspapers and magazines, prompting thousands of women to buy his products to make their own feet look like the American ideal. The signature yellow-and-blue packages containing Dr. Scholl's foot care pads could soon be found in five-and-dime stores and pharmacies across America.

STRANGE FACTS

• Scholl's early advertisements, picturing naked feed adorned only in bunion pads or standing on arch supports, provoked complaints against indecency.

• Scholl urged people to walk two miles a day with "head up, chest out, toes straight forward."

• Scholl advocated that people change their shoes once a day so the perspiration in each pair had time to dry out.

• Scholl ascribed to his own credo: "Early to bed, early to rise, work like hell and advertise."

• While other people claimed they never forgot a face, William Scholl insisted that he never forgot a foot.

Voting with Their Feet

During an election year in the 1970s, the Pulvapies foot powder company ran ads in Ecuador proclaiming, "Vote for any candidate, but if you want well-being and hygiene, vote for Pulvapies." Voters in the town of Picoaza, Ecuador, with a population of four thousand people, elected Pulvapies to be the new mayor.

Freckles

Use Stillman's Freckle Cream

★ In use a half century—that's one recommendation.
★ Sold in over 60 foreign countries—that's another.
★ Over 30 million jars sold. That means something.
★ But—you don't have to depend upon these facts. Try a jar of **Stillman's Freckle Cream** and let your mirror tell you exactly what it will do for you.

If Stillman's Freckle Cream doesn't keep your skin clearer, smoother, softer—give you a lovelier complexion, we will refund your purchase price.

The Stillman Co., Aurora, Illinois

Stillman's FRECKLE CREAM

SINCE 1889

TIRED ALL THE TIME?

Secret Formula
HOMEMADE FOOT POWDER

WHAT YOU NEED

From the supermarket:
- 1/2 cup cornstarch

From the drugstore:
- 1 cup boric acid
- 1/4 cup sodium thiosulfate

WHAT TO DO

In a large mixing bowl, mix the cornstarch, boric acid, and sodium thiosulfate. Blend thoroughly. Pour the mixture into a clean plastic flip-top shaker. Makes 1 3/4 cups.

HOW YOU USE IT

Dust this powerful athlete's foot powder on your feet, between your toes, and in your shoes twice a day (once in the morning, once in the evening) to absorb that clammy moisture and reduce friction between your sweet little tootsies. Let sweaty footwear air out and dry thoroughly (for at least twenty-four hours) before putting it back on.

Those itchy, annoying symptoms will disappear almost overnight! (Well, actually somewhere between two weeks to a month—but it sure will feel like overnight!) If your athlete's foot persists, you'd best consult a doctor—but we doubt you'll have to after using this remedy most people find fit for a queen.

Dumb Mistakes

A HAREBRAINED THEORY

English writer Samuel Johnson claimed, "The cause of baldness in men is dryness of the brain, and its shrinking from the skull."

OOPSY-DAISY

In 1898, Dr. Heinrich Dreser, head of the drug research laboratory at the Bayer Company in Germany, announced that he had developed diacetylmorphine—a "nonaddictive" derivative of morphine with four to eight times the painkilling power. The Bayer Company marketed diacetylmorphine under the brand-name Heroin (derived from the "heroic" state of mind the drug purportedly induced), and the new drug was used in cough syrups and pain remedies, and prescribed by doctors for headaches and menstrual cramps. In 1910, after twelve years on the market, doctors realized that heroin is far more addictive than morphine. In 1924, the United States banned the manufacture of heroin, but by then there were plenty of addicts to create a demand for heroin on the black market.

THE HIPPOCRATIC OATH

The Ancient Greek physician Hippocrates, considered the father of modern medicine, claimed:

- The world is composed of four elements: earth (dry), air (cold), fire (hot), and water (moist).
- You can determine the sex of an unborn child based on which one of the mother's breasts became larger.
- People suffering from jaundice are not susceptible to flatulence.
- People with speech impediments are more likely to get protracted diarrhea.
- Gout only strikes people who have had sexual intercourse.

- South winds cause deafness.
- North winds cause constipation.
- Bald people who get varicose veins regain their hair.

IDENTITY CRISIS

In 1941, when told that the Japanese had destroyed Pearl Harbor, actress Joan Crawford replied, "Oh dear, who was she?"

MODERN QUACKERY

In his 1811 book *The Organon of the Rational Art of Healing*, German doctor Samuel Hahnemann insisted: "A disease can only be destroyed and cured by a remedy which has a tendency to produce a similar disease, for the effects of drugs are in themselves no other than artificial diseases." Hahnemann named this process homeopathy, and this alleged science, lacking scientific proof of its effectiveness, is practiced to this very day.

IT AIN'T NECESSARILY SO

Ancient Greek philosopher Empedocles claimed that everything in the universe is composed of four elements (earth, air, fire, and water), which he insisted were bonded together by love and driven apart by strife.

SOMETHING FISHY

In 1903, British surgeon Sir Jonathan Hutchinson incorrectly insisted that eating bad fish caused leprosy. Hutchinson had clearly failed to keep up with medical advances. In 1865, Louis Pasteur had proven that germs spread from person to person caused infectious diseases, and in 1874, Norwegian bacteriologist Gerhard Hansen identified a bacterium, *Mycobacterium leprae*, as the cause of leprosy.

FROWNIES

In 1889, Margaret Kroesen discovered that she had developed unsightly wrinkles and frown lines. Determined to maintain her youthful beauty, she created "Wrinkle Eradicators," small adhesive patches to diminish wrinkles

naturally by employing the basic principle of fitness to the muscles of the face without chemicals. Margaret created the patches solely for herself, but she soon realized that her amazing invention could benefit women and men everywhere.

Several years later, Margaret's husband died, prompting her to get a job as managing director of the B & P Company, which made barber supplies—straight razors, razor straps, and pomades. When the advent of the safety razor caused sales of straight razors to plummet, Margaret bought the faltering company, phased out the barber supplies, and began selling her wrinkle removers, renamed "Frownies," running small advertisements. Four generations of Margaret Kroesen's female offspring have run the company, helping preserve the faces of men and women everywhere and never altering the Frownies formula.

STRANGE FACTS
• Margaret and her granddaughter (named Margaret in her honor) personally answered the hundreds of letters regarding Frownies that they received from around the world.
• Every month, renowned Hollywood makeup artist Perc Westmore, who advocated Frownies to actresses, sent Margaret and her granddaughter a box of mail from women and men requesting help in eliminating wrinkle and frown lines.
• Many actresses (Olivia de Havilland, Gloria Swanson, Audrey Meadows, and Ursula Andress) used Frownies, as did most of the Kennedy women.
• Frownies starred in the movies *Sunset Boulevard*, *Cocoon*, *Death Becomes Her*, and *Mars Attacks*.

- Frownies were featured in the book *Valley of the Dolls*.
- In *Good Housekeeping* magazine, actress Rene Russo called Frownies her secret weapon.
- According to the company, "Frownies are easy to use and can be applied to your face wherever you have frown or smile lines you wish to reduce. Leave Frownies on while sleeping or relaxing. Used over a period of two to four weeks Frownies will help retrain your muscles and smooth the frown and smile lines in your face. Although you will notice a difference even with overnight use, consistent use is the key to success."

HANFORD'S BALSAM OF MYRRH

At the turn of the nineteenth century in Syracuse, New York, Seth and Betsy Hanford frequently played host to an English physician who traveled from settlement to settlement. Before retiring from his frontier practice, the doctor gave Seth Hanford the recipe for Balsam of Myrrh, a topical antiseptic that he regularly prepared and dispensed and that reduced the risk of infection and gangrene.

Seth and his son George produced the pungent natural antiseptic on his farm, then traveled to nearby communities to sell the cork-sealed bottles. His grandson G. C. took over the business and innovated the idea of hiring employees as traveling salesmen (known as "drummers") to sell Balsam of Myrrh (and "drum up" business). G. C. gradually built the small family business into a thriving industry, turning Balsam of Myrrh into one of America's first widely distributed "patent medicines." G. C., his son, and his grandson added other products to the Hanford line, including tonics, baking powders, and food colorings.

In the mid-twentieth century, the Hanford Company became pioneers in penicillin production. Today, Hanford Pharmaceuticals is a leading producer of sterile injectable antibiotics.

STRANGE FACTS

- Myrrh, an aromatic gum resin secreted by shrubs, has been used as a wound dressing since the dawn of recorded history.
- The Bible frequently refers to myrrh.
- The Smyth Papyrus, an Egyptian medical text dated 1650 B.C.E., describes myrrh as "a most efficacious salve for Pharaoh's soldiers."
- Microbiologists confirm that myrrh inhibits bacterial growth and is bacteriostatic against *Staphylococcus aureus,* the most common bacterial invader.
- Hanford developed Vitaspra— an organic garden insecticide using natural ingredients—fifty years before the American public recognized the importance of environmentally friendly products.

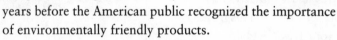

Secret Formula
LEMON-MINT ASTRINGENT

WHAT YOU NEED
From the supermarket:
- 1/2 cup witch hazel
- 1/4 cup lemon juice

From the health food store:
- 5 drops essential oil of mint

WHAT TO DO
Mix the witch hazel, lemon juice, and essential oil of mint, and store in a sterilized glass bottle, tightly capped.

HOW YOU USE IT
Using a cotton ball, apply this tingly lemon-mint astringent to oily skin on your face and neck.

This stimulating and refreshing herbal skin tonic, based on an age-old beauty recipe from the Austro-Hungarian empire, clarifies and balances the skin, leaving your skin feeling exhilarated, lemony, and minty fresh.

Secret Formula

ROSE ASTRINGENT

WHAT YOU NEED

From the supermarket:
- 3 1/2 cups witch hazel
- 5 sprigs fresh rosemary

From the garden:
- 1/2 cup dried rose petals

WHAT TO DO

Mix ingredients together, blending well. Store in an airtight container in a dark place for one week. Strain through a coffee filter and store in a sterilized glass bottle, tightly capped.

HOW YOU USE IT

After cleaning your skin, splash this zesty rose astringent on your face, or dab it on with a cotton ball. The witch hazel cleanses pores, leaving skin feeling soft, moisturized, and refreshed. The rosemary stimulates circulation, revitalizing the skin. And the rose petals give this astringent an invigorating scent that will miraculously remind you of roses. Most women report clearer, smoother, healthier skin just thinking about this all-natural formula.

Secret Formula

SKIN ASTRINGENT

WHAT YOU NEED

From the supermarket:
- 1/4 cup distilled white vinegar
- 3/4 cup distilled water

From a drugstore:
- 1/4 cup isopropyl alcohol
- 1/4 cup tincture of benzoin
- 1 teaspoon camphor

From the health food store:
- 10 drops essential oil of peppermint
- 10 drops essential oil of clove
- 10 drops essential oil of eucalyptus

WHAT TO DO

Using a funnel, mix all of the ingredients (except the distilled water) in a twelve-ounce bottle. Cap tightly and store for ten days. Then add 3/4 cup distilled water and shake well. Makes twelve ounces.

HOW YOU USE IT

After washing your oily skin with soap and warm water, use a cotton ball to apply this delightful astringent to your face to remove oil from your skin (being careful not to get any in your eyes). This penetrating astringent removes trapped oil, dirt, and makeup from pores, leaving your skin oh so invigorated, and enlivening your complexion.

JOHNSON'S BABY POWDER

In 1894, Johnson & Johnson provided small packets of Baby Powder in maternity kits, and public demand for the product compelled Johnson & Johnson to make baby powder available in stores. Johnson's Baby Powder is a refined talcum powder used specifically to absorb moisture from a baby's skin to prevent diaper rash. The fragrance of Johnson's Baby Powder is one of the most recognized scents in the world. Unfortunately, some studies indicate that talc may be carcinogenic if inhaled. Johnson & Johnson now makes a variation of baby powder using nontoxic cornstarch instead of talc, like the formula below.

Gone with the Wind

In the 1939 movie Gone with the Wind, Melanie's pregnancy, when calculated by the dates of the Civil War battles mentioned, lasts twenty-one months.

Secret Formula

ALL-NATURAL BABY POWDER

WHAT YOU NEED

From the supermarket:
- 1 cup cornstarch

From a perfume and cosmetic supply house:
- 4 tablespoons orrisroot (optional)

WHAT TO DO

Mix the ingredients together in a small bowl. Blend well. Fill a plastic flip-top shaker or a old baby powder bottle with the mixture. Makes one cup.

HOW YOU USE IT

It's so simple to prevent diaper rash! Lightly sprinkle this all-natural baby powder on Junior's soft tushy and pat evenly to avoid caking.

The cornstarch absorbs excess moisture so baby's skin stays dry and soft. (If baby does have diaper rash, don't use baby powder. Instead, coat the affected area with a thin coat of Crisco All-Vegetable Shortening to seal in moisture.)

LISTERINE

In 1879, Dr. Joseph Lawrence heard a lecture by Sir Joseph Lister, a nineteenth-century British surgeon who pioneered sanitary operating room procedures. Impressed by Lister's views on germs and his plea for "antiseptic surgery," Lawrence developed an antiseptic in his St. Louis laboratory for safe and effective use in surgical procedures. Lawrence named the new antiseptic Listerine in honor of Sir Joseph Lister.

The local Lambert Pharmacal Company manufactured Listerine exclusively for the medical profession and, in 1895, extended the sale and promotion of Listerine to the dental profession as an antibacterial mouthwash and gargle. In 1914, compelled by popular demand, Lambert made Listerine available to the general public.

STRANGE FACTS

- Listerine should not be swallowed or administered to children under twelve years of age because it contains 26.9 percent pharmaceutical grade alcohol.
- Listerine is the best-selling brand of mouthwash in the United States.
- Listerine can be found in one out of every five homes in the United States.

Secret Formula

CINNAMON MOUTHWASH

WHAT YOU NEED

From the supermarket:
- 8 1/2 tablespoons powdered cinnamon
- 1 cup 100-proof vodka

From the tap:
- 1 cup water

WHAT TO DO

Mix the powdered cinnamon, vodka, and water in an airtight container, seal securely, and let sit for two weeks, shaking the contents twice a day. Strain the liquid through a coffee filter.

HOW YOU USE IT

Mix one tablespoon of this vivacious cinnamon tincture in a glass of warm water, and rinse your mouth to brighten you spirits, kill the bacteria that cause bad breath, and make the woman or man of your dreams definitely want to high-tail it in your direction and get chummy with eyes a-buggin'!

Secret Formula

PEPPERMINT MOUTHWASH

WHAT YOU NEED

From the supermarket:
- 1/4 teaspoon borax

From the drugstore or health food store:
- 1/8 teaspoon menthol
- 1/8 teaspoon essential oil of peppermint

From the liquor store:
- 1/2 teaspoon 100-proof vodka

From the tap:
- 2 cups water

WHAT TO DO

In a small bowl, dissolve the oil of peppermint in the vodka. In a second bowl, mix the borax in the water and add the menthol. Combine the two mixtures. Store in a bottle and cover tightly. Makes sixteen ounces.

HOW YOU USE IT

If you're a gal who likes onions and men, just shake this bottled mixture vigorously, and rinse your mouth with the world's most distinctive mentholated mouthwash so you can start off from third base!

Golly-gosh-a-mighty? You bet! The formula for this mouthwash—a one-of-a-kind blend of menthol and peppermint—has been a closely guarded family secret for over 175 years, until an heiress, unhappy with her inheritance, spilled the beans, giving anyone with discerning taste and foul breath an opportunity to change the winds of fate with this tried-and-true remedy for the heartbreak of halitosis.

Secret Formula

THYME DANDRUFF RINSE

WHAT YOU NEED

From the supermarket:
- 4 heaping teaspoons dried thyme leaves

From the tap:
- 2 cups water

WHAT TO DO

Add the thyme to two cups of water, and bring the solution to a boil for ten minutes. Strain through a coffee filter and let cool. Makes enough rinse for two treatments.

HOW YOU USE IT

Gently pour one cup of the solution over clean damp hair, working well into the scalp. Massage in gently. Do not rinse. Let hair dry.

Thyme, one of the active ingredients in Listerine, is a mild antiseptic that helps reduce dandruff with proven results. You'll be amazed how quickly and easily this revolutionary dandruff rinse acts at once to end the embarrassment of flaking—without a prescription!

At the first sign of infectious dandruff...

LISTERINE!

See how it attacks annoying flakes

When ugly flakes and scales begin to speck your clothes, when your scalp begins to itch annoyingly and inflammation may be present...it's time to act—and act *fast!*

Nature may be warning you that the infectious type of dandruff has set in...may be telling you to do something about it before it gets any worse.

Start now with Listerine Antiseptic. Just douse it on your scalp and hair morning and night and follow with vigorous and persistent massage.

This is the simple medical treatment which has shown such outstanding results in a substantial majority of clinical test cases...the easy method used by thousands in their own homes.

Listerine often brings quick improvement, because it gives both hair and scalp an antiseptic bath. The loosened dandruff scales begin to disappear. Your scalp feels healthier, more invigorated. And meanwhile, Listerine Antiseptic is killing millions of germs on scalp and hair, including the queer "bottle bacillus," recognized by many outstanding authorities as a causative agent of the infectious type of dandruff.

Clinical results of this simple, pleasant treatment have been literally amazing. In a series of tests, 76% of dandruff sufferers who used Listerine and massage twice a day within a month showed complete disappearance of, or marked improvement in, the symptoms.

If you've got the slightest symptom of this trouble, don't waste any time. You may have a real infection, so begin today with Listerine Antiseptic and massage. To save yourself money, buy the large economy-size bottle. Lambert Pharmacal Co., *St. Louis, Mo.*

Feel how it invigorates your scalp

Scalp is healthier, cleaner

THE TREATMENT
that brought improvement to 76% of cases in a clinical test

MEN: Douse full strength Listerine Antiseptic on the scalp morning and night.

WOMEN: Part the hair at various places, and apply Listerine Antiseptic right along the part with a medicine dropper, to avoid wetting the hair excessively.

Always follow with vigorous and persistent massage with fingers or a good hair brush. Continue the treatment as long as dandruff is in evidence. And even though you're free from dandruff, enjoy a Listerine massage once a week to guard against infection. Listerine Antiseptic is the same antiseptic that has been famous for more than 50 years as a mouth wash and gargle.

LISTERINE
ANTISEPTIC

Ben's I.Q. was way up —but the world turned him down

BEN'S PROFESSORS called him "The Brain." Pretty girls called him "The Profile." But the closer Ben got to a girl, the more distant she became. For brains and good-looks go begging—when a man has underarm odor.

IN BUSINESS Ben figured his high-powered brains would zoom him up the hill to success in high. Imagine his embarrassment when he stalled! Ben was going nowhere fast—when a newspaper ad pulled him up—

THINK! YOUR BATH CAN REMOVE ONLY PAST PERSPIRATION! TO PREVENT RISK OF *FUTURE* UNDERARM ODOR— USE *MUM*!

NOW THAT BEN uses Mum every day, he's going places! He always had brains and personality—Mum gave them a chance to get across. Underarm odor keeps many an able citizen down—until he plays safe with Mum!

MUM

In 1888, a Philadelphia man whose name has been lost to history formulated the world's first antiperspirant. The cream, containing zinc, when applied to the underarms, stopped perspiration, preventing odor. He trademarked his clever concoction "Mum" (meaning "to keep silent") and distributed the product through his nurse. In 1931, Bristol-Myers acquired the fledgling Mum manufacturing company.

In the late 1940s, Helen Barnett Diserens joined the Mum production team and, inspired by a suggestion from a colleague, decided to develop an underarm deodorant with an applicator based on the same principal as the newly invented ball-point pen. In 1952, Bristol Meyers launched the product in the United States under the name Ban Roll-On. The product quickly became the best-selling antiperspirant in the country. In 1958, Bristol Meyers launched the product in the United Kingdom as Mum Rollette.

While Mum disappeared from the marketplace in the United States, it remains popular in the United Kingdom as Mum Solid and Mum Pump Spray.

Secret Formula

LOVELY LEMON DEODORANT

WHAT YOU NEED

From the supermarket:
- 1 teaspoon alum
- 2 teaspoons baking soda

From the drugstore:
- 1 cup isopropyl alcohol

From the health food store:
- 5 drops essential oil of lemon

WHAT TO DO

Using a funnel, combine all of the ingredients together in a fine-mist pump spray bottle. Shake well. Makes eight ounces.

HOW YOU USE IT

To keep your underarms bath-time fresh, spray your underarms with this soothing and cool mist after showering. This lovely lemon formula doesn't sting or irritate, and it dries almost instantly, leaving you with cool, dry underarms. More important, it guards your charm so you won't offend.

Secret Formula

DEODORANT CREAM

WHAT YOU NEED

From the supermarket:
- 2 teaspoons baking soda
- 2 teaspoons cornstarch
- 2 teaspoons petroleum jelly

WHAT TO DO

Mix the baking soda, cornstarch, and petroleum jelly well. Heat in a double boiler over low heat and stir until a smooth cream forms. Pour the resulting cream into a small container with a tight-fitting lid and let cool. Makes roughly three ounces.

HOW YOU USE IT

Don't let "B.O." be your one-way ticket to doom as the object of hushed scorn and ridicule! A simple thing like underarm odor can spoil even a pretty girl's charm.

Smear this delightful deodorant cream under your arms and—presto!—all the guys will think you're in the groove, all the other gals will line up to stand in your shoes, and you'll find your name printed on a wedding invitation before you can say, "Honey, let's pick out a china pattern!"

NIVEA

In the second century, Greek physician Galen, having developed beauty formulas for women in Rome, recorded the formula for the first cold cream in his book, *Medical Methods*. Galen's formula called for one part white wax melted into three parts olive oil, in which "rose buds had been steeped and as much water as can be blended into the mass." At the time, many beauty creams contained toxic ingredients, but cold cream has remained pure and simple.

In 1911, scientist Dr. Oscar Troplowitz, inspired by the development of Eucerit, the first stable water-in-oil emulsifier, streamlined Galen's original formula to create the first long-lasting skin cream, which he named Nivea, from the Latin word *nivius* meaning "snow-white." Hamburg pharmacist H. Beiersdorf bought the rights to the product, distributing Nivea, a cold cream that both moisturizes and nourishes the skin.

Secret Formula

SUGAR SCRUB

WHAT YOU NEED
From the supermarket:
- 1 tablespoon granulated sugar

From the tap:
- 1 teaspoon warm water

WHAT TO DO
Place sugar in the palm of your hand. Add water drop by drop to make a paste. Makes about one tablespoon.

HOW YOU USE IT
Use this sweet mixture to exfoliate those dead skin cells that make skin look dull and flaky—unless, of course, you want to look dull and flaky! Gently rub the abrasive scrub over your face and neck (avoiding your eyes), and massage lightly with your fingertips. Rinse with warm water followed by cool water. Just a spoonful of sugar actually helps control oil build-up, cleanses clogged pores, and works as an antibacterial.

Don't Believe Everything You Read

• In *The Aeneid*, the epic poem by Virgil, two characters—Chorinaeus and Numa—die, then later reappear as if nothing happened.

• In the novel *Don Quixote* by Miguel de Cervantes, Sancho Panza sells his donkey, then, without any explanation, is seen riding it again. He loses his coat with food in the pocket, but later, without any explanation, possesses the food. His helmet is shattered into pieces, but later, without any explanation, it reappears in one piece and unscathed.

• In the novel *Robinson Crusoe* by Daniel Defoe, Crusoe takes off his clothes, swims to a wrecked ship, finds some biscuits there, and then, we are told, puts them in his pockets.

• In the novel *Ivanhoe* by Sir Walter Scott, the first name of one of the characters, Richard Malvoisin, inexplicably changes to Philip.

• In the novel *War and Peace* by Leo Tolstoy, Natasha is seventeen years old in 1805. Four years later, in 1809, she is twenty-four years old—having miraculously aged seven years. Also, Prince Andrei's silver icon turns to gold for no apparent reason.

• William Faulkner's last name was actually Falkner. When his first novel, *Soldiers' Pay*, was published in 1926, the printer mistakenly added the letter u to Falkner's name, making it Faulkner. Miffed, the author simply adopted the new spelling of his name.

NOXZEMA

In 1914, pharmacist Dr. George Bunting combined medication and vanishing cream in the prescription room of his Baltimore drugstore at 6 West North Avenue to create "Dr. Bunting's Sunburn Remedy." He mixed, heated, and poured the skin cream into little blue jars from a huge coffee pot. When other druggists began ordering his sunburn remedy for their customers, Bunting decided to devote all his energies to marketing the skin cream—changing the name to Noxzema.

A customer told Dr. George Bunting, "Your sunburn cream sure knocked my eczema," inspiring Bunting to change the name of "Dr. Bunting's Sunburn Remedy" to Noxzema—a clever combination of the misspelled word "knocks" and the last two syllables of the word "eczema."

In 1917, the Noxzema Chemical Company was founded with sales of 5,214 dollars and four employees. Three years later, Bunting opened the first Noxzema "factory" in a tiny house at 102 Lafayette Avenue in Baltimore. Bunting's fellow druggists helped finance the Noxzema company by placing Noxzema in their stores and buying shares of stock in the company—usually for one hundred dollars or less. By 1925, sales reached 100,000 dollars and Bunting launched Noxzema nationally, starting with New York City in 1926, followed by Chicago and the Midwest in 1928, the South and Pacific Coast in 1930, and the Prairie and Rocky Mountain States in 1938.

With national distribution in place, Noxzema began advertising on national radio broadcasts of "Professor Quiz." Sales jumped 40 percent in one season, and Noxzema began expanding into shaving cream, suntan lotions, and cold cream. In 1938, sales reached one million dollars. By 1944, sales skyrocketed to three million dollars. With a new factory completed in 1949, Noxzema improved production, and in 1961, the company launched Cover Girl. In 1966, Noxzema Chemical Company adopted the name Noxell Corporation. In 1989, Procter & Gamble Cosmetics and Fragrances bought Noxell.

STRANGE FACTS

• Noxzema inventor George Bunting worked as a school principal for six years before pursuing a career as a pharmacist by enrolling in the University of Maryland's pharmacy school.

• The little blue jars which Dr. Bunting once filled from a coffee pot are now filled by a machine at the rate of 120 jars per minute.

• During Dr. Bunting's early attempts at financing Noxzema, he was on the verge of bankruptcy several times between 1914 and 1923—the first year he showed a small profit.

• During World War II, the Noxzema Chemical Company manufactured over 63.2 million jars of Noxzema for GIs.

• Noxzema is sold in over one hundred countries and is produced in nine overseas locations.

Perspiration Odor?

NIP IT WITH

ZiP

Cream Deodorant

STOPS PERSPIRATION

A PHYSICIAN'S FORMULA

STOPS PERSPIRATION—and banishes odors for one to three days.

SIMPLE TO USE—just smooth a finger-tip of cream under your arms, and ZIP!—you're free from all danger of offending others.

HARMLESS TO CLOTHING—a snow-white cream. Use freely. Non-irritating. Delightfully refreshing.

ATTRACTIVE JAR—an exquisitely lovely, wide-mouthed urn-shaped container that you'll be proud to have on your dressing table.

MY GUARANTEE—your money refunded if not satisfied that ZiP is the best Cream Deodorant you can buy and the *most* for your money.

Large jar 19¢ — Extra large jar 33¢
At All Good Stores

Madame Berthé
SPECIALIST
608 FIFTH AVE. (49th ST.) NEW YORK

PERCY MEDICINE

In 1898, a young boy named Albert Percy came down with diarrhea while on a train journey from New York to Texas. His father, A. W. Percy, a traveling buggy-whip salesman, took his son to see a country doctor in Kentucky who prescribed a bismuth subnitrate-based medication. Albert recovered, and his father kept a copy of the formula.

When Albert came down with diarrhea again at home in Waco, Texas, his father brought the formula to pharmacist W. S. Merrick and asked him to mix up another batch of the concoction. Again, the medicine cured the young boy.

Percy and Merrick decided to team up and begin selling Baby Percy Medicine, forming the Merrick Medicine Co. in 1904.

Two employees of Behren's Drug Co., Frank J. Trau and Louis Collie, joined the company. Within a few years, the company spent eight

Secret Formula

ORANGE-OIL LAXATIVE

WHAT YOU NEED

From the supermarket:
- ¹/₂ cup olive oil
- ¹/₂ cup orange juice

WHAT TO DO

Mix the olive oil and orange juice in a tall drinking glass. Stir well. Makes one cup.

HOW YOU USE IT

If your "pipes are clogged" or "traffic is jammed," relax and see how fast this tangy Orange-Oil Cocktail "clears the bowling pins from your alley"! The olive oil works like magic as a mild laxative, while the juice gives the oil a terrific orange flavor so you'll be "clean as a whistle" in no time!

"An old maid showed me how to raise my baby"

1. I was unlucky, I guess. Some women go through pregnancy hardly knowing it. Mine was awful. Some mothers have babies good as "gold." Mine used to howl all night long. And was terribly constipated in the bargain.

2. One day an old friend of the family came to visit us. The house was a mess. The baby upset again. And I was on the verge of tears. My friend put her arms around me and said maybe she could help.

3. "I may be an old maid," she said, "but I work for a baby doctor. And he always asks mothers if they use *special* food . . . do they use *special* powder . . . *special* baby medicines. You see, everything a baby gets today should be made *especially* for him."

4. She looked up on the dresser and saw the laxative I was using for the baby. "Now that adult laxative up there," she pointed: "my doctor would advise against it. He would recommend one made *especially* for children . . . one like Fletcher's Castoria."

5. She told me that Fletcher's Castoria was designed especially and *only* for a baby's needs. It's gentle, as a baby's laxative *should* be. Yet very effective. It works mainly in the lower bowel—so it's not so likely to upset the stomach. And above all, she said Fletcher's Castoria is SAFE.

6. So I bought a bottle. It worked like a charm! But one of the pleasantest surprises was its nice taste. If your baby is a medicine-hater, as mine is, you know how important taste can be. So you can bet I keep Fletcher's Castoria always handy. (I honestly couldn't recommend a better laxative.)

Chas. H. Fletcher **CASTORIA**

The modern—SAFE—laxative made especially for children

34

thousand dollars to build a two-story brick factory, painted deep orange like the product's box, on the corner of Eighth Street and Webster Avenue. That building remains the home of Percy Medicine to this day.

After Trau and Collie died in 1946, two other men ran the company for several years. In 1955, William Clayton, Collie's son-in-law, took over the company until his death in 1995. Reese Killion bought Clayton's shares to take charge of the company.

Roughly once a month on a Saturday, the small team of company workers produces about six thousand bottles of Percy Medicine, which has a shelf life of three years, on a small production line on the second floor of the building. While several wholesale drug distributors ship cases of the medicine to a number of cities from Atlanta to San Francisco, Percy Medicine sells best in South Texas. Most American customers have trouble finding Percy Medicine on drugstore shelves.

Unfortunately, the current stockholders lack the capital to invest in wide-scale advertising and promotion of the product, not to mention modernizing the factory to accommodate the subsequent flood of orders. Instead, they just keep plugging away, churning out the three-ounce bottles of Percy Medicine whenever the need arises.

STRANGE FACTS

• The Percy Medicine box features a picture of Albert Percy, a boy cured of diarrhea by the elixir in 1898.

• Percy Medicine helps cure diarrhea, indigestion, and heartburn.

• In 1938, Merrick Medicine Co. dropped the word "Baby" from the name of "Percy Medicine."

• Merrick Medicine Co. holds the Texas Alcoholic Beverage Commission's oldest continuously active industrial alcohol permit, No. 10, issued in 1939. Percy contains 5 percent ethyl alcohol.

• In the 1960s, Merrick Medicine licensed a Mexico City plant to make "Medicina Percy," which accounted for about half the company's sales. Merrick lost control of the plant.

Famous Last Words

"The bullet hasn't been made that can kill me!"
*—Gangster Jack "Legs" Diamond,
just before being shot to death*

"Die? I should say not, dear fellow.
No Barrymore would allow such a
conventional thing to happen to him."
—John Barrymore, last words

"Friends applaud, the comedy is over."
—Ludwig van Beethoven, on his deathbed

"I should never have switched from Scotch to Martinis."
—Humphrey Bogart, on his deathbed

"That was the best ice-cream soda I ever tasted."
—Lou Costello, last words

"That was a great game of golf, fellers."
—Bing Crosby, last words

"Turn up the lights, I don't want to go home in the dark."
*—O. Henry, on his deathbed,
quoting a popular song*

"I wish I'd drunk more champagne."
—John Maynard Keynes, on his deathbed

"Go on, get out. Last words are for
fools who haven't said enough."
—*Karl Marx, on his deathbed*

"I hope I haven't bored you."
—*Elvis Presley,*
concluding what would be
his last press conference

"Nonsense, they couldn't hit an elephant at this distance."
—*John Sedgwick,*
refusing to hide behind a parapet
during the Battle of the Wilderness

"I have just had eighteen whiskeys in a row.
I do believe that is a record."
—*Dylan Thomas, last words*

"Don't let it end like this. Tell them I said something."
—*Francisco "Pancho" Villa, last words*

"This is no time to make new enemies."
—*Voltaire, when asked on his deathbed*
to renounce Satan

"I'd rather be fishing."
—*Jimmy Glass,*
electrocuted in Louisiana in 1987

"How about this for a headline for tomorrow's paper?
French fries."
—*James French,*
electrocuted in Oklahoma in 1966

SLOAN'S LINIMENT

In 1871, twenty-three-year-old Earl Sloan, a native of the village of Zanesfield, Ohio, and the son of a self-taught veterinarian who sold homemade horse liniment, took his father's liniment recipe and moved to Missouri, where his brother traded horses.

Earl began selling the horse tonic locally, and its popularity promoted the two brothers to travel to fairs and carnivals to sell it. When a customer used the liniment on himself to relieve his aches and pains and claimed that it was "Good for Man or Beast," the Sloan brothers adopted the slogan to promote their product.

Encouraged by their success, Earl traveled to Chicago and advertised Sloan's Liniment in newspapers and on streetcars as a remedy for muscle aches, arthritis, and rheumatism, resulting in huge sales. A few years later, he relocated to Boston, added the title "Dr." to his name, and through clever marketing, turned his liniment into a household staple. By 1904, he was a millionaire.

STRANGE FACTS

• Since women did the majority of household shopping, Sloan advertised his liniment primarily in the evening edition of newspapers, convinced that women did not have time to read the morning edition.

• Legend holds that a local librarian refused to loan a book to Sloan when he was a child because he was too poor. Determined to make sure future generations of children would never be denied access to books, Sloan built the Dr. Sloan Library in Zanesfield. Today, money from the Sloan Fund helps to educate the young people of Logan County, Ohio.

• Although he lived on a secluded nine-acre estate in West Roxbury, Massachusetts, Sloan and his wife are buried in the Hicksite cemetery near his hometown of Zanesfield, Ohio.

Secret Formula

HOMEMADE LINIMENT

WHAT YOU NEED

From the supermarket:
- 2 tablespoons Tabasco pepper sauce
- 2 cups apple cider vinegar

From the health food store:
- 2 ounce gum myrrh
- 1 ounce dried goldenseal

WHAT TO DO

Mix the Tabasco pepper sauce, vinegar, myrrh, and goldenseal into a saucepan and boil gently for ten minutes. Let cool, and pour into a sanitized glass bottle, cap tightly, and let sit in dark place for one week, shaking twice a day. Makes about two cups.

HOW YOU USE IT

When applied topically as a rub-down, this powerful liniment helps cure congestion, sprains, muscle aches, back aches, and bruises. Tabasco pepper sauce contains the alkaloid capsaicin, the active ingredient in remedies like Sloan's Liniment and Watkin's Red Liniment. Capsaicin deadens pain when applied topically and provides warm, soothing relief at your fingertips.

SMITH BROTHERS COUGH DROPS

In 1847, after candy maker James Smith moved his family from St. Armand, Quebec, to Poughkeepsie, New York, and opened a restaurant, a customer sold him the formula for a cough remedy for five dollars. Smith cleverly used the formula and his candy-making skills to create a cough lozenge. The lozenges, sold from a large glass bowl on drugstore counters, began to catch on as a remedy for cold symptoms. In 1852, Smith ran his first advertisement for the cough drops in a Poughkeepsie newspaper.

Smith's two sons, William and Andrew, helped him mix the secret formula in his kitchen and busily sold the product in the streets of Poughkeepsie. When their father died in 1866, the two sons inherited the business, officially naming the company Smith Brothers. As sales grew throughout the Hudson Valley, a flurry of imitators jumped on the bandwagon, marketing cough lozenges called "Schmitt Brothers," "Smythe Sisters" and even creating another "Smith Brothers." To beat the competition, the real Smith Brothers decided to use their bearded faces as the company trademark on the glass bowls for counter displays and on the small envelopes shopkeepers used to package the Smith Brothers Cough Drops for their customers.

In 1872, to stop drugstore owners from using the Smith Brothers bowl and envelopes to sell other company's lozenges, Andrew and William Smith designed the first box of Smith Brothers cough drops, featuring their bearded faces. Those two faces appear on boxes of Smith Brothers cough drops to this very day.

Secret Formula

NOSE DROPS

WHAT YOU NEED
From the supermarket:
- 1 teaspoon salt
- 2 cups warm distilled water (If you don't have distilled water, let tap water stand overnight in a shallow pan to allow the chlorine to escape.)

WHAT TO DO
Dissolve the salt in the warm water. Makes two cups.

HOW YOU USE IT
Don't let a nasty stuffed-up nose rain on your pajama party! To clear congested nasal passages, transfer this gentle saline solution to an atomizer and spray into your darling schnozzolla. If you don't have an atomizer, insert a drinking straw into a glass of the liquid, cover the open end of the straw with your finger, insert the straw in your nostril, release your finger from the straw, and inhale the liquid. Repeat several times, then it's tissue time! Blow your nose till your head is as clear as clear can be!

STRANGE FACTS

- Andrew Smith became known as "Trade" and William Smith became known as "Mark" because the word trademark is split into two syllables on the cough drop box, one half of the word under each image.
- Andrew Smith refused to allow ginger ale in his house because, as a fervent prohibitionist, he objected to the alcoholic nature of its name.
- The first newspaper advertisement for Smith Brothers Cough Drops read: "All afflicted with hoarseness, coughs, or colds should test its virtues, which can be done without the least risk."
- A box of Smith Brothers Cough Drops was the first factory-filled candy package in the United States.
- Confectioner William Luden, creator of Luden's Cough Drops in Reading, Pennsylvania, initiated the idea of lining the cough drop box with waxed paper to keep the candies fresh.
- In 1922, Smith Brothers introduced Menthol Cough Drops, followed in 1948 by Wild Cherry Flavor.

A Cough is a Social Blunder

People who know have no hesitation in avoiding the cougher. They know that he is a public menace. They know that his cough is a proof of his lack of consideration of others.

And they know that he knows it too, so they are not afraid of hurting his feelings.

For there is no excuse for coughing. It is just as unnecessary as any other bad habit. For it can be prevented or relieved by the simplest of precautions—the use of S. B. Cough Drops.

S. B. Cough Drops are not a cure for colds. They are a preventive of coughing. True, they often keep a cough from developing into a sore throat or cold. And they are a protection to the public because they keep people who already have influenza, colds and other throat troubles from spreading them through unnecessary coughing. Have a box with you always.

Pure. No Drugs. Just enough charcoal to sweeten the stomach.

One placed in the mouth at bedtime will keep the breathing passages clear.

Drop that Cough
SMITH BROTHERS *of Poughkeepsie*
FAMOUS SINCE 1847

Secret Formula

HOREHOUND COUGH DROPS

WHAT YOU NEED

From the garden or farmer's market:

- 1 quart fresh horehound leaves and stems

From the supermarket:

- 3 cups sugar
- 1/4 cup unsalted butter (1/2 stick)
- Cooking spray

From the tap:

- 2 cups water

WHAT TO DO

Spray a cookie sheet with a thin coat of cooking spray. Wash and chop the horehound leaves and stems. In a medium-size saucepan, boil the horehound leaves in the water for thirty minutes with the cover on to capture the steam.

Strain the resulting liquid and discard the leaves and stems. Stir the sugar into the liquid. Place a candy thermometer in the mixture and boil to the hard crack stage (300 degrees Fahrenheit). Stir in the butter, remove from the heat, and pour the candy solution onto the cookie sheet. Score into pieces with a knife before it sets. Let cool, then crack into pieces. Makes two pounds.

HOW YOU USE IT

Wrap each piece in wax paper, twist the paper at the ends, and store in a tightly covered jar. These potent cough drops immediately relieve your sore, scratchy throat with the full-flavored goodness of horehound herb. Yum!

Secret Formula

BRANDY-ONION COUGH SYRUP

WHAT YOU NEED

From the supermarket:

- 1 diced onion
- 4 ounces honey
- Juice of one lemon (or four tablespoons ReaLemon lemon juice)

From the liquor store:

- 2 jiggers brandy

WHAT TO DO

Place the diced onion in a bowl. Pour the honey over the onion, then add the brandy and lemon juice. Place in the refrigerator and let sit overnight. In the morning, strain the liquid, discard the onion, pour the syrup into a sanitized glass bottle, and cap securely. Makes 3/4 cup. Lasts one week refrigerated.

HOW YOU USE IT

Take two teaspoons of this pungent cough syrup once every three to four hours for instant relief. The onions knock out whatever bug has got you down, the honey soothes your throat, the lemon is an antiseptic, and the brandy—well, let's just say it's for medicinal purposes.

Secret Formula

WILD CHERRY COUGH SYRUP

WHAT YOU NEED

From the supermarket:
- 2 cups granulated sugar
- $1/2$ teaspoon cream of tartar
- 1 teaspoon cherry flavoring
- 2 teaspoons chopped dried marshmallow root

From the tap:
- 2 cups water

WHAT TO DO

Extract the flavor from the marshmallow root by boiling in water for roughly four minutes. Steep the mixture with the cover on the pot for a few minutes. Strain the resulting liquid and discard the root. Slowly stir in the sugar, cream of tartar, and cherry flavoring. Simmer until the mixture becomes thick and the sugar granules completely dissolve. Pour into a sterilized glass bottle, let cool, then cap tightly and store in the refrigerator. Makes roughly two cups.

HOW YOU USE IT

To relieve sore throat and clear congestion, take a maximum of two tablespoons of this tasty elixir once every two hours. Doctors use this trusted cough syrup on themselves. That tasty wild cherry flavor has been a favorite of anyone who feels like a sick tomato. If the symptoms persist for more than a few days, see a doctor, whom you may just find in his office chugging a bottle of this calming libation.

Secret Formula

LEMON-HONEY COUGH SYRUP

WHAT YOU NEED

From the supermarket:
- $1/2$ cup honey
- Juice from one lemon (or four tablespoons ReaLemon lemon juice)

From the drugstore:
- 1 tablespoon glycerin

WHAT TO DO

In a microwave-safe bowl, warm the lemon juice in the microwave for one minute. Add the glycerin and honey, mixing well. Store the syrup in a sterilized glass bottle, tightly capped, in the refrigerator. Good for up to two months. Makes $3/4$ cup.

HOW YOU USE IT

Take two tablespoons of this tangy cough syrup once every two hours to stifle that pesky cough. If the syrup becomes too thick from sitting on a cold shelf, warm the bottle slowly by setting it in a pan of warm water. If those nagging symptoms persist for more than a few days, see a doctor—but chances are you won't have to thanks to this wholesome remedy that soothes your sore throat while it puts that cough to rest.

SMITH'S ROSEBUD SALVE

In 1892, pharmacist George F. Smith, proprietor of an apothecary in Woodsboro, Maryland, invented a salve made from rosebuds. Smith sent out his Rosebud Salve "on trust" to adults and children who sold the product door-to-door for pay or premiums that included cameras, watches, rifles, and lace curtains. Smith got paid after his salespeople sold the product. The salve sold more than two million boxes annually. During the Depression, however, the honor system fell

Secret Formula

ROSE COLD CREAM

WHAT YOU NEED

From the supermarket:
- 1 teaspoon borax

From the drugstore:
- 4 ounces (weight) lanolin
- 2/3 cup mineral oil (or baby oil)

From the health food store:
- 10 drops rose fragrance oil

From a hobby center or candle supply store:
- 1/2 cup beeswax
- 1 tablespoon paraffin

From the tap:
- 3/4 cup water

WHAT TO DO

In the top of a double boiler, melt the beeswax, paraffin, lanolin, and mineral oil to 160 degrees Fahrenheit, stirring well. In a separate pot, heat the borax and water to 160 degrees Fahrenheit, making sure the borax is dissolved, then add the rose fragrance oil. Pour the water mixture into the oil mixture slowly, stirring constantly until a white cream forms. Remove from heat and stir slowly until the mixture cools to 100 degrees Fahrenheit. Pour the cream into small, wide-mouth jars, and cover tightly. Makes 1 1/2 cups.

HOW YOU USE IT

Say "hasta la vista!" to wrinkles with this creamy cold cream that instantly softens and rejuvenates cracked, dry skin. Women report that they can feel this cold cream working even before it touches their face! Now that's strong stuff! You too can have skin as soft as a baby's behind by simply applying this magical cold cream to your face around the clock!

apart. Sellers, unable to make ends meet, neglected to remit the company's share of the proceeds.

The vestiges of Smith's pharmacy, including the mortar and pestle he used to mix remedies, are on display in the company's current headquarters in an old three story hotel across the street from the spot where Smith's pharmacy originally stood in downtown Woodsboro. Today, Rosebud Perfume Company is run by two of Smith's granddaughters.

The salve is now manufactured in Baltimore to Rosebud's specifications and shipped to Woodsboro. The ladies type out mailing labels on a manual Royal typewriter and personally pack boxes full of Rosebud and other salves and send them to customers, including beauty-salon chains in California, Walgreens, the herb shop at the Washington National Cathedral, a London-based concern known as Mister Mustache, and small business owners in small towns across America.

STRANGE FACTS
• Rosebud Salve's red, white, and blue tins decorated with a garland of rosebuds boast "New Package Adopted 1962."
• Rosebud Salve has been touted in articles in magazines including *Glamour*, *Allure*, *Woman's Day*, and *Self*.

THAYERS

In 1847, Dr. Henry Thayer opened a laboratory in Cambridge, Massachusetts, to produce his newly developed line of herbal extracts with standardized strengths for sale to the medical profession. The Henry Thayer & Company grew, becoming the largest manufacturer of pharmaceuticals in America by the time of the Civil War.

By 1875, the company sold over eight hundred different products, including Fluid Extract of Witch Hazel, Lotion for Humors and Eruptions, and Hair Restorative. After Thayer's death in 1902, his great niece, Mrs. Joseph Sturdevant, took over the company and began marketing "patent" medicines, including Slippery Elm Lozenges.

In 1947, Chase, Storrow Co. of Boston, a partnership of former Harvard roommates and recent Navy veterans, bought the company and began an ambitious sales and advertising campaign to expand distribution. Within the next ten years, Thayers Slippery Elm Lozenges, Cough Syrup, Nose Drops, and Cold Sore Balm could be found in drugstores and health food stores across the United States and Canada. In 1989, the company added a line of Witch Hazel products. In 1999, Karen Clarke, who had been managing the business for five years, bought the company.

TIGER BALM

Ancient Chinese herbalists and healers formulated a soothing analgesic balm blended from natural ingredients to treat Chinese emperors who suffered from various aches and pains.

At the turn of the twentieth century, Chinese herbalist Aw Chu Kin, living in Rangoon, Burma, unearthed the recipe for the original balm. He discovered that a salve blended from camphor, menthol, clove oil, and cajaput oil creates a mild topical analgesic that relieves muscular aches and promotes blood flow.

His two sons, Aw Boon Par and Aw Boon Haw, marketed the balm. Aw Boon Haw gave his name, meaning Tiger (an Eastern symbol of strength and vitality), to the remedy. The two brothers moved to Singapore in 1926 and transformed their father's homemade remedy into a world-renowned brand.

Tiger Balm, the world's best known Chinese medicine, is not made from tiger, just as Turtle Wax does not contain turtles, nor horseradish any horses.

Secret Formula

HOMEMADE "TIGER BALM"

WHAT YOU NEED

From the drugstore:
- 2 ounces petroleum jelly

From the health food store or perfume supply house:
- 10 ounces menthol crystals
- 16 ounces camphor blocks
- 2 ounces essential oil of clove
- 2 ounces essential oil of cajuput oil
- 2 ounces essential oil of cinnamon

From the hobby store or candle craft shop:
- 10 ounces beeswax

From the chemical supply store:
- 1 ounce ammonium hydroxide (optional)

WHAT TO DO

Grate the camphor. Melt the beeswax and petroleum jelly in a saucepan over low heat until completely liquefied. Remove from heat, quickly stir in the grated camphor. Add the menthol, clove oil, cajuput oil, cinnamon oil, and ammonium hydroxide (if desired). Stir until the camphor has melted and the mixture achieves a consistent blend. Pour into a sanitized glass jar and let cool. (Adding ammonium hydroxide turns the balm red and adds more heat.) Makes 5 1/2 cups.

HOW YOU USE IT

Massage well into the affected areas two or three times a day. This professional-strength salve, with its brisk aroma, produces dramatic results by sending relieving warmth coursing through achy muscles to revive and enliven your body. Now isn't that worth all the effort?

VASELINE

In 1859, Robert Augustus Chesebrough, a Brooklyn chemist whose kerosene business faced impending closure, traveled to Titusville, Pennsylvania, to enter the competing petroleum business. Intrigued by the jelly residue that gunked up drilling rods, Chesebrough learned from workers that the jelly quickened healing when rubbed on a wound or burn. Chesebrough brought jars of the whipped gunk back to Brooklyn where he purified the petroleum lard into a clear, smooth gel he called "petroleum jelly" and started manufacturing Vaseline in 1887.

Secret Formula

"PETROLEUM" JELLY

WHAT YOU NEED

From the drugstore:
- ¹/₂ cup mineral oil (or baby oil)

From the hobby store or candle craft shop:
- 1 ounce (weight) beeswax

WHAT TO DO

Melt the beeswax in a double boiler. Stir in the mineral oil. Blend well. Remove from heat and stir until cool.

Store in a sealed airtight container. Makes ³/₄ cup.

HOW YOU USE IT

This soothing salve—fortified with the all-natural power of beeswax—works magic on dry hands, small wounds, and burns. Use just as you would any petroleum jelly to speed healing with this fast-acting blend of everything that makes America good and decent.

VICKS VAPORUB

In 1905, Lunsford Richardson, a pharmacist working in his brother-in-law's drugstore in Selma, North Carolina, aspired to create an ointment to decongest sinuses and relieve chest congestion. In the back-room laboratory of the pharmacy, he blended menthol (a newly introduced extract from oil of peppermint), petroleum jelly, and other ingredients from the pharmacy shelf. He named his creation Richardson's Croup and Pneumonia Cure Salve. When rubbed on the forehead and chest, the salve—vaporized by body heat—stimulated blood circulation and decongested blocked sinuses.

Demand for the salve exceeded Richardson's wildest expectations, prompting the pharmacist to market his new remedy. Seeking a catchier name for the product, Richardson decided to name it in honor of his brother-in-law, Joshua Vick. He advertised Vicks VapoRub in local newspapers, with coupons redeemable for a free trial jar. He convinced the United States Postal Service to institute a new policy allowing him to send out advertisements for Vicks VapoRub addressed solely to "Boxholder," effectively creating the concept of junk mail. The 1918 Spanish Flu epidemic—killing 25 million people worldwide—sent sales of Vicks VapoRub skyrocketing, surpassing one million dollars.

Read, Reason & REFLECT!

DR. PARMENTER'S
MAGNETIC OIL!
Will Cure Rheumatism!

TO THOSE AFFLICTED!

This Oil is warranted to ease more pain in less time, than any other medicine now in use. Call and test its Virtue; it removes the worst Rheumatic pain in 30 minutes; pains in the side, breast and back, in 20 minutes; Nervous Headache in 10 minutes; Croup in 20 minutes; Chilblains in one night, and is a sure cure for chapped hands. The Oil acts on the System on the principle of Electricity, regulates the whole system, and is perfectly safe in all cases. **PRICE 25 CENTS PER BOTTLE.**

PRINCIPAL DEPOT,
No. 9 Cooper's Buildings, cor. State & Green Sts.,
ALBANY, N. Y., and for sale by Druggists generally, throughout the United States and the Canadas. Druggists, Merchants and Peddlers supplied at the lowest prices,

By Dr. WM. O. PARMENTER.

BAKER TAYLOR, PRINTER, 60 STATE STREET, ALBANY

WATKINS RED LINIMENT

In 1868, twenty-eight-year-old Joseph R. Watkins of Plainview, Minnesota, hand mixed Asian camphor, extract of capsicum, oil of spruce, and other botanicals in a vat, creating his Red Liniment and giving birth to the J. R. Watkins Medical Company, one of America's first natural remedies companies.

Watkins traveled around the countryside, delivering his liniment door to door from the rear of his horse drawn wagon. Determined to give his customers honest value for their hard-earned money, Watkins offered his customers America's first money-back guarantee. He had a special "Trial-Mark" molded into the bottle of his liniment. He would leave the bottle with the customer upon payment, and if the product

had not been used past the mark by his next visit, Watkins would give the customer a full refund.

When demand for Red Liniment escalated, Watkins hired salesmen to travel by horse and buggy to market his products, founding the direct sales industry. "The Watkins Man," like the latter-day "Avon Lady," became an American icon.

Watkins devoted his energies to creating more remedies for his product line. In 1885, he moved his company headquarters twenty-five miles south to Winona, Minnesota. In 1895, Watkins extended his product line to include such natural foods as vanilla extract, black pepper, and cinnamon. When he died in 1911, Watkins had more than 2,500 people selling his liniment and other products door-to-door.

STRANGE FACTS

• In 1901, Watkins published the first Watkins Almanac, Home Doctor, and Cookbook. A nearly complete collection of Watkins almanacs and calendars are featured in the Watkins museum in Winona, Minnesota.

• Watkins corporate headquarters has been located in the same office building near the banks of the Mississippi River since 1911.

• To this day, the J. R. Watkins Company sells its original Red Liniment.

Secret Formula

MASSAGE OIL

WHAT YOU NEED

From the supermarket:
• 4 cups almond oil

From the health food store:
• 1 ounce dried sage
• 8 drops essential oil of lemon

WHAT TO DO

Combine the almond oil and sage in a saucepan and bring to a slow, rolling boil, then simmer for ten minutes. Let cool, then strain (to remove the sage), and add essential oil of lemon, stirring well. Store this zesty massage oil in a light-proof bottle (such as a dark, clean wine bottle with a cork) and label. Makes one quart.

HOW YOU USE IT

Rub a small amount of this delicious oil on skin and massage into tired muscles to experience true relaxation. The sage rejuvenates sore muscles, the essential oil of lemon reawakens the senses, and the almond oil helps you feel, well, like a nut.

Z-M-O Oil

In the 1800s, pharmacist M. R. "Doc" Zaegel traveled west by covered wagon, brought along his jars and canisters of curing oils and boxes of myrrh and aloes, and settled in Sheboygan, Wisconsin, where he opened a small chemist shop. Doc Zaegel mixed salves, syrups, ointments, and powders, which he administered to patients.

Determined to find one general remedy for all minor aches and pains, Doc Zaegel experimented with various combinations until he formulated a curative oil that he bottled and sold to those seeking relief. Over the years, buyers returned to buy more, reporting the miraculous results achieved with Doc Zaegel's oil.

In the late 1870s, a railroad construction worker laying track in Sheboygan, fell victim to a crushing and painful injury. His fellow workers, convinced that the man would never recover, called for Doc Zaegel, who rushed to the scene. Zaegel cleansed the man's wounds and then gently massaged his oil over the afflicted areas. Remarkably, the victim's pain began to subside, the injuries healed rapidly, and railroad workers began spreading word of Zaegel's Magic Oil along the railroad lines.

Orders for bottles of the oil began pouring in to Zaegel's shop, and the Doc began shipping bottles of his oil across America. Satisfied customers were soon sending in letters testifying to the oil's miraculous properties for treating their own ills and the ills of their livestock, including barbed wire cuts, shipping fevers, and infections.

At the turn of the century, Zaegel began to advertise his "pain relieving oil for man or beast." Early advertisements explained how people could use the oil to "assist nature in the healing of a wound that is better than any salve or ointment because it does not lay on the skin, but penetrates into the wound." Doc Zaegel changed the name of his remedy to "Zaegel's Magnetic Oil" and later shortened the name to "Z-M-O Oil," as the public called it.

STRANGE FACTS

• After the death of Doc Zaegel, Mace Laboratories Inc. of Neenah, Wisconsin, took over the production of Z-M-O.

• In 1965, H. C. Glessner of Findlay, Ohio, purchased the Z-M-O formula and formed the Z-M-O Company, filling mail orders for the many faithful users of Z-M-O.

• In 1976, the family of Ruth and Russell Schaffner bought the company and moved it to Grove City, Ohio. Today, the company is run by the Schaffner's offspring—Ronald and Doris (Schaffner) Johnson and their son, Keith, and Donald and Marie Schaffner and their son, Philip.

• Z-M-O's original formula, patented on October 10, 1899, has never been changed. The ingredients in Z-M-O remain identical to those found in the original oil.

The Rx for Rexall

The Big Boys

In 1903, pharmacist Louis Liggett decided to unite independent pharmacists, then working in concert with the town doctors to provide medical care on an individualized basis, into a national organization called United Drug.

Liggett developed patent medicines that pharmacists could prescribe over-the-counter to their patients. Liggett named his line of patent medicines Rexall Products (short for "Rx to all"). When Rexall became a household word, the stores became Rexall stores.

The Rexall name eventually appeared on some three-hundred company-owned stores and approximately twelve thousand franchised outlets (roughly 20 percent of the drugstores in the United States). In 1977, a group of private investors bought the chain for sixteen million dollars, sold off the stores (allowing former franchisees to continue using the Rexall name), slashed the company's manufacturing capacity, and focused on distributing vitamins, health foods, and health care products.

In 1985, Sundown Vitamins, Inc., a company founded in 1976 by Carl DeSantis, a former executive for Super X Drugstores and Walgreen Drugstores, acquired control of the Rexall name and distribution rights. Five years later, Sundown Vitamins launched Rexall Showcase International (RSI), a direct-marketing ("multilevel") company, to capitalize on the trusted Rexall name to sell weight management products, homeopathic medicines, personal care products, nutritional supplements, and water filtration systems. In 1993, Sundown Vitamins changed its name to Rexall Sundown, Inc.

2

The

CANDY COUNTER

Sweets, Treats, and Old-Time Favorites

Just the thought of a countertop filled with glistening jars of candies of every kind sends children and the young at heart into paroxysms of glee. Country stores sold penny candies— stick candy, rock candy, lemon gum drops, cinnamon red hots, marshmallow drops, cream bonbons, lozenges, candy-coated peanuts, jawbreakers, licorice whips—by weight, carefully measured in a scale, and wrapped in a small paper bag. Many old favorites—Necco Wafers, Tootsie Rolls, Milk Duds—are still around today, but most were lost to history. Come explore the candy counter, and learn how you can make some of your candy favorites by simply dissolving sugar in water at different heating levels.

BABY RUTH

In 1916 during World War I, Otto Schnering founded the Curtiss Candy Company, using his mother's Anglo-sounding maiden name for the company rather than his German-sounding surname. For his first product, Schnering introduced Kandy Kake, a confection with a pastry center topped with nuts and coated with chocolate, which met with moderate success. In 1921, Schnering reformulated Kandy Kake as a bar of caramel and peanuts, covered with chocolate. He renamed his confection the Baby Ruth bar, not after baseball legend Babe Ruth as commonly believed, but in honor of "Baby" Ruth Cleveland, the daughter of former President Grover Cleveland, who had been adored by millions. Priced at a nickel while other candy bars sold for a dime, Baby Ruth was the world's most popular candy by 1926, selling more than five million bars a day.

In 1963, Standard Brands acquired the Curtiss Candy Company, which, in turn, was purchased in 1981 by Nabisco Brands. In 1990, Nestlé bought Baby Ruth brand from Nabisco.

STRANGE FACTS

• In 1904, twelve-year-old Ruth Cleveland died of diphtheria. Seventeen years later, the Curtiss Candy Company produced the first Baby Ruth bar, a year after baseball player Babe Ruth rose to stardom. Skeptics question whether the Curtiss Candy Company capitalized on Babe Ruth's popularity by simply claiming that its candy bar was named for Ruth Cleveland.

• Otto Schnering advertised extensively in magazines, including *The Saturday Evening Post,* and *Open Road for Boys,* trumpeting the new candy bar with slogans like "The Favorite Candy of Over Fifty Million People!"

• Schnering chartered planes to drop thousands of Baby Ruth bars with tiny parachutes over various cities across forty states.

• In 1937, Admiral Richard Byrd and his team brought thousands of Baby Ruth bars on their expedition to the South Pole.

• When a competing candy company introduced the "Babe Ruth Home Run Bar," with the full approval of Babe Ruth, the Curtiss Candy Company threatened legal action and forced the Babe Ruth Home Run Bar off the market.

BIT-O-HONEY

In 1924, the Schutter-Johnson Company in Chicago introduced Bit-O-Honey, a honey-flavored taffy bar made with bits of almond. Bit-O-Honey provides a unique honey taste with a long-lasting chew. In the 1960s, Chunky Corporation acquired Bit-O-Honey. In 1984, Nestlé bought Bit-O-Honey, which it now markets through its Sunline Brands division.

Do-It-Yourself Recipe

HOMEMADE "BIT-O-HONEY"

WHAT YOU NEED

From the supermarket:

- 1/2 cup honey
- 1/2 cup sugar
- 1 ounce almond paste
- 1 cup dry powdered milk

WHAT TO DO

Melt honey, sugar, and almond paste together, stirring with a wooden spoon, until reaching the soft-crack stage at 270 degrees Fahrenheit. Let cool to 180 degrees Fahrenheit. Add dry powdered milk and mix well with the wooden spoon. Let cool to 110 degrees Fahrenheit and roll out on a cutting board. Cut into rectangular chunks about one inch long. Let harden. Wrap in wax paper to store. Makes approximately three dozen chunks.

BOBS PEPPERMINT STICKS

In 1918, returning World War I veteran Lieutenant Bob McCormack decided to start a candy factory. The following year, he opened the Famous Candy Company in the small town of Albany, Georgia, with five employees.

Working as salesman, bookkeeper, and plant manager, McCormack soon renamed his company after himself, since everyone referred to his confections as "Bobs Candies." He specialized in pecan candy and also made fudges, stick candy, coconut bars, and peanut candies.

In the 1950s, McCormack's brother-in-law Gregory Keller, a Catholic priest, invented and patented the first machine to automatically make stick candy. Bobs Candies then developed and patented box and case designs that made possible the safe shipment of fragile candy canes. These innovations catapulted Bobs Candies to the forefront of the confections industry, making the company the world's largest producer of candy canes. To this day, Bobs Candies remains a family-run business.

STRANGE FACTS
• In the 1920s, Bobs Candies became the first candy manufacturer to wrap its product in the newly developed transparent paper called Cellophane.
• During World War II, sugar rationing compelled Bobs Candies to develop other products, including peanut butter and cracker sandwiches.
• During World War II, the United States military issued Bobs specially formulated hard candies in soldiers' ration kits.

CHICLETS

When Mexican dictator General Antonio de Santa Anna went into exile, he lived with photographer and tradesman Thomas Adams at his home in Staten Island, New York. Santa Anna suggested that Adams attempt to develop a synthetic rubber tire by vulcanizing rubber with chicle from Mexican sapota trees, supplied by Santa Anna's friends in Mexico. Adams, having failed in his attempts to make synthetic rubber from chicle, planned to throw the remaining chicle into the East River—until he heard a little girl ask for chewing gum in a local corner drugstore. Adams suddenly recalled that native Mexicans used chicle as a chewing gum and realized that he could use his supply of chicle to make chewing gum. Adams and his son, Tom Jr., having been chewing the chicle while experimenting on the rubber-blending project, made up a few boxes of chicle chewing gum, named it Adams New York Gum No. 1, and wrapped the little penny sticks in different colored tissue papers.

STRANGE FACTS

• In 1899, five of the largest chewing gum manufacturers in the United States and Canada, which included Adams, combined to form a dominant conglomerate in the chewing gum industry.

• General Antonio de Santa Anna ruled Mexico as president three times and was overthrown three times. He defeated Texan troops in the Battle of the Alamo at San Antonio, resulting in the deaths of James Bowie and Davy Crockett, and giving rise to the battle cry, "Remember the Alamo!"

CRACKER JACK

In 1872, German immigrant F. W. Rueckheim opened a popcorn stand in Chicago, Illinois. Brisk business soon enabled Rueckheim to send to Germany for his brother, Louis. F. W. Rueckheim & Bro. soon expanded into candy making and, at the 1893 World's Columbian Exposition, the duo introduced a unique popcorn-and-peanut molasses-coated candy—the forerunner of Cracker Jack caramel-coated popcorn and peanuts. Unfortunately, the original candy kernels, while popular, stuck together in blocks—until 1896, when Louis discovered a secret process to keep them separate. Louis gave the molasses-covered treat to a salesman, who after tasting it, exclaimed "That's crackerjack!" F. W. Rueckheim immediately embraced the slang word (meaning excellent) and had it trademarked. In 1899, the Rueckheim brothers packaged Cracker Jack in wax-sealed boxes that preserved the candy's freshness, enabling the brothers to ship their product to stores nationwide.

In 1912, the Rueckheim brothers added "a prize in every box" of Cracker Jack. Over the years, the "toy surprise inside" has included rings, yo-yos, whistles, charms, tops, plastic toys, miniature storybooks, super-hero stick-ons, and tiny tattoos.

In 1964, Borden, Inc., based in Columbus, Ohio, bought the Cracker Jack Company. In 1997, Frito-Lay of Dallas, Texas, purchased Cracker Jack from Borden.

STRANGE FACTS

• The 1902 Sears & Roebuck catalogue included Cracker Jack.
• In 1908, Jack Norworth wrote the lyrics to song "Take Me Out to the Ball Game" during a thirty-minute subway ride, immortalizing Cracker Jack brand in the third line, "Buy me some peanuts and Cracker Jack." Albert Von Tilzer, who composed the music to the song, did not see a baseball game until more than twenty years after the song's release. Norworth witnessed his first baseball game in 1940 when the Brooklyn Dodgers honored him at Ebbets Field.
• In 1918, Sailor Jack and his dog Bingo first appeared on the Cracker Jack box. Sailor Jack was modeled after F. W. Rueckheim's grandson Robert, who had a dog named Bingo. Robert, who died of pneumonia shortly after the new box appeared, is buried in St. Henry's cemetery, near Chicago, under a headstone with a depiction of him in his sailor suit.

- In the 1961 movie *Breakfast at Tiffany's,* Holly Golightly, played by Audrey Hepburn, pays Tiffany's to engrave initials on a ring from a Cracker Jack box.
- The Cracker Jack Company maintains an archive of all the toys ever put in Cracker Jack boxes and displays some of the best toys at its Chicago headquarters.
- Since 1912, Cracker Jack has given out more than twenty-three billion toys.
- The secret process for keeping the molasses-covered popcorn morsels from sticking together, discovered by Louis Rueckheim in 1896, is still used to produce Cracker Jack and remains a company secret to this very day.

Do-It-Yourself Recipe

HOMEMADE "CRACKER JACK"

WHAT YOU NEED

From the supermarket:
- 6 cups popped corn
- 1 cup roasted, unsalted peanuts
- 1 tablespoon butter
- $1/2$ cup molasses
- $1/4$ cup sugar

WHAT TO DO

Pour the popcorn and peanuts into a large pan. Melt the butter in a saucepan, then add the molasses and sugar, blending the ingredients together. Heat to the soft-crack stage at 290 degrees Fahrenheit. Pour the liquid candy over the popcorn and peanuts, stirring the mixture with a wooden spoon to make sure the popcorn and peanuts are evenly coated with candy. Lay on wax paper to dry. Makes six cups.

DOTS

In 1864, Joseph Mason and Ernest von Au founded Mason & Au confectioners in Brooklyn, New York. In 1883, Emil Zollinger joined the company, which became Mason, Au & Zollinger. The next year, Louis Magenheimer joined the company, which eventually became Mason, Au & Magenheimer. The confectionery company made Mason Peaks, a coconut candy bar covered with chocolate, and Mason Mints, a chocolate-covered mint patty.

In 1890, company founders Ernest von Au and Joseph Mason introduced a candy intended to be called Black Rose, but the printer heard the name as Black Crows and so he printed up wrappers with the wrong name for the candy. Rather than forcing the printer to reprint the wrappers, Mason kept the name Crows.

In 1945, the company formally introduced and trademarked Mason Dots, a soft gumdrop in assorted fruit flavors.

In 1949, Mason, Au & Magenheimer relocated to Long Island, New York. The business was sold in the 1960s to Bayuk Cigar, then to the Candy Corporation of America, and in 1972 to Tootsie Roll Industries, which continues to make Mason Dots and Crows.

DR PEPPER

In 1885, Charles Alderton, a young pharmacist working at Wade Morrison's Old Corner Drugstore in the central Texas town of Waco, also served carbonated drinks at the soda fountain. Realizing that customers were tired of drinking the same old fruit flavors, he began experimenting with flavors of his own until he hit upon one he liked—which he tested on Wade Morrison, who also liked the new soft drink.

Alderton then offered his new drink to some of his soda-fountain customers. They liked it, too. Word spread, and soon everyone at Morrison's soda fountain was ordering the new soft drink, called a "Waco," because Waco was the only place it was available. Patrons suggested that Morrison name the new bittersweet fountain drink Dr. Pepper, after Dr. William R. Pepper, the Virginia physician who purportedly refused to let him marry his daughter, Minerva. (The period after "Dr" was dropped in 1950.) Legend holds that Wade Morrison returned to Virginia and finally won the hand of Dr. Pepper's daughter, but in fact he married Carrie B. Jeffress in 1882 and remained married to her until his death in 1924.

Soon other soda-fountain operators in Waco began buying the syrup from Morrison and serving it. Morrison decided to bottle the drink, and in 1891 formed the Artesian Manufacturing and Bottle Company (named after the many artesian wells in the area that supposedly supplied healthful water). Robert S. Lazenby, a young beverage chemist hired to run the plant, perfected and stabilized the formula for bottling. Alderton, the soft drink's

Candy Is Dandy

• The first sweet treat was discovered when cavemen ate honey from bee hives.

• Ancient Egyptians, Arabs, and Chinese prepared the first confections by candying fruit and nuts with honey.

• During the Middle Ages in Europe, only the wealthy could afford sugar candy due to the high cost of sugar.

• Hot temperatures yield hard candy, medium heat makes soft candy, and cool temperatures create chewy candy.

• The Mayan and Aztec civilizations of Central America used to make a drink from the beans of the cacao tree. In 1528, Spanish colonists brought the cocoa drink back to Europe. Three hundred years later, a method was found to produce solid chocolate.

• In 1868, Richard Cadbury invented the first "chocolate box" by decorating a candy box with a painting of his young daughter holding a kitten in her arms. Cadbury also introduced the first Valentine's Day candy box.

• Fake glass windows and fake glass bottles broken over the heads of movie stars in Hollywood films were originally made from sugar.

• Sugar, the main ingredient in candy, is also used for mixing cement.

• During World War II, soldiers called a letter from one's sweetheart a "sugar report."

• In his address before the Canadian Senate and House of Commons in 1941, Winston Churchill said, "We have not journeyed all this way across the centuries, across the oceans, across the mountains, across the prairies, because we are made of sugar candy."

• During World War II, women working on the Whitman's Sampler production line secretly slipped notes to soldiers in those boxes destined for military shipment. The notes resulted in several long-term friendships and even a few marriages.

• The average American uses ninety pounds of sugar every year.

• Americans spend more than one billion dollars each Valentine's Day on candy, making it the fourth biggest holiday for confectionery purchases (after Halloween, Christmas, and Easter).

originator, remained more interested in the pharmacy than the soft-drink business.

In 1904, Lazenby introduced Dr. Pepper to almost twenty million people attending the 1904 World's Fair Exposition in St. Louis. In 1923, Lazenby and his son-in-law, J. B. O'Hara, moved the company to Dallas and changed the name to the Dr. Pepper Company. O'Hara eventually became president of the company and expanded sales throughout the United States. In 1986, the Dr Pepper Company merged with the Seven-Up Company to form Dr Pepper/Seven-Up Companies, Inc., which was acquired in 1995 by Cadbury Schweppes.

STRANGE FACTS

• Dr. Pepper was invented one year before Coca-Cola (1886) and six years before Pepsi-Cola (1901).

• The original formula for Dr. Pepper did not contain caffeine or cocaine because some researchers at the time considered caffeine and cocaine dangerous, even though both substances were legal.

• In 1917, Robert Lazenby, president of the company, decided to add caffeine to Dr. Pepper. In 1939, Dr. Pepper executives took the caffeine out and added vitamin B-1, reasoning that the drink would be healthier and therefore more popular. Unfortunately, the vitamin caused the soft drink to go bad and changed the taste. Vitamin B-1 was promptly taken out of Dr. Pepper.

• The original advertising slogan for Dr. Pepper was "Liquid Sunshine."

• Twenty-three fruit flavors make up Dr. Pepper.

• When Dr. Pepper made its debut at the 1904 World's Fair Exposition in St. Louis, the exposition also marked the first time in history that hamburgers and hot dogs were served on buns. The exposition also witnessed the introduction of the edible ice cream cone.

• In 1906, the Dr. Pepper Company bought the Freckleater Company, which manufactured an ointment for removing freckles from the skin. In 1907, Dr. Pepper sold the Freckleater Company back to its original owner for the same price it was purchased.

• During the 1920s and 1930s, while Dr. Pepper was sold by "Old Doc," a typical country-doctor character with monocle and top hat, Dr. Walter Eddy, a professor at Columbia University, discovered that the average person experiences a slump of energy during the normal day at 10:30 A.M., 2:30 P.M., and 4:30 P.M. Since research also showed that the sugar in Dr. Pepper provided energy, J. B. O'Hara originated the famous advertising slogan, "Drink a bite to eat at 10, 2, and 4," which was eventually abbreviated to the mysterious "10-2-4" on the bottles.

• Dr. Pepper's advertising slogans have included "If Atlas were on earth, he would recommend Dr. Pepper," and "It leaves a pleasant farewell and a gracious call back."

• In 1963, Dr Pepper introduced "Dietetic Dr Pepper," but changed the name three years later after realizing that people confused the word dietetic with diabetic.

• Dr Pepper went from being "the most misunderstood soft drink" in the 1960s, to "the most original soft drink ever" in the 1970s.

• In 1991, the Dr Pepper Museum and Free Enterprise Institute opened in the classic 1906 "Richardsonian Romanesque" building in downtown Waco, Texas, that served as the national headquarters for Dr. Pepper until 1922. The building stands three blocks from the original site of Morrison's Old Corner Drugstore, where Dr. Charles Alderton first created Dr. Pepper in 1885. The building is the only surviving early headquarters for a major American soft drink. Aside from showcasing the history of Dr Pepper, the museum boasts one of the largest soft-drink collections in the world, a working antique soda fountain, and a gift shop with a catalog offering more than 1,500 items.

DUBBLE BUBBLE

In 1928, twenty-three-year-old Walter E. Deimer, an accountant working for the Fleer Chewing Gum Company in Philadelphia, tinkered with new gum recipes in his spare time. One batch turned out less sticky and more elastic than regular chewing gum, stretching easily. "It was an accident," admitted Deimer. "I was doing something else and ended up with something with bubbles."

Envisioning the possibilities, Deimer brought a five-pound chunk of the pink, popping bubble gum to a grocery store to be sold in small pieces. The gum sold out by the end of the afternoon.

The Fleer Chewing Gum Company marketed Deimer's invention as Dubble Bubble for a penny a piece. Deimer taught the company's salesmen how to blow bubbles so they could demonstrate the gum's unique property. The innovative accountant rose to become senior vice president of the company. While he never received any royalties for his invention, he felt tremendously rewarded knowing he had created something that made kids happy around the world.

STRANGE FACTS

• The National Association of Chewing Gum Manufacturers reports that children in North American spend 500 million dollars each year to chew 100,000 pounds of bubble gum.
• During World War II, the United States military issued Dubble Bubble in soldiers' ration kits.
• In 1962, 106-year-old Mary Francis Stubbs became the oldest bubble-gum chewer in the world.

GOOD & PLENTY

In 1893, the Quaker City Confectionery Company in Philadelphia introduced Good & Plenty candy, the oldest branded candy still being marketed in the United States. In 1950, the company began running advertisements featuring the cartoon character Choo Choo Charlie, an engineer who fueled his train with Good & Plenty. Television commercials for Good & Plenty featured the Choo Choo Charlie Good & Plenty theme song.

Warner-Lambert acquired Good & Plenty candy in 1973 and sold the operation to Beatrice Foods in 1982. A year later, Huhtamaki Oy of Finland purchased Leaf Brands, the confectionery division of Beatrice Foods, acquiring the Good & Plenty brand. In 1996, Hershey Foods Corporation bought Leaf's North America confectionery operations, capturing the Good & Plenty brand.

Choo Choo Charlie Good & Plenty Theme Song

Once upon a time there was an engineer,
Choo Choo Charlie was his name, we hear;
He had an engine and he sure had fun,
He used Good & Plenty candy to make his train run.
Charlie says, "Love my Good & Plenty!"
Charlie says, "Really rings my bell!"
Charlie says, "Love my Good & Plenty!
Don't know any other candy that I love so well!"

HERSHEY'S KISSES

In 1887, Milton S. Hershey, a thirty-year-old Pennsylvania Dutchman who had worked as an apprentice to a candy maker, founded Lancaster Caramel Company and began manufacturing caramels. In 1900, inspired by a new chocolate-making machine he had seen at the 1893 Chicago Exposition, he sold his caramel company for one million dollars to start a chocolate factory in Derry Church, Pennsylvania, to manufacture America's first mass-marketed five-cent chocolate bar. In 1905, the factory was completed and Hershey began producing individually wrapped Hershey's milk chocolate bars, followed by Hershey's Kisses Milk Chocolates in 1907.

Legend holds that Hershey's Kisses were named for the sound or motion that the machine nozzles make as they squeeze out a dollop of chocolate on the steel plate beneath them. Hershey's employees individually wrapped each Hershey's Kisses Chocolate until August 1921 when the company developed a single-channel machine to wrap the chocolates and insert a new element: the now familiar Hershey's Kisses flag.

Three years later, company founder Milton Hershey established a registered trademark for the "plume" extending out of the wrapper.

The machines that make Hershey's Kisses Chocolates now deposit the dollops of chocolate on a continuously moving stainless steel belt. The chocolate moves through a cooling tunnel for approximately eighteen minutes before emerging as a solid product. Machinery wraps

A Kiss for You

HERSHEY'S SWEET MILK CHOCOLATE KISSES

the Hershey Kisses in aluminum foil and bags the chocolates by weight. Hershey's quality assurance specialists check all Hershey's Kisses and reject all imperfectly wrapped chocolates.

STRANGE FACTS

• Derry Church, Pennsylvania, the home of Hershey's Foods, was renamed Hershey in 1906.

• In 1909, Milton Hershey and his wife founded the Milton Hershey School, a school for orphaned children, near the chocolate plant. In 1918, Hershey donated his entire interest in Hershey's Chocolate Corporation to the Milton Hershey School. Although Hershey Foods is now publicly traded, the Milton Hershey School still controls the company. Former Hershey's Food chairman William Dearden (1976–84) was a Hershey School graduate, as are many Hershey employees.

• Hershey has produced variations on Hershey's Kisses Chocolates using different chocolate formulas: Sweethearts (1900 to 1918), made with vanilla sweet chocolate and imprinted with a heart; Silvertops (1909 to 1931), Hershey's Kisses sold individually; and Silverpoints (1918 to 1929), made with a chocolate paste containing more milk.

• During the Depression, Milton Hershey put people to work by building a hotel, golf courses, a library, theaters, a museum, a stadium, and other facilities in Hershey, Pennsylvania.

• Hershey's ceased production of Hershey's Kisses from 1942 to 1949 due to the rationing of silver foil during and after World War II.

• In 1962, Hershey's introduced Hershey's Kisses wrapped in red and green foil for the Christmas season.

• In 1968, Hershey's introduced Hershey's Kisses in pastel blue and pink and followed in 1993 by Hershey's Hugs (mini Hershey's Kisses Chocolates coated with white chocolate) and Hershey's Hugs With Almonds.

• Hershey introduced Valentine's Hershey's Kisses with red and silver foil in 1986 and Fall Harvest Hershey's Kisses in 1991.

• Today's wrapping machines can wrap up to 1,300 Hershey's Kisses Chocolates a minute. That's equal to roughly 33 million Hershey's Kisses Chocolates every day (or more than twelve billion a year).

• Hershey Foods produces Hershey's Kisses at its plants in Hershey, Pennsylvania, and Oakdale, California.

• The street lights on Chocolate Avenue in Hershey, Pennsylvania, look like wrapped and unwrapped Hershey's Kisses Chocolates.

Do-It-Yourself Recipe

HOMEMADE CHOCOLATE KISSES

WHAT YOU NEED

From the supermarket:
• 1 cup sweetened chocolate chunks
• Wax paper

From a baking supply store:
• Candy molds

WHAT TO DO

Place an inch of water into the bottom section of a double boiler. Heat the water on the stove to a gentle simmer. Do not let the water boil. With a sharp knife, cut the chocolate into very small pieces or grate it with a grater. Place the chocolate pieces all at once into the top of the double boiler. Stir the chocolate constantly with a spoon until the chocolate melts. Remove the chocolate from the heat the instant it melts (otherwise the chocolate may scorch).

With a spoon, gently pour the melted chocolate into the candy molds. Gently tap the molds a few times on the countertop to eliminate air bubbles in the candy.

Carefully place the filled molds in the refrigerator until the bottom of the candy mold appears frosted.

Place a sheet of wax paper on the countertop, turn the mold upside-down about an inch above the paper, and gently flex the mold to remove the chocolate kisses. Makes approximately two dozen kisses.

JUJYFRUITS

In 1920, Henry Heide, Inc.—based in New Brunswick, New Jersey, and founded by German immigrant Henry Heide in 1869—introduced JuJyFruits. The chewy candy does not contain or get its name from the jujube, an edible plum-like fruit that grows in the tropics. Instead, JuJyFruits were named for one of its basic ingredients: ju-ju gum.

This small ju-ju candy comes in seven assorted shapes: asparagus, banana (embossed with the Heide name), grapes, pea pod, pineapple, raspberry, and tomato. They come in five flavored colors: lemon (yellow), licorice (black), lime (green), orange (orange), and raspberry (red).

When chewed, JuJyFruits frequently get stuck in teeth, much to the delight of true JuJyFruits aficionados who enjoy

Do-It-Yourself Recipe

HOMEMADE "JUJYFRUITS"

WHAT YOU NEED

From the supermarket:
- 3 teaspoons dry fruit pectin (with citric acid)
- 1/3 teaspoon baking soda
- 1 cup sugar
- 1 cup Light Karo Corn Syrup
- Crisco All-Vegetable Shortening
- Peppermint oil or cherry extract
- Food coloring

From the tap:
- 1/4 cup water

From a baking supply store:
- Candy mold

WHAT TO DO

Lightly grease the candy molds with shortening. In a small pan, mix together the pectin, water, and baking soda. Bring to a rolling boil, then reduce heat, stirring alternately until foam subsides in the pectin solution.

In a second larger pan, mix together the sugar and Light Karo Corn Syrup. Heat to the hard-ball stage at 250 degrees Fahrenheit.

Pour the pectin mixture into the sugar and corn syrup solution in a slow, steady stream.

Remove from the heat and stir in one teaspoon flavoring and food coloring as desired. Pour into prepared molds. Let set for twenty-four hours, then remove from the molds.

the challenge of a long-lasting chew, delivered by a flavorful candy that seems to bite you right back.

Farley's & Sathers Candy Company, Inc. acquired Heide brands and currently manufacturers JuJyFruits.

JUNIOR MINTS

In 1949, James Welch, the brother of Sugar Daddy originator Robert Welch, created Junior Mints, small chocolate-covered mint patties. Welch named the candy after the Broadway play Junior Miss.

The James O. Welch Company, which introduced the candies, was sold to Nabisco. Later, the Warner-Lambert Company acquired Junior Mints, and in 1993, the company sold the business to Tootsie Roll Industries, which now markets the tasty mint candies.

STRANGE FACTS

• Tootsie Roll Industries produces an average of fifteen million Junior Mints per day.

• The Broadway play Junior Miss inspired a magazine series, had a second run on Broadway in the 1940s, and was adapted into a popular radio show starring Shirley Temple.

• In an episode of the television comedy Seinfeld, while Kramer eats a Junior Mint in an operating room, Jerry pushes his hand, causing the Junior Mint to go flying into Elaine's boyfriend's open incision. The patient's miraculous recovery from surgery is credited to the Junior Mint.

LIFE SAVERS

In 1912, Cleveland-based chocolate maker Clarence A. Crane came up with the idea for white-circle mints with a hole in the center—as something different. He had a pharmaceutical manufacturer produce them on his pill machine and named the mints Life Savers because they resembled the flotation device. Crane created a label depicting an old sailor tossing a life preserver to a beautiful lady swimmer. The type read: "Crane's Peppermint Life Savers—5¢—For that Stormy Breath." The original package was a small cardboard tube with paper caps on each end.

In 1913, New York advertising salesman Edward John Noble tried to convince Crane to let him advertise the product. Instead, Crane sold the rights to Life Savers to Noble and his boyhood friend, J. Roy Allen, for 2,900 dollars. Realizing that the mints soon lost their flavor and absorbed the odor of the cardboard package, Noble switched to the tin foil wrapping and paper band label still used to this day. He paid six women five dollars a week each to hand wrap the mints, refusing to quit his advertising job until the Life Savers business took off. Noble told his customers to place the rolls of Life Savers next to the cash register with a big five-cent price card and to then make sure all customers received a nickel with their change. Within a few years, Noble's company had made a quarter of a million dollars from sales of the minty impulse item.

STRANGE FACTS

• In 1913, the company had costumed women hand out Life Savers for free on streets and in office building lobbies.
• The most popular flavor Life Saver is Pep-O-Mint.
• Edward Noble designed a cardboard display rack to be placed next to the register to hold Life Savers and other manufacturer's chewing gum and candy bars.
• In 1934, Life Savers introduced the popular five-flavor roll.
• An estimated 75 percent of Life Savers are purchased by people who did not plan on buying them until they saw the display.
• Advertisements for Life Savers have included the corny puns hole-some, enjoy-mint, refresh-mint, and content-mint.
• The world's record for keeping a Life Saver in the mouth with the hole intact is seven hours, ten minutes.
• If you bite into a Wint-O-Green Life Saver in a dark room, a quick burst of

When Was It Invented?

1854	Whitman's Chocolates
1861	CIVIL WAR BEGINS
1880s	Candy Corn
1890	Black Crows
1893	Juicy Fruit Gum
	Wrigley's Spearmint Gum
	Good & Plenty
1896	Tootsie Rolls
	Cracker Jacks
1899	Liquorice Allsorts
1900	Chiclets
1901	King Leo Pure Peppermint Stick
	Necco Wafers
1902	Necco Sweethearts
1903	WRIGHT BROTHERS INVENT THE AIRPLANE
1905	Popsicle
	Hershey Milk Chocolate Bar
1907	Hershey's Kisses
1912	Goo Goo Clusters
	Life Savers
	Whitman's Sampler
1914	WORLD WAR I BEGINS
	Mary Janes
1917	Clark Bar
1920	PROHIBITION BEGINS
	Mounds
1921	Chuckles
1922	Goldenberg's Peanut Chews
	Charleston Chew
1923	Milky Way

	Reeses Peanut Butter Cups
1924	Bit-O-Honey
	Mr. Goodbar
1926	Milk Duds
1928	Crunchy Heath Bar
	Dubble Bubble
1929	STOCK MARKET CRASHES
1930	Snickers
1931	Tootsie Pops
	Valomilk Candy Cups
1932	FDR ELECTED PRESIDENT
	Katherine Beecher Butter Mints
	Mars Almond Bar
	Red Hots
	3 Musketeers Bar
	Sugar Daddy
1936	5th Avenue Bar
1938	Bartons Almond Kisses
1939	WORLD WAR II BEGINS
	Hershey's Miniatures
1940	York Peppermint Pattie
1941	M&M's Plain Chocolate Candies
1945	Dots
1947	Bazooka Bubble Gum
1949	El Bubble Bubble Gum Cigars
	Jolly Rancher Hard Candies
	Junior Mints
	Smarties
	Whoppers
1950	Bobs Candy Canes
1952	Pez
1954	Marshmallow Peeps
1960	Lemonheads
1963	SweeTarts

bluish-green light flashes the moment the wintergreen candy is crushed. Crushing a crystalline substance, in this case the synthetic wintergreen—methyl salicylate—emits light. This phenomenon is called triboluminescence.

• In a letter published in the *New England Journal of Medicine,* two Illinois physicians, Dr. Howard Edward, Jr., and Dr. Donald Edward, warned that biting a Wint-O-Green Life Saver while in an oxygen tent, operating room, or space capsule could be life-threatening. The journal declared Wint-O-Green Life Savers safe for oxygen tents and gas stations.

• In 2003, Life Savers replaced the lemon-, lime-, and orange-flavored candies in its classic five-flavor roll with blackberry, raspberry, and watermelon. Cherry and pineapple remained unchanged. The change marked the first time the flavors in the five-flavor roll had been altered since the product's introduction in 1935.

• Every day, people consume more than 125 million Life Savers candies.

LIQUORICE ALLSORTS

In the late 1890s, British confectioner Charlie Thompson created several different types of flavorful licorice candies—Buttons, Chips, Cubes, Nuggets, Plugs, Rocks, and Twists. In 1899, while trying to sell his sweets to store owners, he met with constant rejection—until he accidentally dropped his case of samples, creating a colorful assortment of licorice treats on the floor. The store owner, entranced by the  colorful mixture of candies, immediately ordered a batch, inspiring Thompson to name his accidental combination of confections "Liquorice Allsorts."

LITTLE DEBBIE

In the Depression year of 1933, unemployed O. D. McKee asked a man selling Virginia Dare nickel cakes from his car how he could get a job like that. McKee soon found himself selling cakes from his 1928 Whippet throughout the Chattanooga territory in Tennessee. Convinced he could prosper in the baked goods

industry, McKee and his wife, Ruth, bought a small Chattanooga bakery in 1934, Jack's Cookie Company on Main Street.

When McKee's father-in-law, a partner in the venture, refused to agree to expand the business, O. D. took some of the cash and moved his family to Charlotte, North Carolina, where he and Ruth opened a new bakery, designed by McKee himself and featuring highly advanced automated equipment. In the late 1940s he oversaw the building of a new bakery. A few years later, they sold the Charlotte bakery and made plans to retire, but moved back to Chattanooga to run the family bakery in the early 1950s.

When the woodwork shop at Southern Missionary College burned down in 1957, McKee Baking Company moved to Collegedale, Tennessee, to give the dispossessed students work opportunities.

In 1960, the company introduced individually wrapped

Little Debbie snack cakes, named after O. D. and Ruth McKee's granddaughter Debbie McKee, and used a photo taken of Debbie at 3½ years for the artwork that appears on all the Little Debbie packaging.

STRANGE FACTS

• Company co-founder O. D. McKee suffered from dyslexia.

• Little Debbie is the best-selling snack cake brand in the United States.

• In 1991, McKee Baking Company changed its name to McKee Foods Corporation.

• McKee Foods was the first bakery to sell individually wrapped cakes in a multi-pack carton.

• McKees Foods sells sixty-six varieties of Little Debbie snack cakes, including seasonal products.

Do-It-Yourself Recipe

HOMEMADE "LITTLE DEBBIE" CAKES

WHAT YOU NEED

From the supermarket:

• 5 egg whites
• 5 egg yolks, beaten
• 2 cups sifted confectioners' sugar
• 4 tablespoons regular cocoa
• Crisco All-Vegetable Shortening
• All-purpose flour
• Wax paper
• 3 tablespoons milk
• 1 cup heavy cream, whipped and flavored with sugar and vanilla

WHAT TO DO

Beat egg whites until frothy. Add one cup confectioners' sugar and beat until stiff. Add three tablespoons cocoa and mix well. Fold in egg yolks. Grease a ten-by-fifteen inch jelly roll pan with vegetable shortening. Line the bottom of the pan with a sheet of wax paper, then grease and flour the wax paper and the inside of the rest of the pan. Spread the cake mixture evenly in the pan and bake twenty minutes at 375 degrees Fahrenheit.

While the cake bakes, combine the milk, one cup confectioners' sugar, and one tablespoon cocoa to make icing. Blend until smooth.

Sprinkle confectioners' sugar over a clean dish towel, and turn out the baked cake on it. Cover the cake with a second dish towel dampened with water until the cake cools. Spread with whipped cream over the top of the cake. Roll up both ends of the cake toward the center, creating two rolls. Cut the rolls apart, cut each roll in half, and frost with icing. Makes four cakes.

Do-It-Yourself Recipe

LOLLIPOPS

WHAT YOU NEED

From the supermarket:
- 2 cups sugar
- $^3/_4$ cups Light Karo Corn Syrup
- 1 tablespoon butter
- $^1/_2$ teaspoon peppermint or cherry extract
- Green or red food coloring

From a baking supply store:
- Lollipop or Popsicle sticks
- Lollipop bags or wax paper

From the tap:
- 1 cup water

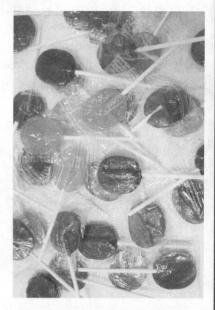

WHAT TO DO

Boil water. Add sugar, corn syrup, and butter, and bring to boil. Cook mixture until candy thermometer registers 300 degrees Fahrenheit or a drop of the mixture placed in cold water produces a brittle strand of candy. Remove from heat, place the pot in a pan of cold water to prevent the temperature from exceeding 300 degrees Fahrenheit, and let cool to 160 degrees Fahrenheit. Stir in the peppermint (or cherry) extract and several drops of green (or red) food coloring. On a lightly oiled marble slab or cooking sheet, pour the syrup into small circles, and position a paper lollipop stick in each circle. Or pour the syrup into lightly oiled small cupcake tins, and position a lollipop stick in each cup. Let harden, then carefully lift each lollipop and individually wrap in plastic wrap, lollipop bags, or wax paper to prevent them from sticking together. Makes two dozen small lollipops or one dozen large lollipops.

The Lollipop Guild

In the 1939 movie The Wizard of Oz, Dorothy travels by way of tornado to the strange and unusual Munchkinland where three members of the Lollipop Guild present her with a huge lollipop—indicating that even Munchkins living in the Land of Oz know how to make lollipops.

M&M'S
CHOCOLATE CANDIES

After his graduation from Yale University, Forrest Mars went to work for his father, Frank Mars, the inventor of the Snickers bar and the Milky Way bar. After several arguments, Forrest moved to England and started his own Mars candy company in the 1930s, also making pet food. According to legend, Forrest traveled to Spain during the Spanish Civil War where he discovered soldiers eating pellets of chocolate encased in a hard sugary coating to keep them from melting. Inspired, Forrest returned to England and purportedly concocted the recipe for M&M's Chocolate Candies in his kitchen. During World War II, Forrest did return home with the rights to market British Smarties in the United States—as M&M's.

M&M's are the combined initials of Forrest E. Mars and his associate Bruce Murrie. In 1954, Mars introduced M&M's peanut Chocolate Candies, and with the advertising slogan "Melts in your mouth, not in your hands," sales of M&M's skyrocketed. Forrest took over the company when his father died, and in 1973, he turned over the reigns of the family-run business to his two sons, Forrest Jr. and John.

STRANGE FACTS
• More than 300 million individual M&M's chocolate candies are made every day.
• To make M&M's Chocolate Candies, chocolate is poured into tiny molds to create the chocolate centers. After they harden, the chocolates are rotated in large containers as several coatings of liquid candy are sprayed onto them. The single-colored batches of red, yellow, blue, green, brown and orange candy are mixed together and then sifted to eliminate misshapen pieces. A conveyor belt carries each piece in its own little indentation past rubber etch

rollers that gently touch each candy, printing that distinctive "m" on its shell. A packaging machine then weighs the M&M's, pours the proper amount into each bag, and heat-seals each package.

• The average bag of M&M's Plain Chocolate Candies contains 30 percent browns, 20 percent each of yellows and reds, and 10 percent each of oranges, greens, and blues.

• In 1976, after scientists determined that Red Dye Number 2 caused cancer in rats, M&M's Chocolate Candies stopped making red M&M's (which did not contain Red Dye Number 2) and replaced them with tan M&M's, sparking protests from the Society for the Restoration and Preservation of Red M&M's. In 1987, the company brought back red M&M's, using FD&C Red Number 40.

• In the movie *Peggy Sue Got Married,* Peggy Sue gets sent back in time to the 1950s, where she sees her younger sister eating M&M's Chocolate Candies and exclaims "Don't eat the red ones."

• In 1994, M&M's Chocolate Candies became certified Kosher.

• Green M&M's are considered to be an aphrodisiac. At wedding showers, guests often present the future bride with a bag of M&M's with all the green candies carefully removed and placed in a second bag specifically reserved for the wedding night. An M&M/Mars brochure states: "Although many consumers ask us about the special qualities of green M&M's Chocolate Candies, we cannot explain any extraordinary 'powers' attributed to this color, either scientifically or medically."

Do-It-Yourself Recipe

GORP (GOOD OLD RAISINS AND PEANUTS)

WHAT YOU NEED
From the supermarket:
• 1 cup raisins
• 1 cup salted peanuts
• 1 cup M&M's chocolate candies

WHAT TO DO
Combine the raisins, peanuts, and M&M's in a Ziploc Storage Bag and shake well to mix up the ingredients. Makes three cups.

For a more eclectic mixture, add almonds, chopped walnuts, chopped dates, roasted cashews, dried banana chips, or sunflower seeds.

MILK DUDS

In 1926, F. Hoffman & Company in Chicago attempted to develop a perfectly round chocolate-covered caramel morsel made with a large amount of milk. The resulting lopsided "duds" tasted wonderful, and the company decided to market the misshapen morsels under the name Milk Duds.

In 1928, Milton J. Holloway took over F. Hoffman & Company, and under his leadership, sales of Milk Duds went through the roof. Milk Duds became a staple of movie theater candy counters. In 1969, Holloway sold the company to Beatrice Foods. In 1986, Leaf purchased the company, and six years later moved the production of Milk Duds to its candy factory in Robinson, Illinois. In 1996, Hershey Foods Corporation bought Leaf's North America confectionery operations, acquiring the deformed chocolate balls still marketed today as Milk Duds.

NECCO WAFERS

In 1847, candy maker Oliver R. Chase of Boston created round pastel wafers made from sugar, corn syrup, and dextrose. Tired of cutting the candy wafers by hand, Chase invented and patented the first American candy machine—a lozenge cutter. At the time, candy makers had to pulverize sugar by hand to make finely ground powdering sugar. To do away with this tedious chore, the enterprising Chase invented and patented a machine in 1850 for pulverizing sugar.

In 1866, Chase's brother Daniel invented the Lozenge Printing Machine to print mottoes directly on lozenges. His highly popular "Conversation Candies" and "Wedding Lozenges" featured such couplets and conundrums as "Married in pink, he will take a drink." In 1901, Chase and Company merged with Fobes, Hayward and Company (founded by Daniel Fobes in 1848) and Wright and Moody (begun in 1856) to form the New England Confectionery Company. The newly formed company, known by the acronym Necco, renamed Chase and Company's 1847 wafer candy Necco Wafers.

STRANGE FACTS

• In 1913, explorer Donald MacMillan took Necco Wafers on his Arctic expedition.

• The New England Confectionery Company factory, located in Cambridge, Massachusetts, was the largest factory in the world devoted entirely to the manufacture of candy when it was built in 1927.

• Necco Wafer rolls contain eight flavors and colors: lemon yellow, orange orange, lime green, clove purple, cinnamon white, wintergreen pink, licorice black, and chocolate brown.

• In very low humidity, Necco Wintergreen Wafers spark when broken in the dark. Crushing a crystalline substance, in this case the synthetic wintergreen—methyl salicylate—emits light. This phenomenon is called triboluminescence.

• If the more than four billion Necco Wafers sold each year were placed edge to edge, they would encircle the world twice.

• In the 1930s, Admiral Richard Byrd brought 2.5 tons of Necco Wafers to the South Pole to help his men endure their two-year stay in Antarctica.

• Necco also manufactures eight billion Sweethearts, the small heart-shaped candies printed with romantic phrases and sold between January 1 and February 14, each year.

OH HENRY!

Contrary to popular belief, the "Oh Henry!" candy bar was not named after author O. Henry, best known for his short-story "The Gift of the Magi." In 1921, a young man named Henry (whose last name has been lost to history) frequented the Williamson Candy Store in Chicago and flirted with the young women who made the candy. After awhile, the girls began asking Henry to do errands and favors. Whenever the young ladies needed something done, they would call out, "Oh Henry, do this" or "Oh Henry, will you get me that?" Later that year, Williamson named his new candy bar, "Oh Henry!"

Do-It-Yourself Recipe

HOMEMADE "OH HENRY!"

WHAT YOU NEED

From the supermarket:

- Crisco All-Vegetable Shortening
- 4 cups quick-cooking Quaker Oats
- 1/2 cup granulated sugar
- 1 cup brown sugar (packed)
- 1 cup butter
- 6 ounces chocolate chips
- 1 cup crunchy peanut butter

WHAT TO DO

Preheat the oven to 350 degrees Fahrenheit. Grease a nine-inch by thirteen-inch pan. Mix the oats, granulated sugar, and brown sugar in a large bowl. Melt the butter, pour into the bowl, and mix the ingredients well. Press the mixture into the pan, bake at 350 degrees Fahrenheit for twenty minutes, then let cool for twenty minutes.

Melt the chocolate chips and peanut butter in a saucepan over medium heat, stirring to blend. Spread over cooked base. Refrigerate for one hour. Cut into rectangular bars. Makes two dozen.

POPSICLE

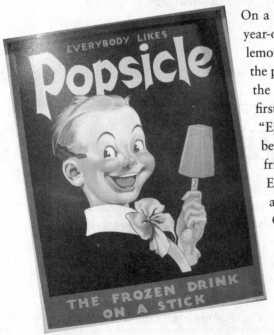

On a cold winter night in 1905, eleven-year-old Frank Epperson left a glass of lemonade with a spoon in it outside on the porch. In the morning, he pulled on the spoon and out came the world's first ice pop, which Epperson named "Epsicle." The enterprising young man began selling his ice pop to his school friends. Eighteen years later in 1923, Epperson, who ran a lemonade stand at an amusement part in Alameda, California, applied for a patent for "frozen ice on a stick," which his children re-named Popsicle. By 1928, Epperson had earned royalties on more than sixty million Popsicle ice pops.

During the Depression, Epperson created the twin Popsicle ice pop so two children could split it for a nickel. Epperson also created the Fudgsicle, Creamsicle, and Dreamsicle brands. In the 1950s, when Popsicle ice pops boxed in a multi-pack were introduced to grocery stores, sales skyrocketed into the millions. As of 2002, there were more than thirty variations on the original Popsicle ice pop.

STRANGE FACTS
• Popsicle sticks are made from birch wood.
• During World War II, the Eighth Air Force unit chose the Popsicle ice pop as a symbol of American life.
• There have been more than one hundred different Popsicle ice pop flavors.
• The most popular Popsicle ice pop flavors are orange, cherry, and grape.
• It takes 275 writers to come up with the riddles printed on Popsicle sticks.
• If all the sticks from Popsicle ice pops eaten in one year were laid end-to-end, they would circle the earth three times.
• In 1997, Americans ate more than 1.2 billion Popsicle ice pops. That's 2,220 Popsicle ice pops every minute.

Do-It-Yourself Recipe
HOMEMADE "POPSICLE" ICE POPS

WHAT YOU NEED
From the supermarket:
• 1 cup sugar
• 1/2 cup Light Karo Corn Syrup
• 3/4 cup lemon juice
From a baking supply store:
• Popsicle sticks
From Tupperware:
• Tupperware Ice Tups molds
From the tap:
• 2 cups water

WHAT TO DO
In a pitcher, mix the sugar, corn syrup, lemon juice, and water. Stir well to dissolve all the sugar.

Pour the solution into the Popsicle molds, insert Popsicle sticks through the lids, and seal the lids in place. Place in the freezer for twenty-four hours. Makes six ice pops.

These tangy ice pops are sure to help you keep your cool.

ORANGE DREAM BARS

WHAT YOU NEED

From the supermarket:
- 1 box orange Jell-O (4-serving size)
- 2 cups vanilla ice cream (softened)
- 12 paper Dixie Cups
- Reynolds Wrap aluminum foil

From a baking supply store or craft store:
- Popsicle sticks

From the tap:
- 1 cup water

WHAT TO DO

In a large bowl, dissolve the Jell-O powder in one cup boiling water, then let cool to room temperature. Stir in ice cream. Pour $1/4$ cup of the mixture into each one of the paper cups. Cover each cup with a piece of aluminum foil. Push a Popsicle stick through the center of the foil and into the orange mixture, and place the cups in the freezer overnight. Peel off the paper cups and enjoy. Makes twelve ice cream pops.

RED HOTS, BOSTON BAKED BEANS, AND LEMONHEAD

In 1908, Salvatore Ferrara, an Italian immigrant skilled in the art of making Italian pastries and sugar-coated candy almonds known as "confetti," founded Original Ferrara Bakery, a retail pastry and confection shop, in Chicago, Illinois.

Ferrara's sugar-coated almond business boomed, and in 1919, he teamed up with his brothers-in-law, Salvatore Buffardi and Anello Pagano, to build a factory to manufacture a wide range of confections now known as Ferrara Pan Candy Company.

The word "pan" in the company name refers to the candy-making process of tossing nuts or candy centers into revolving pans and then adding flavor, color, and other candy ingredients until the pieces grow to the desired size. In the early 1930s, Ferrara Pan

Candy Company used this cold-panned candy method to create its famous Red Hot candies, based on the traditional cinnamon hard candy known to confectioners as "cinnamon imperials."

Using this same method, Ferrara Pan Candy Company developed its Boston Baked Beans, a generic name used throughout the candy industry for sugar-coated peanuts, in the early 1930s. Other companies tried to compete with Ferrara Pan's Boston Baked Beans, but Ferrara Pan's high-quality sugar-coated peanuts remain the best-selling Boston Baked Beans in the world.

In 1962, using the same cold-panned process, Ferrara Pan Candy Company created and named Lemonhead—a unique, round, sour candy—as a counterpart to Red Hots. The Lemonhead became the most successful candy of its time.

STRANGE FACTS

• Salvatore Ferrara, fluent in both English and Italian, worked for four years as an interpreter for the Santa Fe Railroad to help foremen communicate with their crews.

• Original Ferrara Bakery still operates from the original factory located at 2200 West Taylor Street in Chicago. The same families (Ferrara, Buffardi, and Pagano) own and operate the Ferrara Pan Company in Forest Park, Illinois.

• Ferrara Pan Candy Company produces approximately 500 million Lemonheads per year.

• Based on the success of Lemonhead, Ferrara Pan Candy Company created a number of other product lines, including Black Forest Gummies and Atomic Fireballs.

Do-It-Yourself Recipe

ROCK CANDY

WHAT YOU NEED

From the supermarket:
- 2 cups sugar

From the kitchen:
- Pot
- Clean, empty glass jar
- Candy thermometer

From the workshop:
- 1-inch metal washer
- String
- Pencil

From the tap:
- Water

WHAT TO DO

Boil a pot of water, drop the metal washer and the string in the boiling water, and let boil for five minutes to sterilize both items.

Dissolve the sugar in $^3/_4$ cup water and, using the thermometer, heat to 250 degrees Fahrenheit, without stirring. Fill the jar with the solution. Attach the washer to one end of the string and the pencil to the other end of the string so when you rest the pencil on the mouth of the jar, the washer hangs down into the thick sugar water without touching the bottom of the jar. Place the jar in a warm place and let stand for up to one week. The water evaporates and rocky sugar crystals form on the string.

SUGAR DADDY

In 1926, Robert Welch, a street vendor who sold chocolates in Cambridge, Massachusetts, invented and launched a caramel lollipop he named Papa Sucker. In 1932, Welch changed the name of the candy to Sugar Daddy, inspired by a popular term at the time, suggesting a wealth of sweetness.

In 1935, Welch used the success of Sugar Daddy as a springboard to introduce Sugar Babies, named after the popular song "Let Me Be Your Sugar Baby." Today, Tootsie Roll Industries owns Sugar Daddy and Sugar Babies, producing both candies in their hometown of Cambridge, Massachusetts. Welch's brother, James, created Junior Mints (see page 72).

TOOTSIE ROLLS AND TOOTSIE POPS

In 1896, Austrian immigrant Leo Hirshfield founded a small candy store in New York City, where he hand-rolled and hand-wrapped a chocolate candy created from a recipe he had brought from his home country. Hirshfield named the candy after his five-year-old daughter, Clara, nicknamed Tootsie. The Tootsie Roll became the first penny candy in America to be individually wrapped in paper.

By 1905, Hirshfield produced Tootsie Rolls in a four-story candy factory in New York City. In 1917, he renamed his enterprise Sweets Company of America and began to advertise Tootsie Rolls nationally. In 1931, the company introduced the Tootsie Pop, a lollipop with hard candy on the outside and chewy, chocolaty Tootsie Roll on the inside. Seven years later, growing sales compelled the company to relocate to a larger factory in Hoboken, New Jersey, fitted with conveyor belt systems to mass produce Tootsie Rolls and Tootsie Pops.

In 1966, the company changed its name to Tootsie Roll Industries, Inc., and today the company is headquartered in Chicago, with factories in Massachusetts, New York, Tennessee, Wisconsin, and Mexico.

STRANGE FACTS

• The Tootsie Roll today still looks and tastes remarkably like the original chewy, chocolaty Tootsie Roll and still sells for the original price of one penny.
• In 2002, Tootsie Roll Industries sold more than 393 million dollars worth of Tootsie Roll products and produced more than sixty million Tootsie Rolls and twenty million Tootsie Pops every day.

- During World War II, the United States military put Tootsie Rolls in GI ration kits because the candy could withstand severe weather conditions and gave soldiers a burst of "quick energy."
- Tootsie Rolls sponsored the television shows *Howdy Doody, Rin Tin Tin,* and *Rocky & Bullwinkle.*
- Tootsie Roll Industries produces more than twenty million lollipops a day, making the company the world's largest lollipop producer.
- In the 1970s television police drama *Kojak,* actor Telly Savalas, starring as Kojak, always sucked on a Tootsie Pop as he solved crimes.
- Advertisements and commercials for Tootsie Pops asked, "Mr. Owl, how many licks does it take to get to the Tootsie Roll center of a Tootsie Pop?"
- Tootsie Roll Industries has received more than 25,000 letters from people around the world who counted how many licks it took them to get to the center of a Tootsie Pop. Tootsie Roll Industries responds to every letter and sends out a "Clean Stick Award" certificate to each person who mails in a letter revealing how many licks it took. Most children report a range from 600 to 800 licks. A chemical engineering doctorate student at the University of Michigan reported that his licking machine required an average of 411 licks per Tootsie Pop.

Do-It-Yourself Recipe
HOMEMADE "TOOTSIE ROLLS"

WHAT YOU NEED
From the supermarket:
- 1 cup powdered sugar
- 1/2 cup Light Karo Corn Syrup
- 2 1/2 tablespoons Crisco All-Vegetable Shortening
- 4 teaspoons cocoa
- 2 tablespoons evaporated fat free milk
- 1/2 teaspoon vanilla extract

WHAT TO DO
Mix the sugar, corn syrup, shortening, and cocoa in a medium saucepan over medium/high heat. Bring to a boil, then reduce heat to medium, and simmer until mixture reaches soft crack stage at 275 degrees Fahrenheit. Remove from heat. When bubbling ceases, add the evaporated milk and beat in the pan with electric mixer for approximately thirty seconds. Add vanilla, then continue to beat until the mixture firms up. Pour onto a well-greased pan. When cool, divide the roll into ropes approximately 1/2 inch thick, and slice with a knife into pieces roughly 1 1/8 inches long. Place on a plate and let sit overnight to firm up. Makes approximately sixty candies.

Who Is the Dairy Queen?

The Big Boys

In 1938, J. F. McCullough, owner of the Homemade Ice Cream Company of Green River, Illinois, developed a new frozen dairy dessert—soft ice cream. The next year he and his son Alex tested the new soft ice cream by convincing one of their best customers, Sherb Noble, to host the first "All the Ice Cream You Can Eat for only 10 Cents" at his ice cream shop in Kankakee, Illinois. On August 4, 1938, lines of customers stretched for blocks. Noble served the soft ice cream to more than 1,600 people in two hours.

The McCulloughs then teamed up with Harry Oltz, who had developed a freezer capable of keeping the ice cream at a constant 23 degrees Fahrenheit, the temperature needed to keep the ice cream soft. The trio launched Dairy Queen, but instead of operating restaurants, sold franchisees the right to use their freezers, collecting royalties on the number of gallons of soft ice cream produced.

Sherb Noble, who had hosted the first "All You Can Eat" sale, opened the first Dairy Queen franchise at 1700 West Jefferson in Joliet, Illinois, on June 22, 1940. Ten years later, there were 1,156 Dairy Queen stores.

Menus varied from store to store, and franchise operators created such menu items as the Banana Split, the Dilly Bar, The DQ Sandwich, and the Buster Bar. In 1957, a territory operator in Georgia added hamburgers, hot dogs, and French fries to his menus, starting the Brazier food line.

By 1960, there were three thousand Dairy Queens in twelve countries, but the chain remained a disorganized group of territory operators and franchisees who happened to be working under the same trade name.

Finally, in 1962, a group of territory operators formed International Dairy Queen.

STRANGE FACTS
• Company founder J. F. McCullough, eager to convey the real dairy freshness of his new soft ice cream, named his company Dairy Queen, in honor of the queen of the dairy industry—the cow.
• The first Dairy Queen shop in Joliet, Illinois, was flanked by two funeral parlors.
• Aside from being the home of the first Dairy Queen, Joliet, Illinois, is also home to Joliet Prison.

3

Toys,

GAMES, & BRAINTEASERS

You've Got to Be Kidding

The action in a typical country store centered around a traditional board game. Next to the cast-iron stove, customers sat in rocking chairs around a checkerboard, coaching the players. Country stores also stocked homemade three-dimensional puzzles fashioned by local blacksmiths and welders from metal loops, rings, nails, and horseshoes. The challenge? To take apart and then reassemble these deceptively simple yet infuriating puzzles that leave you either deeply baffled or feeling like a genius. Rediscover the joys of Raggedy Ann dolls, balsa wood planes, Mr. Potato Head, Scrabble, elaborate doll houses, Lionel Trains, and other amusements that provided—and still provide— hours of family fun.

BALSA WOOD PLANES

In 1926, Paul K. Guillow, a former World War I Navy pilot who loved aviation, created a line of toy model construction kits so hobbyists could build models of famous World War I combat aircraft from balsa wood and tissue paper. He founded his Nu Craft Toys company in the barn of his family home in Wakefield, Massachusetts. The following year, Charles Lindbergh made the first successful solo airplane flight across the Atlantic, triggering a surge of interest in aviation. Sales of Guillow's model airplane kits took off for the skies.

Demand for the model airplanes soon compelled Guillow to move his company to a larger facility in downtown Wakefield. He renamed his business Paul K. Guillow, Inc.

STRANGE FACTS

• The original line of Guillow balsa shelf model kits consisted of twelve different World War I biplane fighters with six-inch wing spans that sold for ten cents each. Each kit contained a three-view plan, balsa wood cement, two bottles of colored glue, and a strip of bamboo for wing and landing gear struts.

• Paul Guillow published four books on aviation: *Tom's Book of Flying Models, Flying Models: How to Build Them, Building An Airplane,* and *Flying Model Airplane Plans.*

• During World War II, the United States military diverted most balsa wood to produce rafts and life jackets. Guillow supplied his customers with model kids that used paper cardboard and pine to build World War II aircraft.

• Balsa wood, the lightest wood for commercial use, comes from the balsa tree, which grows in Latin America. Ecuador produces the most balsa wood, followed by Costa Rica.

• During World War II, Guillow supplied the United States military with drone aircrafts to help gunners sharpen their skills.

• After World War II, when the advent of plastic model airplane kits killed sales of balsa wood kits, Guillow began producing inexpensive hand-launched and rubber-powered balsa-wood gliders.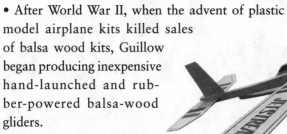

• When Guillow died in 1951, his widow Gertrude ran the company.

• In addition to the traditional line of hobby and toy airplanes, Guillow's also makes promotional products by custom-printing messages on the wings of inexpensive hand-launched gliders.

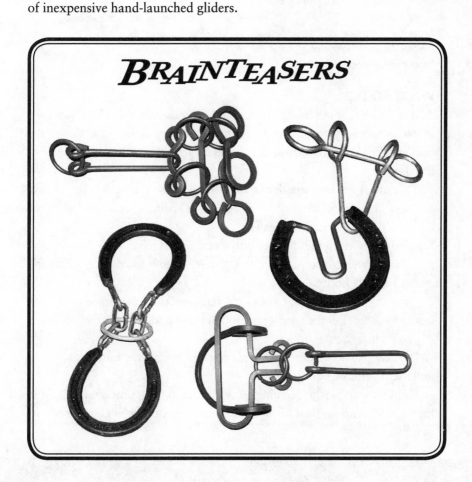

BRAINTEASERS

Bubble Making

WHAT YOU NEED

From the supermarket
- Two 90-fluid-ounce bottles of Ultra Dawn dishwashing liquid
- Plastic bucket
- Two plastic drinking straws
- String
- An eighteen-inch square plastic container

From the drugstore:
- Six 4-ounce bottles of glycerin

From the toy store:
- Plastic children's wading pool
- Hula hoop
- Swimming mask

From the tap:
- 1 gallon water

From the kitchen:
- 12-inch square piece of cardboard
- Plastic holder from a six pack of soda cans

From the closet:
- Wire clothes hanger

WHAT TO DO

Add the dishwashing liquid, water, and glycerin in the bucket. Swirl the ingredients gently to mix them without creating soap suds. Cover the bucket with the cardboard square and let the mixture sit undisturbed for five days.

Thread a three-foot length of string through two plastic drinking straws as if beading a necklace. Knot the ends of the string together and glide the knot inside one of the two straws.

Bend the wire clothes hanger into a circle with a handle.

Tie four twelve-inch pieces of string to make four handles equidistantly around a Hula hoop.

Place the plastic wading pool on a flat surface in the shade and away from any wind. Fill the pool with enough bubble solution to reach a depth of one inch.

Dip the plastic holder from a six pack of soda cans into the solution and use it to blow bubbles.

Hold the two plastic drinking straws apart so the string is taut, dip it in the bubble solution, then lift up while simultaneously bringing the straws together.

Submerge the wire clothes hanger into the bubble solution, then lift up, swishing through the air.

Place the Hula hoop in the pool. Place the eighteen-inch square plastic container in the center of the pool. Have an assistant put on the swimming mask (to avoid getting soap in his or her eyes) and stand inside the plastic container in the pool. With a second assistant, slowly lift the Hula hoop from the pool and over the victim's head.

STRANGE FACTS

• A soap bubble is a drop of water that has been stretched out into a sphere by using soap to loosen the magnetic attraction that exists between water molecules. Glycerin helps gives the walls of the bubble strength. When you wave the wire coat hanger through the air, for instance, the air pushes apart the molecules in the soapy film, but the molecules, attracted to each other, contract, forming the smallest surface possible to contain the largest volume of air possible—a sphere.

• Bubbles filled with carbon dioxide (blown from your mouth) last longer than bubbles filled with air.

• Bubbles made from a warm soapy solution last nearly twice as a long as bubbles made from a cold soap solution. Warmth sustains the surface tension of the bubbles. You can warm the bubble solution by placing it in a pot and heating it to 120 degrees Fahrenheit.

Bubble, Bubble, Toil and Trouble

Making monster bubbles successfully depends upon several variables, including air temperature and humidity. The more humidity in the air, the easier it is to make large bubbles. Bubbles also tend to burst quickly in direct sunlight.

• The more detergent used to make the bubble solution, the larger the bubbles will be. If you use more detergent than water (as instructed above), you can create monstrous bubbles.

• Adding glycerin slows down the evaporation of the water in the bubble.

• By wetting one end of a plastic straw in bubble mix, you can gently push it through a large bubble and then blow a second bubble inside the first bubble.

• The study of bubbles is called bubbleology.

CRAYOLA CRAYONS

In 1864, Joseph W. Binney began the Peekskill Chemical Works in Peekskill, New York, producing hardwood charcoal and a black pigment called lampblack. In 1880, he opened a New York office and invited his son, Edwin Binney, and his nephew, C. Harold Smith, to join the company. The cousins renamed the company Binney & Smith and expanded the product line to include shoe polish, printing ink, black crayons, and chalk. In 1903, the company made the first box of Crayola crayons costing a nickel and containing eight colors: red, orange, yellow, green, blue, violet, brown, and black. Alice Binney, wife of company co-owner Edwin Binney, coined the word Crayola by joining craie, from the French word meaning chalk, with ola, from oleaginous, meaning oily.

In 1958, Binney & Smith introduced the now-classic box of sixty-four crayons, complete with built-in sharpener. Hallmark Cards, Inc., the world's largest greeting card manufacturer, acquired Binney & Smith in 1984.

STRANGE FACTS

• Crayola crayons are made from paraffin wax, stearic acid, and colored pigment.

• In 1949, Binney & Smith introduced another forty colors: Apricot, Bittersweet, Blue Green, Blue Violet, Brick Red, Burnt Sienna, Carnation Pink, Cornflower, Flesh (renamed Peach in 1962, partly as a result of the civil rights movement), Gold, Gray, Green Blue, Green Yellow, Lemon Yellow, Magenta, Mahogany, Maize, Maroon, Melon, Olive Green, Orange Red, Orange Yellow, Orchid, Periwinkle, Pine Green, Prussian Blue (renamed Midnight Blue in 1958 in response to teachers' requests), Red Orange, Red Violet, Salmon, Sea Green, Silver, Spring Green, Tan, Thistle, Turquoise Blue, Violet Blue, Violet Red, White, Yellow Green, and Yellow Orange.

• In 1958, Binney & Smith

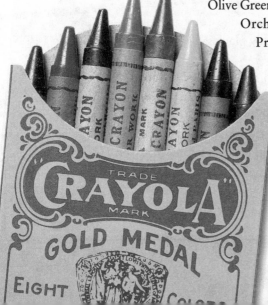

added sixteen colors, bringing the total number of colors to 64: Aquamarine, Blue Gray, Burnt Orange, Cadet Blue, Copper, Forest Green, Goldenrod, Indian Red (renamed Chestnut in 1999 in response to educators' requests), Lavender, Mulberry, Navy Blue, Plum, Raw Sienna, Raw Umber, Sepia, and Sky Blue. The company also debuted the now-classic box of sixty-four crayons, complete with built-in sharpener.

• In 1972, Binney & Smith introduced eight fluorescent colors: Chartreuse, Ultra Blue, Hot Magenta, Ultra Lemon, Ultra Orange, Ultra Green, Ultra Pink, and Ultra Red. (In 1990, the company changed the names to Atomic Tangerine, Blizzard Blue, Hot Magenta, Laser Lemon, Outrageous Orange, Screamin' Green, Shocking Pink, and Wild Watermelon.)

• Hallmark Cards, Inc., the world's largest greeting card manufacturer, acquired Binney & Smith in 1984.

• In 1990, the company introduced eight more fluorescent colors: Electric Lime, Magic Mint, Purple Pizzazz, Radical Red, Razzle Dazzle Rose, Sunglow, Unmellow Yellow, and Neon Carrot.

• In 1990, Binney & Smith retired eight traditional colored crayons from its 64-crayon box (Green Blue, Orange Red, Orange Yellow, Violet Blue, Maize, Lemon Yellow, Blue Gray, and Raw Umber) and replaced them with New Age hues (Cerulean, Vivid Tangerine, Jungle Green, Fuchsia, Dandelion, Teal Blue, Royal Purple, and Wild Strawberry). Retired colors were enshrined in the Crayola Hall of Fame. Protests from groups such as RUMPS (The Raw Umber and Maize Preservation Society) and CRAYON (The Committee to Reestablish All Your Old Norms) convinced Binney & Smith to release one million boxes of the Crayola Eight in October 1991.

• In 1993, Binney & Smith introduced sixteen more colors, all named by consumers: Asparagus, Cerise, Denim, Granny Smith Apple, Macaroni and Cheese, Mauvelous, Pacific Blue, Purple Mountain's Majesty, Razzmatazz, Robin's Egg Blue, Shamrock, Tickle Me Pink, Timber Wolf, Tropical Rain Forest, Tumbleweed, and Wisteria.

• In 1998, Binney & Smith introduced twenty-four new colors, bringing the total number of colors to 120: Almond, Antique Brass, Banana Mania, Beaver, Blue Bell, Brink Pink, Canary, Caribbean Green, Cotton Candy,

Cranberry, Desert Sand, Eggplant, Fern, Fuzzy Wuzzy Brown, Manatee, Mountain Meadow, Outer Space, Pig Pink, Pink Flamingo, Purple Heart, Shadow, Sunset Orange, Torch Red, and Vivid Violet.

• Washington Irving used the pseudonym Geoffrey Crayon when he published *The Sketch Book,* a collection of short stories and essays, including "The Legend of Sleepy Hollow" and "Rip Van Winkle."

• On average, children between the ages of two and seven color 28 minutes every day.

• The average child in the United States will wear down 730 crayons by his or her tenth birthday.

• The scent of Crayola crayons is among the twenty most recognizable scents to American adults.

• The Crayola brand name is recognized by 99 percent of all Americans.

• Red barns and black tires got their colors thanks in part to two of Binney & Smith's earliest products: red pigment and carbon black. Red and black are also the most popular crayon colors, mostly because children tend to use them for outlining.

• Binney & Smith produces two billion Crayola crayons a year, which, if placed end to end, would circle the earth 4.5 times.

• Crayola crayon boxes are printed in eleven languages: Danish, Dutch, English, Finnish, French, German, Italian, Norwegian, Portuguese, Spanish, and Swedish.

DOLLHOUSES

Albert V, Duke of Bavaria between 1550 and 1579, owned the first dollhouse in recorded history. The dollhouse, a miniature copy of the duke's residence, became known as his "baby house."

Dollhouses became popular in Germany, Holland, and England in the seventeenth and eighteenth centuries. Craftsmen usually made the houses with interiors, fixtures, and furnishings that reflected the lifestyle of the owners and contained many collector's pieces. In England, craftsmen built "baby houses" that replicated the owner's home both inside and out.

Craftsmen also made single rooms, such as miniature Nuremberg kitchens,

market stalls, and butcher shops, as teaching tools to instruct young women in the skills of housewifery.

In his 1845 novel *The Cricket on the Hearth,* Charles Dickens describes the workshop of a toy maker named Caleb: "There were houses in it, finished and unfinished, for Dolls of all stations of life."

At the beginning of the twentieth century, commercial production of dollhouses expanded with finely made houses reflecting suburban architecture with plumbing and electrical fittings. The advent of technology also launched the introduction of plastics dollhouses, including the popular Barbie Dream House. Fine craftsmen continue to build exquisite dollhouses, and many dollhouses can be built from kits. Most dollhouse collectors today are adults.

ERECTOR SET

A. C. Gilbert, a native of Salem, Oregon, worked his way through Yale University Medical School by performing as a magician at parties and by founding the Mysto Manufacturing Company to sell magic kits for children. After his graduation in 1909, Gilbert decided to expand his toy company rather than practice medicine.

In 1911, while traveling aboard a train from New Haven, Connecticut, to New York City, Gilbert looked out the window and spotted workmen constructing an electrical power-line tower by positioning and riveting steel beams to one another. Inspired, Gilbert decided to create a children's construction set containing metal beams of various shapes made with evenly spaced holes for bolts to pass through, screws, bolts, pulleys, gears, and crank shafts.

Two years later, Gilbert introduced the "Mysto Erector Structural Steel Builder" and launched the first major American advertising campaign for a toy, making his Erector Set one of the most popular toys of all time. Around 1930, Gilbert purchased the rights to produce Meccano, a similar metal toy construction set first produced about 1900 in England by Frank Hornby, in the United States. After 1938, Gilbert stopped manufacturing Meccano. During World War II, Gilbert ceased manufacturing Erector Sets because all steel was needed for the war effort. After the war, Gilbert resumed production of Erector Sets until his death in 1961. To pay estate taxes, Gilbert's son sold his majority holding in the company. Although Gilbert's son served as president, the new majority owners drove the company into bankruptcy in 1966. Gabriel Toys acquired the A. C. Gilbert and Erector names, eventually selling the company to Ideal Toys. Gilbert and Erector went through several other owners. Finally, in the 1980s, Meccano, now manufactured in Calais, France, purchased the rights to the company and began distributing the construction toy throughout the world under the brand name Meccano.

In the early 1990s, Meccano started selling its Mecanno sets in the United States as Erector Sets. In 2000, Nikko Toys of Japan purchased Meccano. Today, the BRIO Corporation, based in Germantown, Wisconsin, distributes Erector Sets in the United States.

What Every Kid Wants

The No. 12½ deluxe Erector Set kit came with blueprints for building the "Mysterious Walking Giant" robot.

FINGER PAINTS

WHAT YOU NEED

From the supermarket:
- One package Knox plain gelatin
- $1/2$ cup cornstarch
- Joy dishwashing liquid
- Six clean, empty 4-ounce baby food jars
- Food coloring

From the kitchen:
- Two mixing bowls
- Spoon
- Measuring cup
- Pot

From the tap:
- Water

WHAT TO DO

In a mixing bowl and using a spoon, mix the packet of powdered gelatin mix with $1/4$ cup water until dissolved. Set aside.

In a pot, mix the cornstarch with $3/4$ cup water. Add 2 cups hot water and mix well. Heat the pot on a stove, bringing the mixture to a boil while stirring constantly. When the mixture becomes clear and thick (after one to two minutes), remove the pot from the heat. Pour in the gelatin mixture. Mix well, then pour equal amounts of the mixture into the six baby food jars. Add one drop of Joy dishwashing liquid to each jar.

In the first jar, add five drops of yellow food coloring and mix well. In the second jar, add five drops of red food coloring and mix well. In the third jar, add five drops of green food coloring and mix well. In the fourth jar, add five drops of blue food coloring and mix well. In the fifth jar, add four drops of yellow food coloring and one drop red food coloring, and mix well. In the sixth jar, add three drops red food coloring and two drops blue food coloring, and mix well. Let cool.

You've created finger paints that can be used on heavy white paper. To store, seal the lids on the jars.

STRANGE FACTS

- Finger paint can also be made by mixing food coloring with shaving cream, condensed milk, or plain yogurt.
- Chinese artists created finger paintings as early as 750 C.E.
- In 1845, Peter Cooper, inventor of the Tom Thumb locomotive, patented the first clear powdered gelatin mix. Fruit-flavored gelatin was invented in LeRoy, New York, fifty-two years later by carpenter Pearl B. Wait.
- Gelatin, a colorless protein derived from the collagen contained in animal skin, tendons, bone, and hooves, is extracted by treating hides and bones with lime or acid. The material is then boiled, filtered, concentrated, dried, and ground into granules that dissolve in hot water and congeal into a gel.

Secret Formula

FLUBBER

WHAT YOU NEED

From the supermarket:
- 50 drops green food coloring
- 1 teaspoon 20 Mule Team Borax
- 4-ounce bottle of Elmer's Glue-All

From the kitchen:
- Two large glass bowls
- Large spoon
- Measuring cup
- Ziploc storage bag or airtight container

From the tap:
- 1 1/2 cups warm water

WHAT TO DO

Empty the bottle of Elmer's Glue-All into the first bowl. Fill the empty glue bottle with water and then pour it into the bowl of glue. Add 10 drops food coloring and stir well. In the second bowl, mix the borax with 1 cup water. Stir until the powder dissolves.

Slowly pour the colored glue into the bowl containing the borax solution, stirring as you do so. Remove the thick glob that forms, and knead the glob with your hands until it feels smooth and dry. Discard the excess water remaining in the bowl. Store the Flubber in the Ziploc bag or airtight container.

HOW TO USE IT

The resulting soft, pliable, rubbery glob snaps if pulled quickly, stretches if pulled slowly, and slowly oozes to the floor if placed over the edge of a table.

STRANGE FACTS

- According to legend, borax was used by Egyptians in mummification.
- Flubber is a non-Newtonian fluid—a liquid that does not abide by any of Sir Isaac Newton's laws on how liquids behave. Quicksand, gelatin, and ketchup are all non-Newtonian fluids.
- A non-Newtonian fluid's ability to flow can be changed by applying a force. Pushing or pulling on the slime makes it temporarily thicker and less oozy.
- Increasing the amount of borax in the second bowl makes the slime thicker. Decreasing the amount of borax makes the slime more slimy and oozy.

The Elmer Story

In 1936, Borden launched a series of advertisements featuring cartoon cows, including Elsie, the spokescow for Borden dairy products. In 1940, compelled by Elsie's popularity, Borden dressed up "You'll Do Lobelia," a seven-year-old, 950-pound Jersey cow from Brookfield, Massachusetts, as Elsie for an exhibit at the World's Fair. She stood in a barn boudoir decorated with whimsical props including churns used as tables, lamps made from milk bottles, a wheelbarrow for a chaise lounge, and oil paintings of Elsie's ancestors—among them Great Aunt Bess in her bridal gown and Uncle Bosworth, the noted Spanish-American War admiral. This attracted the attention of RKO Pictures, which hired Elsie to star with Jack Oakie and Kay Francis in the 1940 movie *Little Men*. Borden needed to find a replacement for Elsie for the World's Fair exhibit. Elsie's husband, Elmer, was chosen, and the boudoir was converted overnight into a bachelor apartment, complete with every conceivable prop to suggest a series of nightly poker parties. In 1951, Borden chose Elmer to be the marketing symbol for all of Borden's glue and adhesive products. Elsie the Cow and her husband Elmer have two calves, Beulah and Beauregard.

- 20 Mule Team Borax is named for the twenty-mule teams used during the late nineteenth century to transport borax 165 miles across the desert from Death Valley to the nearest train depot in Mojave, California. The twenty-day round trip started 190 feet below sea level and climbed to an elevation of over 4,000 feet before it was over.

- Between 1883 and 1889, the twenty-mule teams hauled more than twenty million pounds of borax out of Death Valley. During this time, not a single animal was lost nor did a single wagon break down.

- Today it would take more than 250 mule teams to transport the borax ore processed in just one day at Borax's modern facility in the Mojave Desert.

- Although the mule teams were replaced by railroad cars in 1889, twenty-mule teams continued to make promotional and ceremonial appearances at events ranging from the 1904 St. Louis World's Fair to President Woodrow Wilson's inauguration in 1917. They won first place in the 1917 Pasadena Rose Parade and attended the dedication of the San Francisco Bay Bridge in 1937.

- 20 Mule Team Borax was once proclaimed to be a "miracle mineral" and was used to aid digestion, keep milk sweet, improve the complexion, remove dandruff, and even cure epilepsy.

FRISBEE

In the 1870s, William Russell Frisbie opened a bakery called the Frisbie Pie Company in Bridgeport, Connecticut. His lightweight pie tins were embossed with the family name. In the mid-1940s, students at Yale University tossed the empty pie tins as a game. In the 1950s, Walter Frederick Morrison, a Los Angeles building inspector determined to capitalize on Hollywood's obsession with UFOs, designed a lightweight plastic disk, based on the Frisbie bakery's pie tins, but changed the name to Flyin' Saucer to avoid legal hassles. Morrison sold the rights to the Wham-O Manufacturing Co. of San Gabriel, California, and on January 13, 1957, Americans were introduced to the Frisbee (a name inspired by the Frisbie Pie Company, but with a different spelling to avoid legal issues). The Frisbie Pie Company went out of business in 1958. In 1994, Mattel acquired Wham-O.

STRANGE FACTS

• The Wham-O Company, founded in 1948, was named after the sound of a slingshot, one of its first products, missile makes when it hits a target.
• In May 1989, Middlebury College in Vermont unveiled a bronze statue of a dog jumping to catch a Frisbee to commemorate the alleged fiftieth anniversary of the Frisbee. According to Middlebury legend, five undergraduates driving through Nebraska in 1939 suffered a flat tire. As two boys changed the tire, a third found a discarded pie tin from the Frisbie Pie Company near a cornfield and threw the circular disk in the air. Middlebury President Olin Robison told *Time* magazine, "Our version of the story is that it happened all over America, but it started here."

• In the United States, more Frisbee discs are sold each year than baseballs, basketballs, and footballs combined.

Gone Batty

In 1920, Boston Red Sox owner Harry Frazee sold Babe Ruth to the New York Yankees for a purported 100,000 dollars, and used the money to finance the Broadway musical *No, No, Nanette*. While *No, No, Nanette* became a hit, the Yankees won four World Series during the fifteen years Babe Ruth was in their line-up. As of 2003, the Boston Red Sox had never won the World Series.

HULA HOOP

Children in ancient Egypt played with hoops made from dried grapevines and other plants by rolling and throwing them or twirling them around their waist and limbs. Over time, children started playing with hoops made out of wood or metal.

In 1957, an Australian visiting California told Richard Knerr and Arthur "Spud" Melin, founders of the Wham-O Company, that Australian children twirled bamboo hoops around their waists in gym class. Knerr and Melin, envisioning the popularity of such a toy in America, created a hollow plastic prototype and tested it on local school children, winning enthusiastic approval.

The following year, Wham-O began marketing the Hula Hoop, named after the Hawaiian dance its users seemed to imitate by gyrating their hips to keep the hoop rotating around the waist. Wham-O sold twenty-five million brightly colored plastic hoops within four months and created a national craze.

STRANGE FACTS

• In ancient Greece, physicians recommended hoop twirling to adults to lose weight.

• In the fourteenth century, English doctors denounced hoop twirling as a cause of sprains, dislocated backs, and heart attacks.

• South American cultures made hoops from sugarcane plants.

• The hula was originally a religious dance performed by Hawaiians to promote fertility.

• Wham-O, unable to patent an ancient toy, reinvented the hoop for the modern world by using Marlex, a lightweight plastic invented by Phillips Petroleum.

• You can make a Frisbee golf course by hanging a Hula hoop from a tree branch. Designate a tee-off spot and toss the Frisbee toward the "hole," pick it up wherever it lands, and continue tossing until you get the Frisbee through the Hula hoop. Set up nine different holes and keep score. The player with the fewest tosses to get through all the holes wins.

Jacks

WHAT YOU NEED
- A small, bouncy rubber ball
- 10 jacks
- A hard, smooth, level playing surface (floor, sidewalk, patio, or blacktop)

HOW TO PLAY

Sit on the ground and toss the jacks gently onto the playing surface.

Using one hand, gently toss the ball into the air, letting it bounce on the playing surface. With the same hand, pick up one jack and catch the ball before it bounces again.

Repeat until you have picked up all ten jacks. This round is called "onesies."

Toss the ten jacks on the playing surface again.

Toss the ball into the air, letting it bounce once on the playing surface, and pick up two jacks at the same time. Repeat until you have picked up all ten jacks, two at a time. This round is called "twosies."

Increase the number of jacks you pick up during each round until you pick up all ten jacks at once and catch the ball.

If you fail to pick up the correct number of jacks, fail to catch the ball, or drop the jacks from your hand, your turn is over and the next player goes.

When you get another turn, continue where you left off. If you went out during "threesies," toss the ten jacks, and start with "threesies."

To make the game more challenging, forbid players from touching jacks other than the ones being picked up and require players to place the jacks in their free hand before catching the ball.

The first player to complete "onesies" through "tensies" wins the game. For a variation on the game, require all players to go from "onesies" to "tensies" and then back down to "onesies" again.

Kite Making

WHAT YOU NEED

From the hardware or hobby store:

- One pine or cedar 26-inch long stick $1/4$ inch by $1/4$ inch
- One pine or cedar 22-inch long stick $1/4$ inch by $1/4$ inch
- Coping saw
- Scissors
- Yardstick or tape measure
- Pencil
- A sheet of paper 22 inches wide by 26 inches long (gift wrapping or tissue paper for color or white wrapping paper for strength)
- Rubber cement or homemade flour paste (for paper)
- Elmer's Glue-All (for wood)
- Kite string

WHAT TO DO

Mark $1/2$ inch from the ends of each stick. Using a saw, carefully cut a narrow slit $1/2$ inch long in each end.

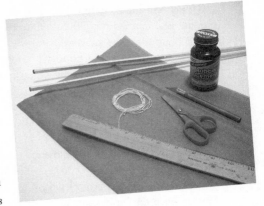

From the end of the 26-inch stick (the spine), measure 7 and $7^{1/4}$ inches from the top and mark.

From each end of the 22-inch stick (the cross), measure $10^{7/8}$ inches and mark.

Apply a thin coat of glue between the marks on both sticks and adhere the sticks perpendicular to each other.

Use a piece of string to securely tie the sticks together at the intersection, keeping the sticks perpendicular to each other.

Cut four pieces of string eight inches long, and wrap each piece twice just below the slit at the ends of each stick, tie a double knot, and let the ends hang free.

Create a diamond framework for the kite by slipping a long piece of string through each of the four slits, pulling the string taut (without bending the sticks), and tying the string ends together. Make certain the two sticks remain perpendicular to each other.

Finish tying the four pieces of string at the end of each stick by wrapping them around the stick to hold the framing string in the notch. Knot securely, and cut off the loose ends.

Place a sheet of paper on a table, place the kite frame spine-side down on the paper, and with a pencil, trace a ³/₄-inch margin around the kite frame, so when the paper is cut, the margin will fold over the framing string.

Safety Rules

• Never fly a kite near electric wires, transmission towers, ditches, or ponds.
• Never fly a kite in a thunderstorm.
• Never make a kite with any metal.
• Never use wire or wet string for a kite line.
• Never fly a kite on a public street, highway, or railroad tracks.
• Never attempt to remove a kite entangled in electrical wires, treetops, roofs, or high poles.

Cut along the outline. Fold the margins so the paper will fit over the framing string without pulling the string out of place and without covering the sticks. Apply glue along the margins, fold in place, then let sit until dry.

When the kite is dry, run a piece of string between the slits in the cross in the back of the kite, pull tautly until the kite bows approximately three to four inches from the spine, and knot securely.

Run a four-foot piece of string from the slits in the spine in the front of the kite and knot securely. Tie the end of the ball of string to the center of this vertical line.

You're ready to fly your kite. A bow kite does not need a tail for balance. Should you feel the need for a tail, attach an

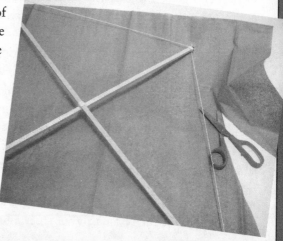

18-inch-long by 2-inch-wide piece of plastic (cut from a plastic trash bag) to the bottom of the kite.

STRANGE FACTS

• Around 3000 B.C.E., the ancient Chinese invented kites as military signaling devices to send coded messages based on the kite's color, painted pattern, and controlled movements in the sky. During the Han Dynasty, the Chinese military attached small bamboo tubes to kites, which, when flown over enemy troops, produced whistling sounds in the wind, frightening away the enemy. The ancient Chinese even tried to use kites made from bamboo and paper to send people airborne. Children in ancient China also flew cleverly designed kites with tails.

• The science of kite building and flying slowly made its way to India and onward to Europe, where people embraced the kite's military applications for sending signals. In the twelfth century, European children flew kites punctured with small holes to make the kites whistle and "sing."

• In 1752, Benjamin Franklin flew a kite during a thunderstorm with a metal key attached to the wire he used as line, to prove that lightning is electricity, conducting the most famous and most dangerous kite experiment in history.

• Kites have also been used to construct bridges, study aerodynamics, and measure the weather.

• In 1847, engineers used a kite to carry a cable across the Niagara River between the United States and Canada to build a suspension bridge.

• In 1893, Australian Lawrence Hargrave invented the box kite, the first truly three-dimensional kite, which the Wright Brothers then used to test their ideas about wing warping, enabling them to make their historic flight in 1903.

• Early meteorologists used kites to carry weather-measuring devices.

• Today kites are used primarily for entertainment.

LINCOLN LOGS

In 1916, John Lloyd Wright, inspired by the interlocking building system used to construct Tokyo's earthquake-proof Imperial Hotel (designed by his father, architect Frank Lloyd Wright), developed a toy building set comprised of sturdy, interlocking logs made from real wood. Wright

named the construction set Lincoln Logs after President Abraham Lincoln, in honor of the fiftieth anniversary of the end of the Civil War. Lincoln Logs® building sets, with their simple building system, became an instant success. After World War II, the resulting baby boom caused sales of Lincoln Logs building sets to skyrocket. Postwar parents bought Lincoln Logs building sets for their children because the educational construction set, unlike ordinary building blocks, captured children's imaginations and forced them to focus their concentration and develop better hand-eye coordination.

LIONEL TRAINS

In 1884, seven-year-old Joshua Lionel Cohen, who was born on New York City's Lower East Side, whittled a miniature locomotive from wood and fit it with a tiny steam engine. It exploded.

As a student at Cooper Union College, Cohen invented what was perhaps the first electric doorbell, but when his instructor insisted that the ringing contraption was impractical, Cohen dropped the idea.

While working at the Acme Electric Light Company as an assembler, Cohen, who changed his last name to Cowen, worked on his inventions on the side. He invented the flashlight to illuminate flowerpots and sold the patent rights to his employee, Russian immigrant Conrad Hubert, who started the company that became the Eveready Battery Company and became a multimillionaire.

Cowen turned his attention to electric fans and soon perfected a miniature motor. When his fan failed to produce a significant breeze, twenty-two-year-old Cowen fitted the small motor beneath the floor of a model railroad flatcar (built by the Converse toy company), giving birth to the electric toy train in 1890. He used his middle name to market the electric flatcar and thirty feet of track for six dollars as the Lionel "Electrical Express" train.

Cowen thought the motorized train, powered by wet-cell batteries wired to the simple thirty-foot loop of 27.8-inch-gauge brass track, made an excellent store window display to attract shoppers. A store commissioned Cowen to build the train layout in its window to showcase its products, but instead onlookers favored the train rather than the goods. When a Rhode Island company placed an order for twenty-five sets, Cowen founded the Lionel Manufacturing Company in lower Manhattan and focused all his energies on producing model railroads. Realizing that accessories could turn the toy train into a hobby, Cowen introduced a suspension bridge in 1902, followed by dozen of other

LIONEL TRAINS
"The Trains Railroad Men Buy for their Boys"

unique accessories, and a sixteen-page Lionel catalog. To sell hobbyists more than one train, Cowen created realistic train models painted to represent different railroad companies (such as locomotive used by the Baltimore & Ohio Railroad and the New York Central Railroad) and developed electronically activated action cars (such as the Mechanical Derrick Car) that duplicated freight-loading operations.

Cowen also designed his detailed locomotives to last a lifetime—making the locomotive bodies from sheet steel, coating the cars with heavy enamel, and casting the wheels from nickeled steel.

Since batteries had a short life span, in 1906 Cowen invented a transformer to modify household electricity to power the trains through the train tracks. To enable his locomotives to pick up electrical power from the rails

more efficiently, Cowen replaced his two-rail track with a three-rail track that he named "Standard Gauge." A metal roller on the bottom of the engine picked up current from the center rail. Current flowed back out through the engine's wheels. Competing model railroad manufacturers copied this new design, inspiring Cowen to advertise Lionel trains as "Standard of the World."

In 1910, the Ives Company introduced O gauge trains (half the size of the Standard gauge trains), enabling model railroad enthusiasts to build train layouts in the half the space. Realizing the advantages of smaller trains, Cowen launched a line of O gauge Lionel trains, tracks, and accessories in 1915. Within two years,

Lionel trains were the best-selling model trains in the United States, and within twenty years, the less expensive O gauge trains outsold the larger Standard gauge trains (which Lionel would phase out in 1939).

The company continued making innovations. In 1935, Lionel introduced the steam whistle, mounted in the tender of select locomotives and activated by a push of a button. In 1945, Lionel came out with the magnetic coupler, and the following year, the company introduced locomotives whose smoke stacks bellow forth real smoke. By 1953, Lionel had firmly established itself as the largest toy maker in the world.

Spiked

On May 10, 1869, the Union Pacific and Central Pacific railways were linked together with two golden spikes during a well-publicized ceremony at Promontory, Utah. Although the builders immediately replaced the golden spikes with steel spikes to avoid theft, within a few days souvenir hunters disconnected the transcontinental railroad at the historic spot, stealing twelve spikes, six ties, and two pairs of rails.

Today, Lionel remains one of the world's leading marketers of model trains, the most widely recognized brand in the toy train industry, and one of the most recognized brands in America.

STRANGE FACTS

• The "Lionel Boy" featured on most prewar Lionel packaging was Joshua Cowen's son Larry.

• In 1912, Cowen produced one of the first model race cars using a form of slotted track. When the product failed to sell well, Lionel stopped making it.

• During World War I, the United States government contracted Lionel to produce periscopes, compasses, and navigation instruments for the Signal Corps.

All-Time Lionel Favorites

• **Coal Elevator.** This building accepts loads of artificial coal into its receiving bin, hoists it up to the elevator's storage bin, one bucket at a time, and, at the push of button, releases the coal into waiting hoppers on a parallel track.

• **Bascule Bridge.** This drawbridge rises open and drops back down automatically.

• **Gateman.** A small gateman automatically pops out from his shack and swings a lantern whenever a train passes by.

• **Log Loader.** This loading dock accepts a load of wooden-dowel logs, conveys them into a loading bin, and, at the push of a button, dumps them into a waiting car on a parallel track.

• **Milk Car.** When parked in front of a loading dock, the door to this white refrigerator car swings open, and a small man unloads a metal milk can onto the adjoining platform.

• **Coal Loader.** This loading dock accepts loads from ore-dump cars and carries the dumped ore up a conveyer belt and into a waiting ore-dump car or hopper.

• **Searchlight Car.** A flatcar with a depressed-center holds a powerful electric searchlight.

• **Cattle Car.** When this car is parked next to the cattle stockade, a push of a button causes the car's doors to open and cattle to exit the car into the corral.

• **Switch Tower.** Two railroad workers emerge from this building (one holding a lantern, the other descending a flight of stairs) whenever a locomotive passes by.

Marbles

WHAT YOU NEED
- Large and small marbles
- Chalk, string, or a stick

HOW TO PLAY

Draw a circle two feet in diameter. Use chalk on asphalt or concrete, a stick in dirt, or a loop of string on a carpet or tile floor.

Each player chooses an easily identifiable marble to use as a shooter and places an equal number of marbles inside the circle. Ideally, shooters should be larger marbles.

Kneeling on the ground outside the circle, hold the shooter in your fist and flick your thumb to shoot it at any marble(s) inside the circle, trying to knock as many marbles as possible outside the line.

Collect any marbles you knock out of the circle.

Continue shooting until you fail to knock any marbles out of the circle or your shooter remains in the circle—in which case your turn is over and the next player shoots.

Players continue shooting in turn until all the marbles have been knocked from the circle. Whoever has the most marbles at the end of the game is the winner.

STRANGE FACTS

• Marbles can be played for fun, returning the marbles to each original owner at the end of the game, or as a gambling game called "keepsies," in which each player keeps the marbles won.

• The phrase "losing your marbles," derived from playing "keepsies," means losing your mind.

• Almost every ancient culture independently developed the game of marbles.

• Primitive man used chestnuts, hazelnuts, and olives as marbles.

• Ancient Egyptian children played marbles with semiprecious stones as early as 3000 B.C.E.

• As early as 1435 B.C.E., children on the Greek island of Crete played with marble balls made from jasper and agate.

• The word marble is derived from the Greek word *marmaros* (meaning polished white agate).

• Ancient Romans made clear glass marbles from silica and ash.

• The British Museum contains a collection of marbles from ancient Egypt and Rome.

• Ancient Saxons and Celts used ordinary stones and pellets of clay as marbles.

• The 1560 painting "Children's Games" by Flemish painter Pieter Brueghel depicts children shooting marbles.

• Although marbles have been made from clay, stone, wood, glass, and steel, most marbles today are made from glass.

• When a German glassblower invented a tool called marble scissors in 1846, the manufacture of glass marbles became economically feasible.

• World War I cut off the supply of marbles from Europe to North America.

• Most glass marbles in the United States are made at a plant in Clarksburg, West Virginia, which makes millions every year.

• A variety of colors and intricate patterns create a wide range of glass marbles, including the Cat's Eye, First American, Genuine Carnelian, Immy, Japanese Cat's Eye, Marine, Moonstone, Peppermint Stripe, Rainbow, and Scrap Glass.

• Marble games include Archboard, Bounce About, Bounce Eye, Conqueror, Die Shot, Dobblers, Eggs in the Bush, Handers, Hundreds, Increase Pound, Lag Out, Long Taw, Odds or Even, One Step, Picking Plums, Pyramid, Ring Taw, Spanners, and Three Holes.

• Marbles are often used at the bottom of clear glass vases to support flowers or at the bottom of fish tanks as decorative gravel.

• The most common method of shooting a marble is known as *fulking*.

MONOPOLY

When Charles B. Darrow, a heating engineer in Germantown, Pennsylvania, lost his job during the Depression, he lifted his flagging spirits by devising board games at home to entertain himself. Fantasizing about easy money and frightfully aware of how easily an amassed fortune could be wiped out overnight by the fickle finger of fate, Darrow began creating a game based on buying and trading real estate deeds, building houses and hotels, and getting rich through a toss of the dice. In 1933, Darrow fondly remembered a vacation to Atlantic City, New Jersey, and named the playing squares on his board game after the streets in the resort town.

In 1934, encouraged by his friends and family who loved playing the game, Darrow brought it to the Parker Brothers Company in Massachusetts. After playing the Monopoly® game, Parker Brothers executives rejected the game, citing "52 design errors," including a dull premise, slow action, and overly complicated rules.

Undaunted, Darrow convinced Wanamaker's department store in Philadelphia to sell the game. He borrowed money from family and friends, and with help from a printer, produced five thousand sets of the Monopoly game. When demand outpaced Darrow's ability to produce the game, he reapproached Parker Brothers in 1935. Impressed by Monopoly® game sales, Parker Brothers executives reversed their previous assessment of the game, copyrighted the name Monopoly, and were soon producing twenty thousand Monopoly sets a week. The Monopoly game quickly became the best-selling game in the United States, turning Charles Darrow, who received a royalty for every game sold, into a millionaire.

STRANGE FACTS

• In 1936, convinced that the public's fascination with the Monopoly game was a short-lived fad, company president George Parker ceased production of the game. The company soon resumed production because that anticipated slump in sales has yet to occur.

• Monopoly is the best-selling board game in the world, sold in eighty countries and produced in twenty-six languages.

• More than 200 million Monopoly sets have been sold worldwide.

• Since 1935, Parker Brothers has manufactured more than eight billion little green houses.

• The longest Monopoly game ever played lasted 1,680 hours (equal to seventy consecutive days).

• During World War II, Americans smuggled contraband material into POW camps inside Germany by inserting escape maps, compasses, and files into Monopoly game boards and by slipping genuine currency into the packs of Monopoly money.

• The largest outdoor Monopoly game ever played used a game board 938 feet wide by 765 feet long.

• In 1975, two students at Cornell University, Jay Walker and Jeffrey Lehman, co-authored the book, *1000 Ways to Win Monopoly Games*. Jay Walker went on to found Priceline.com, and Lehman currently serves as president of Cornell University.

• Parker Brothers prints approximately fifty billion dollars worth of Monopoly money every year.

• Each Monopoly set contains 15,140 dollars in Monopoly money.

• The price values on the Monopoly game board remain the same as they were in 1935 (with the exception of the taxes, which were changed in 1936).

• Boardwalk is called *Rue de la Paix* in France, *Schlossallee* in German, *Kalverstraat* in the Netherlands, and *Mayfair* in the United Kingdom.

• The name of the cartoon character on the Monopoly board, Chance cards, and Community Chest cards is Mr. Monopoly.

MR. POTATO HEAD

Shortly after World War II ended, inventor George Lerner created a set of plastic noses, ears, eyes, and mouth parts that could be pushed into fruits or vegetables to create comical food characters. Toy companies, however, rejected Lerner's new toy, convinced that American consumers, still clinging to a World War II mentality to conserve resources, would refuse to buy any toy that wasted food.

Lerner eventually sold the rights to the toy for five thousand dollars to a cereal company that planned to use the pieces as a premium giveaway in cereal boxes. Regretting the move and confident that his new toy had much greater potential, Lerner showed his creation to a New England manufacturer. With shared enthusiasm, Lerner and the manufacturer bought back the rights from the cereal company for seven thousand dollars.

In 1952, Hasbro, Inc., a toy company based in Pawtucket, Rhode Island, launched Mr. Potato Head® toy character, a box of plastic parts (eyes, ears, noses, and mouths) that children could use to adorn a real potato (provided by mom and dad). When Mr. Potato Head became the very first toy to be advertised on television, sales skyrocketed.

STRANGE FACTS

- One year after introducing Mr. Potato Head, Hasbro launched his wife, Mrs. Potato Head. On February 11, 1985, after twenty-three years of marriage, Hasbro introduced the first Tater Tot of Mr. and Mrs. Potato Head—Baby Potato Head.
- In 1960, Hasbro added a hard plastic potato "body" to Mr. Potato Head.
- In 1987, Mr. Potato Head surrendered his signature pipe to United States Surgeon General C. Everett Koop and became the spokespotato for the American Cancer Society's annual "Great American Smokeout" campaign.

PLAY-DOH

In 1956, brothers Noah and Joseph McVicker of the Rainbow Crafts Company, a soap company in Cincinnati, Ohio, received United States patent number 3,167,440 for a soft, reusable, nontoxic modeling compound cleverly named Play-Doh®. According to the patent office, the McVicker brothers originally invented Play-Doh as a wall-paper cleaner. The McVicker brothers obviously realized  their invention made a better children's toy. In 1955, they tested Play-Doh modeling compound in nursery schools, kindergartens, and elementary schools in Cincinnati.

First sold and demonstrated in the toy department of Woodward & Lothrop Department Store in Washington, D.C., the original cream-colored Play-Doh, packaged in a twelve-ounce cardboard can, became an immediate hit. In 1957, the Rainbow Crafts Company introduced Play-Doh in blue, red, and yellow. Three years later, the company introduced the Play-Doh Fun Factory.

In 1965, General Mills bought the Rainbow Crafts Company, folding Play-Doh into its Kenner Toy Company in 1970. The Tonka Corporation purchased Kenner in 1987, and four years later, Hasbro acquired Tonka and transferred Play-Doh to its Playskool division.

STRANGE FACTS
• The patent for Play-Doh explains how Play-Doh modeling compound is made: "We are unable to state definitely the theory upon which this process operates, because the reactions taking place in the mass are complicated."
• One of the most recognized scents in the world is the smell of Play-Doh.
• The Play-Doh boy, pictured on every can of Play-Doh, is named Play-Doh Pete and was created in 1960.
• In 1986, the cardboard Play-Doh can, used for thirty years, was replaced with a tightly-sealing, easy-to-open plastic container to ensure the modeling compound a longer life.
• Kids eat more Play-Doh than crayons, finger paint, and white paste combined.

- The formula for the original Play-Doh® modeling compound still remains top secret.
- Today, Play-Doh is sold in more than seventy-five countries.
- If rolled together, all the Play-Doh manufactured since 1956 would make a ball weighing more than 700 million pounds.
- More than two billion cans of Play-Doh have been sold since 1956.
- If all the Play-Doh made since 1956 were squeezed through the Fun Factory®, it would make a snake that would wrap around the earth nearly three hundred times.

Secret Formula
HOMEMADE PLAY-DOUGH

WHAT YOU NEED

From the supermarket:
- Food coloring
- 2 cups flour
- 1 cup salt
- 1 teaspoon alum
- 1 teaspoon 20 Mule Team Borax
- 1 tablespoon canola oil

From the kitchen:
- Large glass bowl
- Frying pan
- Wooden spoon
- Cutting board
- Ziploc storage bag or airtight container

From the tap:
- 2 cups water

WHAT TO DO

In the bowl, combine the water and fifty drops of food coloring. (For blue Play-Dough, use 45 drops blue food coloring and 5 drops green. For orange, use 15 drops red, 30 drops yellow.) Then add the flour, salt, alum, borax, and canola oil. Mix well. Cook and stir in the frying pan over medium heat for three minutes (or until the mixture holds together). Turn onto the cutting board and knead to proper consistency. Store in the Ziploc bag or airtight container. (After you make Play-Dough in an old pan, the pan will be sparkling clean. The combination of flour and salt cleans the pan.)

HOW TO USE IT

Mold as you would Play-Doh. If molding compound hardens, add one drop of water at a time to restore pliable consistency. To remove from carpet or fabrics, allow the dough to dry, then loosen with a stiff brush and vacuum.

RADIO FLYER WAGONS

In 1917 in a small town outside of Venice, Italy, the Pasin family sold their mule to help raise enough money to send their sixteen-year-old son, Antonio, on a ship to the United States. Pasin made his way to Chicago, and unable to find work as a cabinet-maker like his father and grandfather before him, saved enough money working odd jobs to buy some used wood-working equipment and rent a one-room work-shop. At night he built coaster wagons for children and sold them by day.

By 1923, Pasin had sev-eral employees working for his Liberty Coaster Company, named after the Statue of Liberty. They soon created the No. 4 Liberty Coaster, a hand-crafted wooden wagon for children which Pasin personally sold directly to stores. Inspired by the automotive industry, Pasin began using metal-stamping technology to produce steel wagons, embracing mass-production techniques to create the Radio Flyer line of affordable, high-quality wagons "For every boy. For every girl." Pasin named the Radio Flyer in honor of the invention of the radio by fellow Italian, Guglielmo Marconi, and his fascination with flight.

In 1930, Pasin renamed his company Radio Steel & Manu-facturing. The company, already the world's largest producer of toy coaster wagons, partici-pated in the 1933 World's Fair in Chicago, making Radio Flyer world renowned. Soon afterwards, the company in-troduced the Streak-O-Lite, a classic red wagon with sleek

Blitz Cans

During World War II, Radio Flyer ceased all wagon production to focus all of its manufacturing efforts on mak-ing five-gallon steel "Blitz Cans" to be mounted on the backs of jeeps, trucks, and tanks to transport fuel and water to troops stationed overseas.

styling modeled after the popular Zephyr streamline trains, complete with control dials and working headlights.

Today, the company is run by Antonio Pasin's grandsons, Robert and Paul Pasin. In 1997, to celebrate the eightieth anniversary of the company, Radio Flyer introduced the world's

largest wagon, measuring 27 feet long, 13 feet wide, and weighing 15,000 pounds.

RAGGEDY ANN

In 1906, Marcella Gruelle, daughter of author and illustrator Johnny Gruelle, found a worn rag doll in her grandmother's attic. After her mother, Myrtle, patched and re-stuffed the doll, her father, Johnny, painted new facial features on the doll, including a unique triangular nose.

Marcella named the doll Raggedy Ann®, combining the names of the main characters from two of her favorite poems, "The Raggedy Man" and "Little Orphan Annie" by James Witcomb Riley, a friend of the family. When Marcella fell ill as a child, her father would entertain her by inventing stories about Raggedy Ann and her adventures.

When Marcella died in her early teens, Johnny Gruelle coped with his daughter's death by compiling and illustrating all the Raggedy Ann stories he had told Marcella over the years.

He patented the Raggedy Ann doll in 1915, published the stories in 1918, produced handmade Raggedy Ann dolls, and, in 1920, introduced a second doll, the brother of Raggedy Ann—Raggedy Andy®.

STRANGE FACTS

• John Barton Gruelle, born on December 24, 1880, in Arcola, Illinois, worked as a newspaper cartoonist in Indianapolis, Indiana, and later moved to Norwalk, Connecticut, where he created the popular "Mr. Twee Deedle" comic strip.

• Marcella Gruelle's original Raggedy Ann doll purportedly contained a heart-shaped candy imprinted with the words "I Love You." Today, a heart with the words "I Love You" is silk-screened on every Raggedy Ann doll.

• Raggedy Ann is the longest-running character license in the toy industry.

• Gruelle wrote and illustrated an average of one Raggedy Ann and Raggedy Andy book every year.

• After Johnny's death in 1901, his widow, Myrtle, ran the company, then passed the reins to her two sons, Worth and Richard, who sold the company to Hasbro.

ROADMASTER LUXURY LINER

In 1936, the Cleveland Welding Company introduced Roadmaster Bicycles. Fifteen years later, the Cleveland Welding Company merged with Junior Toy Company after a parent company acquired both firms. The following year, the company introduced the 1952 Roadmaster Luxury Liner, designed by Brooks Stevens, the industrial designer who coined the phrase "planned obsolescence." Stevens envisioned "better, more desirable products each season so customers can't resist upgrading." The 1952 Roadmaster Luxury Liner featured a Shockmaster coiled-sprint front fork, a chrome-trimmed horn tank, a rear carrier with taillights, and a powerful Searchbeam headlight that enabled children to continue riding the bicycle after dark. The Roadmaster Luxury Liner became the best-selling bicycle the Cleveland Welding Company ever produced.

SCRABBLE

In 1931, Alfred Mosher Butts, a New England architect who lost his job during the Depression, entertained himself at home by trying to figure out how to turn the popular crossword puzzle into a viable board game. After calculating how often each of the twenty-six letters of the English language appeared on the front page of the *New York Times,* Butts decided how many of each letter to include in his game and assigned a different point value to each letter.

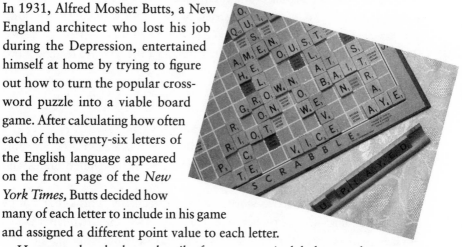

He cut one hundred wooden tiles from quarter-inch balsa wood and hand-lettered each one with a letter of the alphabet and its point value. To limit the use of plural words, Butts decided to include only four of the letter S in the game. Using his architectural drafting tools, Butts drew a grid of boxes and reproduced the board by blueprinting his original and pasting it on folding checkerboards.

He originally named the game Lexico, but eventually changed the name to "Criss-Cross Words." Over the next ten years, Butts played the game with his family and friends, fine-tuning the rules and each letter's point value.

In 1948, one of his friends, James Brunot of Newton, Connecticut, persuaded Butts that the game had vast commercial potential. Butts and Brunot refined the game, copyrighted it as Scrabble®, and brought it to game manufacturers. When major game manufacturers rejected the game, Brunot set up the first Scrabble factory in an abandoned schoolhouse in Dodgington, Connecticut, where he and friends made twelve sets of the game per hour, stamping the letters on wooden tiles one at a time. The Scrabble game slowly gained popularity, and in the early 1950s, the president of Macy's purportedly discovered Scrabble while on vacation and ordered some for his store.

In 1952, Brunot, unable to make the games fast enough to meet rising demand, licensed the rights to market and distribute the Scrabble game to Selchow and Righter Company, the maker of Parcheesi and a well-known game manufacturer founded in 1867.

Scrabble became the second best-selling American board game, behind

Monopoly and ahead of third-place Parcheesi. In 1972, Selchow and Righter bought the trademark Scrabble® from Brunot, giving them the exclusive rights to all Scrabble-brand products and entertainment services in the United States and Canada. In 1986, Coleco Industries, maker of the Cabbage Patch dolls, purchased Selchow & Righter. When Coleco went bankrupt three years later, Hasbro Inc., owner of Milton Bradley Company, the nation's leading game company, bought Scrabble.

STRANGE FACTS
• The word Scrabble means "to grope frantically."
• The National Scrabble Association sanctions more than 175 Scrabble tournaments and more than 200 Scrabble clubs in the United States and Canada every year.
• Learning the 96 two-letter words and the three-letter words that can be formed by adding a letter to either to the front or back of these two-letter words can help increase your Scrabble scores by at least fifty points per game.
• A Scrabble game can be found in one out of every three homes in America.
• The letter Q can be used without the letter U to form the following eleven words and their plural forms: faqir, qaid, qanat, qat, qindar, qindarkas, qintar, qoph, qwerty, sheqel, and tranq.

SILLY PUTTY

In the 1940s, when the United States War Production Board asked General Electric to synthesize an inexpensive substitute for rubber, James Wright, a company engineer, was assigned to the project in New Haven, Connecticut. Unfortunately, the pliant compound mixed from boric acid and silicone oil, dubbed "nutty putty," offered no advantages over synthetic rubber.

In 1949, Paul Hodgson, a former advertising copywriter running a New Haven toy store, happened to witness a demonstration of the "nutty putty" at a party. He bought twenty-one pounds of the putty for 147 dollars, hired a Yale student to separate it into half-ounce balls, and marketed the putty inside colored plastic eggs as "Silly Putty," a name he came up with off the top of his head while playing with the pink polymer.

When Silly Putty outsold every other item in his store, Hodgson mass-produced Silly Putty as "the toy with one moving part," selling up to three hundred eggs a day. He shipped Silly Putty in egg cartons purchased from the Connecticut Cooperative Poultry Association. *The New Yorker* featured a short piece on Silly Putty in "Talk of the Town," launching an overnight novelty in the 1950s and 1960s.

STRANGE FACTS

• In 1961, Silly Putty attracted hundreds of Russians to the United States Plastics Expo in Moscow.

• The astronauts on Apollo 8 played with Silly Putty during their flight and used it to keep tools from floating around in zero gravity.

• In 1981, the Columbus Zoo used Silly Putty to take hand and foot prints of gorillas for educational purposes.

• Geology and Astronomy professors often use Silly Putty to demonstrate the gradual movement of large masses of Earth.

• Non-smoking groups recommend Silly Putty to their members to give their hands something to do.

• Americans buy more than two million eggs of Silly Putty every year.

• While the average fad lasts six months, demand for Silly Putty has continued for more than fifty years.

SLINKY

In 1943, Richard James, a twenty-nine-year-old marine engineer working in Philadelphia's Cramp Shipyard, tried to figure out how to use springs to mount delicate meters for testing horsepower on World War II battleships. When a torsion spring fell off his desk and tumbled end over end across the floor, James realized he could create a new toy by devising a steel formula that would give the spring the proper tension to "walk."

After James found a steel wire that would coil, uncoil, and recoil, his wife, Betty, a graduate of Penn State University, thumbed through the dictionary to find an appropriate name for the toy. She choose Slinky because it meant "stealthy, sleek, and sinuous."

In the summer of 1945, the Jameses borrowed five hundred dollars to pay a machine shop to make a small quantity of Slinkys. During the Christmas shopping season, they convinced a buyer from Gimbel's Department Store in downtown Philadelphia to provide counter space for four hundred Slinkys and let them demonstrate the new toy to customers. Richard James went alone, carrying a small demonstration staircase. Much to his astonishment, he sold all four hundred Slinkys in ninety minutes.

The Slinky became the hit of the 1946 American Toy Fair, and Slinky sales soared. The Jameses founded James Industries with a factory in Philadelphia to market their product. Richard James invented machines that could coil eighty feet of steel wire into a Slinky in less than eleven seconds.

In 1960, Richard James abandoned his business and family to join a religious cult in Bolivia, leaving his wife, Betty, behind with six kids, a floundering Slinky business, and a huge debt (largely rung up by his donations to his spiritual leaders). Betty James relocated the Slinky factory to her hometown of Hollidaysburg, Pennsylvania, devised a unique co-op advertising plan for the toy, and began marketing the Slinky with a simple jingle that infected the collective consciousness of the Baby Boom.

STRANGE FACTS

• The original Slinky has seen only two changes since its inception in 1943. The prototype blue-black Swedish steel was replaced with less expensive, silvery American metal (specially coated for durability), and in 1973, the Slinky's ends were crimped for safety reasons.

• Slinky sales have totaled more than 250 million. That's roughly one Slinky for every man, woman, and child in the United States.

• The metal coil of a standard Slinky stretched out straight measures eighty-seven feet in length.

• The Slinky jingle, broadcast on television continuously since 1962, is now one of the most recognizable toy jingles in America, recognized by nearly 90 percent of all adults.

• More than three million miles of wire have been used to make the classic Slinky since its inception. That's enough wire to make a Slinky big enough to hold the earth and stretch to the moon and back.

• The Slinky is sold on every continent of the world except Antarctica.

• Slinkys are on exhibit in the Smithsonian Institute and in the Metropolitan Museum of Art.

Slinky Dog

In 1952, seven years after the first Slinky appeared on the scene, Mrs. Helen Malsed of Seattle, Washington, sent an idea to Richard and Betty James. Later that year, Slinky Dog was on toy store shelves across America. Slinky Dog was eventually discontinued, but reappeared on the scene after he made a strong supporting role in the 1995 Disney movie *Toy Story* and the 1999 Disney sequel *Toy Story 2*. The voice of Slinky Dog was provided by Jim Varney, better known as Ernest P. Worrell in the movies *Ernest Goes to Camp*, *Ernest Saves Christmas*, and *Ernest Goes to Jail*.

• United States soldiers using radios during combat in Vietnam tossed the Slinky into trees to act as a makeshift antenna.

• In 1985, Space Shuttle astronaut Jeffrey Hoffman became the first person to play with a Slinky in space. He used the Slinky to conduct zero-gravity physics experiments while in orbit around the earth.

• The Slinky helps scientists understand the supercoiling of DNA molecules. Slinky and Shear Slinky, two computer graphics programs developed at the University of Maryland, use a Slinky model to approximate the double helix coiling of DNA molecules.

• Betty James ran the company until 1998 when, at the age of eighty-three, she sold James Industries to Poof Products so she would have more time to spend with her six children and sixteen grandchildren.

• In 1999, the United States Postal Service introduced a Slinky stamp.

TEDDY BEARS

In 1902, President Theodore Roosevelt traveled south to negotiate a border dispute between the states of Mississippi and Louisiana. During a break from the negotiations, Roosevelt accepted an invitation to join a hunting expedition in Smedes, Mississippi. After ten days of hunting, Roosevelt failed to spot a single bear. His hosts, hoping to please the President, searched the woods, found a small bear cub, tethered it to a tree outside Roosevelt's tent, and cried "Bear!" to beckon the president. Roosevelt emerged from his tent, took one look at the frightened cub, and refused to kill such a young animal.

Newspapers reported the event. In the *Washington Star*, political cartoonist Clifford K. Berryman drew a caricature of Roosevelt with his hand upraised, refusing to shoot the cuddly bear cub. The caption read "Drawing the Line in Mississippi," cleverly referring to the unresolved border dispute.

Inspired by the cartoon, toy store owner Morris Michtom, a thirty-two-year-old Russian immigrant, made a stuffed bear cub and displayed it alongside the political cartoon in his store window in Brooklyn to generate attention. When customers wanted to buy their own "Teddy's Bear," Michtom began making them, founding the Ideal Toy Company. Meanwhile in Germany, Richard Steiff, a nephew of stuffed toy maker Margarete Steiff, similarly inspired by Berryman's political cartoon, created his own stuffed bear toy. Launched at the 1903 Leipzig Trade Fair, Steiff's bears also began selling quickly. In 1906, guests at a White House wedding reception for Roosevelt's daughter discovered tables decorated with Steiff bears dressed as hunters and fishermen as a tribute to the President's love for the outdoors. While mulling over the possible breed of the animals, a wedding guest cleverly labeled them "Teddy Bears." In 1907 alone, Steiff produced more than 974,000 Teddy Bears.

TINKERTOY

Around 1910, Charles Pajeau, a stonemason from Evanston, Illinois, discovered that his children built structures by sticking pencils and sticks into empty spools of thread. Inspired by his children's ingenuity, Pajeau worked in his garage to create a shorter, wheel-like spool with a series of holes running around the circumference and several other basic wooden parts so his children could build a wide variety of three-dimensional structures.

Realizing he had created a marketable construction toy that let kids tinker for hours, Pajeau teamed up with Robert Pettit to found the Toy Tinkers of Evanston, Illinois, and the two men displayed Tinkertoy®, packaged in a cardboard canister with a metal lid and bottom, at the 1914 American Toy Fair. Unfortunately, Tinkertoy went unnoticed. Undaunted, Pajeau and Pettit built an elaborate Tinkertoy display in the pharmacy of Grand Central Station in New York City so passersby would see how children could play with the creations they built with Tinkertoy parts. Within days, the display generated thousands of sales.

At Christmas time, Pajeau and Pettit hired several little people, dressed them in elf costumes, and had them play with Tinkertoy in a display window of a Chicago department store as a publicity stunt. Within a year, over a million Tinkertoy sets had been sold.

In 1985, Playskool acquired Tinkertoy.

Do-It-Yourself
TRIANGLE PEG GAME

WHAT YOU NEED

From the hardware store:
- Equilateral triangle of $3/4$-inch pine wood with a base $5^1/2$ inches long and height $4^7/8$ inches long
- Sandpaper

From the sporting goods store:
- 14 golf tees

From the workshop:
- Electric drill with $1/16$-inch bit
- Ruler
- Pencil

WHAT TO DO

Using the ruler, draw a line down the center of the triangle. Measure $1/4$ inch from the base of the triangle and draw a line parallel to the base. On the intersection of the two lines, make a dot and mark four more dots along the horizontal line, each one inch apart. From that first line, measure up $7/8$ inch and draw a second line parallel to the base.

Where the second line intersects the height line, measure $1/2$ inch from both sides of the height line and make two dots. Measure one inch from each of those dots and make two more dots.

From that second line, measure up $7/8$ inch and draw a third line parallel to the base. On the intersection of the third line and the height line, make a dot and mark two more dots along the horizontal line, each one inch apart.

From that third line, measure up $7/8$ inch and draw a fourth line parallel to the base. Where the fourth line intersects the height line, measure $1/2$ inch from both sides of the height line and make two dots.

From that fourth line, measure up $7/8$ inch and draw a fifth line parallel to the base. Make a dot where the fifth line intersects the height line.

Drill a hole through each one of the fifteen dots. Sand the triangle of wood and each of the drilled holes.

HOW TO PLAY

Place all the golf tees in the holes, leaving one hole empty anywhere on the board. Some people prefer to start with the missing peg in a corner of the triangle. Jump pegs one at a time by moving an adjacent peg to the open hole directly across from it and then remove the jumped peg. You can only remove pegs by jumping them. See if you can leave only one peg on the board. For a more difficult challenge, see if you can leave the one peg in the hole that began the game empty.

Do-It-Yourself
Wooden Train

WHAT YOU NEED

From the craft store or hardware store:

- One $7^1/_2$-inch length of $1^3/_4$- by $2^1/_2$-inch pine
- One $4^1/_2$-inch length of $1^3/_4$- by $2^1/_2$-inch pine
- Four $6^1/_2$-inch lengths of $1^3/_4$- by $2^1/_2$-inch pine
- One $8^1/_2$-inch length of $^1/_2$- by $4^1/_4$-inch pine
- One $5^1/_2$-inch length of $^1/_2$- by $4^1/_4$-inch pine
- Four $7^1/_2$-inch lengths of $^1/_2$- by $4^1/_4$-inch pine
- Three 6-inch lengths of $1^1/_2$- by 2-inch pine, with two edges of the 2-inch height rounded
- One $3^1/_2$-inch length of $1^3/_4$- by $3^1/_2$-inch pine, with one end of the $3^1/_2$-inch length rounded
- One $1^1/_2$-inch length of $^3/_4$-inch diameter hardwood dowel
- One $5^1/_2$-inch length of $1^3/_4$- by $4^1/_4$-inch pine
- Two 7-inch lengths of $1^3/_4$- by $2^1/_4$- inch pine
- Two 7-inch lengths of $^3/_8$- by 1-inch pine
- Two $3^3/_4$-inch lengths of $^3/_8$- by 1-inch pine
- One $7^1/_2$-inch length of 2- by $2^3/_4$- inch pine
- Eight $^3/_4$-inch diameter hardwood knobs
- 24 hardwood wheels ($1^3/_4$-inch diameter)
- 12 hardwood dowels $4^1/_8$-inch length ($^1/_8$-inch diameter)
- Five pairs of eye hooks

WHAT TO DO

To make the locomotive engine: On the $7^1/_2$-inch length of $1^3/_4$- by $2^1/_2$-inch pine, measure in one inch from each end of the $1^3/_4$-inch wide side of the block and $^3/_8$-inch from the bottom of the block. Using a $^3/_8$-inch drill bit, drill two holes for the axles. Glue the $8^1/_2$-inch length of $^1/_2$- by $4^1/_4$-inch pine on top of the wheel block. Glue a 6-inch length of $1^1/_2$- by 2-inch pine (with two edges of the 2-inch height rounded) and the $3^1/_2$-inch length of $1^3/_4$- by $3^1/_2$-inch pine into place on top of the wheel block to create the locomotive engine. Drill a $^3/_4$-inch hole $^1/_2$ inch deep in the top of the 6-inch length of $1^1/_2$- by 2-inch pine (toward the front of the engine). Glue the $1^1/_2$-inch length of $^3/_4$-inch diameter hardwood dowel

into the hole. Drill six holes in the top of the front of the engine to attach the hardwood knob (as pictured above). Drill a ³/₄-inch hole in the two sides of the cabin (as pictured above).

To make the locomotive tender: On the 4¹/₂-inch length of 1³/₄- by 2¹/₂-inch pine, measure in one inch from each end of the 1³/₄-inch wide side of the block and ³/₈-inch from the bottom of the block. Using a ³/₈-inch drill bit, drill two holes for the axles. Glue the 5¹/₂-inch length of ¹/₂- by 4¹/₄-inch pine on top of the wheel block. From the 5¹/₂-inch length of 1³/₄- by 4¹/₄-inch pine, cut a 5- by 3³/₄-inch block. Glue the remains of the 5¹/₂ inch length to the top of the wheel block to create the locomotive tender.

To make the box car, coal car, oil tanker, and caboose: On each one of the four 6¹/₂-inch lengths of 1³/₄- by 2¹/₂-inch pine, measure in one inch from each end of the 1³/₄-inch wide side of the block and ³/₈-inch from the bottom of the block. Using a ³/₈-inch drill bit, drill two holes for the axles. Glue each one of the four 7¹/₂-inch lengths of ¹/₂- by 4¹/₄-inch pine on top of each of the four wheel blocks.

For the box car, take the first 6¹/₂-inch length wheel block, glue the two 7-inch lengths of 1³/₄- by 2¹/₄-inch pine together to create the box car top 3¹/₂ inches wide. Cut a square in the bottom of the wood block to create a box car door (see picture). Glue the box car top to the wheel block.

For the coal car, take the second 6¹/₂-inch length wheel block, use glue and small nails to attach the two 7-inch lengths of ³/₈- by 1-inch pine (top coal car) and the two 3³/₄-inch lengths of ³/₈- by 1-inch pine to create the walls of a coal car.

For the oil tanker, take the third 6¹/₂-inch length wheel block, use glue to attach the two remaining 6-inch lengths of 1¹/₂- by 2-inch pine (with two edges of the 2-inch height rounded) to create the dual oil tanker. Drill

six holes in the top of the oil tankers to attach the hardwood knobs (as pictured on page 140).

For the caboose, take the fourth 6$\frac{1}{2}$-inch length wheel block, cut the 7$\frac{1}{2}$-inch length of 2- by 2$\frac{3}{4}$-inch pine to match the caboose cabin in the picture. Drill two $\frac{3}{4}$-inch holes for windows. Glue the cabin on the wheel block. Drill one hole in the top of the caboose to attach the hardwood knob (as pictured on page 140).

Insert the hardwood dowels through the axle holes of every wheel block and glue on the hardwood wheels. Screw the eye hooks into the front and back of each car (with the exception of the front of the engine and the back of the caboose) to attach the cars into a train.

STRANGE FACTS

• British civil engineer Sir Thomas Bouch designed a two-mile-long bridge to cross the Tay River in Scotland from Newport to Dundee. The bridge was opened in 1878, and Bouch was knighted in June 1879. Unfortunately, Bouch failed to calculate the effects of wind pressure on the bridge or provide any continuous lateral wind bracing below the deck. On December 28, 1879, a hurricane hit the bridge, blowing thirteen spans of wrought-iron lattice girders into the river, bringing the Edinburgh mail train with them, killing all seventy passengers aboard.

• During World War I, German spy Carl Hans Lody, based in England, received reports of troop trains traveling with the window blinds shut. Lody received a follow-up report that a soldier aboard one of those trains, when asked where he was from, replied "Russia." Unbeknownst to Lody, the blinds on the troop trains in England had been shut so the Scottish soldiers from Ross Shire (not "Russia") could sleep. Lody wired his German

superiors, informing them that large numbers of Russian troops stationed in England were about to be sent to France. In response, the German army held back two divisions from the Western front to combat the impending Russian invasion, possibly contributing to Germany's defeat at the Battle of the Marne, a major turning point in the war.

• On April 12, 2000, *The Wall Street Journal* reported that Amtrak's online reservation system designed itineraries that sent passengers far out of their way. "Instead of traveling from Houston to Austin via San Antonio, a 12-hour trip," explained the *Journal*, "Amtrak's Web site planned a four-and-a-half day journey through Jacksonville, Florida; Washington, D.C.; and Chicago—for a round-trip price of 359 dollars, compared with eighty dollars for the direct route." Not programmed to alert customers that certain trains do not run on certain days, the Web site could only generate the best route available on the date requested.

• Trains departing Liverpool Street station in London go to East Anglia, not Liverpool.

• All the trains in the New York subway system pass through the island of Manhattan—except the G train, which passes between Brooklyn and Queens.

• The longest railway in the world is the Trans-Siberian line from Moscow to Nakhoda, Russia, spanning 5,864.5 miles. The journey takes just over eight days.

WOOLY WILLY

In the 1930s, brothers Don and Jim Herzog frequently went to work with their father, Ralph Herzog, the owner and founder of the Smethport Specialty Company, a toy factory in Smethport, Pennsylvania. The two boys loved watching idle factory workers use magnets to play with iron-ore shavings.

While attending a trade show in the 1940s, Don and Jim Herzog, then in their twenties, noticed a display on vacuum encasing. Realizing that this new technology would enable them to encase loose iron-ore shavings safely behind a plastic window, the Herzog brothers designed a chubby cartoon face with a bald head and a red nose and launched Wooly Willy in 1950.

With the attached magnet, children and the young at heart could move around the iron-ore shavings to give Wooly Willy a head of hair, a moustache, a beard, a patch over his eye, or dark sunglasses. Should anyone's imagination need a kick-start, illustrations on the back of the package suggested nine ways to disguise Wooly Willy, including "Pete the Pirate" and "Dick the Dude."

The Herzog brothers quickly discovered that children nationwide shared their fascination with moving iron-ore filings with a magnet, and sales of Wooly Willy went through the roof, turning the toy into an American icon.

The Smethport Specialty Company created an entire line of magnet/iron-ore toys, including Wooly Willy's girlfriend, Hairdo Harriet, but Wooly Willy remains the Smethport Specialty Company's best-selling toy.

YO-YO

Around 1000 B.C.E., the ancient Chinese originated a toy made from two disks sculpted from ivory, connected by a central peg, and wound with a silk cord. The toy made its way to Europe, where Europeans created yo-yos decorated with jewels and painted patterns to create whirling shapes when the toy spun up and down. The oldest surviving yo-yos, discovered in Greece and dating from 500 B.C.E., are terra-cotta disks, decorated with paintings of mythological figures. The French called the toy a *bandalore*, and a 1789 painting of French Prince Louis XVII portrays him playing with the toy. The British named the toy a quiz.

The name yo-yo originated in the Philippines, where, in the sixteenth century, hunters used a large yo-yo wrapped with a long piece of heavy twine to capture their prey. The hunter would hold the free end of the twine and, from a safe distance, hurl the yo-yo at the unsuspecting animal. The yo-yo would ideally wrap around the animal's legs, entangling the creature in twine, which the hunter would then tug, pulling the animal off its feet. The Filipinos named the weapon "yo-yo" (Tagalog—the Filipino language—for "come-come"), and eventually turned it into a children's toy. In 1916, *Scientific American* published a story on the yo-yo as a Filipino toy.

In 1923, Pedro Flores, a Filipino living in the United States, made a yo-yo in the tradition of his Filipino forefathers. Five year later, Flores opened a yo-yo factory in Santa Barbara, California, and began running yo-yo contests, creating a yo-yo craze. When American entrepreneur Donald F. Duncan took notice of the yo-yo, he bought out Flores, trademarked the word yo-yo, and began promoting yo-yo contests in cities through the United States, turning his Duncan Toy Company into the leading yo-yo company in the world.

In 1965, Duncan lost a landmark court battle with Royal Tops Company over Duncan's trademark on the word "yo-yo." The court ruled that yo-yo is a generic term, and legal costs forced both companies into bankruptcy.

The World's Largest Yo-Yo

On March 29, 1990, the woodworking class of Shakamak High School in Jasonville, Indiana, launched a yo-yo measuring six feet in diameter and weighing 820 pounds from a 160-foot crane. It "yo-yoed" twelve times.

Why Toys "R" Us Doesn't Want to Grow Up

The Big Boys

In 1948, Charles Lazarus took two thousand dollars of his own money and a two-thousand-dollar bank loan to convert his father's Washington, D.C., bicycle-repair shop into a children's furniture store. After customers convinced him to add toys, Lazarus renamed the store Children's Supermart and opened a second store. His third store, opened in 1958, was a 25,000-square-foot discount toy store offering a wider variety of toys than other retailers with prices twenty to fifty percent lower.

By 1966, Lazarus had sales in excess of twelve million dollars. Eager to build more stores, Lazarus sold his company to Interstate Stores, a large discount-store operator, for 7.5 million dollars but retained control of the toy division. Although Lazarus had forty-seven stores and 130 million dollars in sales by 1974, Interstate Stores, facing competition from Kmart and other discount stores, filed for bankruptcy. To save his toy division, Lazarus pleaded with the court to let him run Interstate. The court agreed. Lazarus immediately sold off all of the company's non-toy holdings.

In 1978, Lazarus changed the company's name to Toys "R" Us, with the backwards R. With seventy-two toy stores (and ten department stores remaining from Interstate), Toys "R" Us sold 349 million dollars worth of toys that year.

The advertising jingle "I Don't Want to Grow Up, I'm a Toys "R" Us Kid," created by J. Walter Thompson, catapulted sales further. By 1983, there were 169 Toys "R" Us stores, and the company opened two Kids "R" Us children's discount clothing stores. By 1986, Toys "R' Us had almost 2.5 billion dollars in annual sales, four times the sales of its nearest competitor.

Before Toys "R" Us, toy stores were small, business was seasonal, and department stores expanded their toy departments around Christmas and shrank them back down in January. Toys "R" Us features supermarket-style shopping, everyday low prices, and an enormous selection of toys all year round. Today, one out of every five toys purchased in the United States comes from Toys "R" Us.

143

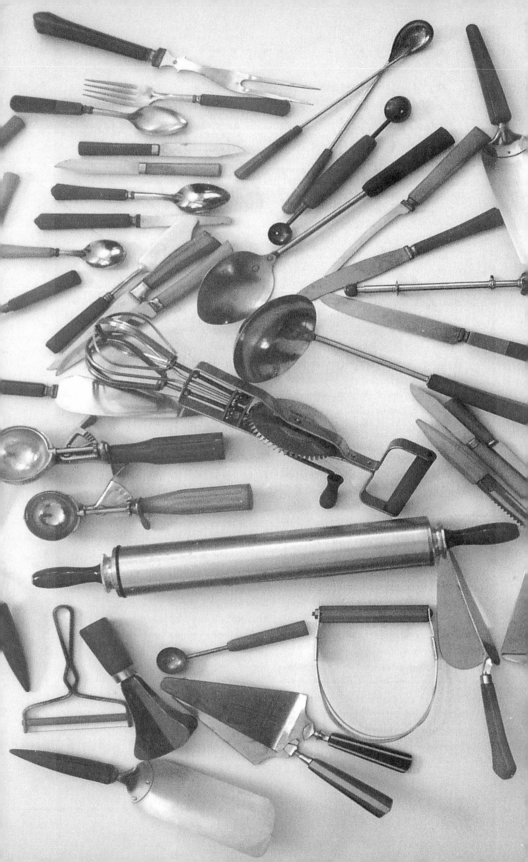

4

GADGETS & GIZMOS

Old-Fashioned Ingenuity and Insanity

The shelves and display cases of country stores overflowed with the most ingenious gadgets and gizmos—coffee grinders, spice mills, nutmeg graters, oil lamps, apple peelers, potato peelers, cheese graters, bottle openers, hand-cranked pencil sharpeners, electric irons, and toasters. The word *gadget* purportedly originated in 1886 when a Monsieur Gaget, a partner in Gaget, Gauhier & Cie., the French company that built the Statue of Liberty, came up with the idea of selling miniature replicas of the statue in Paris. Americans supposedly called the souvenirs "gadgets," mispronouncing Gaget's name. The word *gizmo* originated in 1942, not for anyone named Gizmo, but as United States Navy and Marine Corps slang for a gadget or machine part.

BAKELITE

In 1907, American chemist Leo Hendrik Baekeland, a Belgian immigrant and former organic chemistry professor at the University of Ghent, began his attempts to synthesize a rubber substitute in his home laboratory. He combined phenol and formaldehyde to make the first synthetic resin that could be substituted for hard rubber. He called his discovery Bakelite, and Baekeland became known as the "father of plastics."

Once shaped under heat and pressure, Bakelite, tinted in a variety of colors, became rock solid, resisting heat, acids, and electric currents. Unlike rubber, which dried out and cracked, Bakelite endured, making the perfect synthetic polymer from which to mold bracelets, pot and pan handles, the heads of electrical plugs, and radio dials.

In 1927, the Catalin Corporation acquired Bakelite, selling the bracelets through upscale department stores like Saks Fifth Avenue, B. Altman, and Bonwit Teller, but also through F. W. Woolworth and Sears. During the Depression, socialites who could no longer afford to buy jewelry at Tiffany's and Cartier, embraced vibrantly colored Bakelite bracelets adorned with rhinestones and costing between twenty cents and three dollars. In 1942, Bakelite and Catalin stopped making colorful costume jewelry and instead concentrated their efforts on manufacturing telephones, aviator goggles, and other products for use by the military. By the end of the war, manufacturers switched to newly developed injection-molded plastics, like Lucite, Fiberglass, vinyl, and acrylic, making Bakelite obsolete. Today, Bakelite is prized solely by collectors who scour flea markets, swap meets, and antique shows.

• Baekeland developed a superior emulsion for photographic paper that allowed artificial light to be substituted for sunlight in developing film. He sold the paper to Kodak founder George Eastman in 1899 for 750 thousand dollars.

• In 1924, *Time* magazine featured Leo Hendrik Baekeland on the cover of its September issue.

BLENDER

In 1915, Stephen J. Poplawski, a Polish-American from Racine, Wisconsin, began designing a gadget to mix his favorite drink—malted milk shakes. Seven years later, Poplawski patented the "vibrator," the first mixer with a wheel of blades mounted inside the bottom of a pitcher and activated only when the pitcher is placed in a base containing the motor. Picturing every soda fountain in America using his mixer, Poplawski struck a deal with the Racine-based Horlick Corporation, the largest manufacturer of the powdered malt used in soda fountain shakes. Obsessed with malted milk shakes, Poplawski never thought of using his mixer to blend fruits and vegetables.

In 1936, Fred Waring, the famous bandleader of the "Pennsylvanians," witnessed a demonstration of one of Poplawski's blenders. Impressed, he decided to finance the development of a competing food liquefier to be marketed to bartenders to mix daiquiris. The Waring Blendor would be spelled with the letter o to make the blender stand out.

At the 1936 National Restaurant Show in Chicago, the Waring Mixer Corporation demonstrated how the new Waring Blendor could mix daiquiris and other drinks and gave out sample drinks, making the blender accessible to a wider audience than Poplawski had ever imagined. Soon afterwards, the Ron Rico Rum Company launched an advertising campaign showing how

Do-It-Yourself

CHOCOLATE MALT SHAKE

WHAT YOU NEED

From the supermarket:
- 4 tablespoons chocolate syrup
- 2 cups milk
- 1 cup chocolate malted milk powder
- 1 scoop chocolate ice cream

WHAT TO DO

In a blender, combine the chocolate syrup, milk, and malted milk powder. Blend until smooth, then add one scoop chocolate ice cream. Makes one tall serving.

the Waring Blendor could be used to make exotic rum drinks easily and effortlessly.

In 1955, to promote blenders for use in the kitchen, Waring introduced blenders in designer colors. Meanwhile, Poplawski sold his company to Oster Manufacturing. Oster doubled the number of speeds of its blender from two ("Low" and "High") to four (adding "Medium" and "Off"), inadvertently launching a "Battle of the Buttons." Competitors began adding more buttons, including "Chop," "Dice," "Grate," "Liquefy," "Puree," and "Whip." By 1968, blenders boasted as many as fifteen different buttons, despite the fact that most people use only two or three speeds.

CAN OPENER

In 1810, British merchant Peter Durand invented the metal can so he could supply rations to the Royal Navy. Unfortunately, Durand failed to invent a device to open the cans. During the war of 1812, British soldiers used pocketknives or bayonets to tear open canned rations—sometimes resorting to gunfire. The war of 1812 popularized the metal can in England, despite the lack of an efficient can opener. Americans, while familiar with the can, had little use for it—until 1861, when soldiers fighting the Civil War needed preserved rations, necessitating canned foods.

In 1858, Ezra J. Warner of Waterbury, Connecticut, invented and patented the first can opener—a fierce-looking device with a large curved blade like a sickle that the user stabbed into the can and then worked around the rim.

In 1870, American inventor William W. Lyman developed a can opener with a cutting wheel that rolls around the rim of the can. In 1925, the Star Can Opener Company of San Francisco added a serrated "feed wheel" to Lyman's can opener so the can rotated against the wheel—the design used to this very day.

STRANGE FACTS

• On an Arctic expedition in 1824, British explorer Sir William Parry carried a can of veal printed with the instructions: "Cut round on the top with a chisel and hammer."
• Some warfare historians claim that the bayonet was originally designed by a blacksmith in the French city of Bayonne as a can opener.
• The electric can opener was invented in 1931.

Silly Willy

• In his play *King John*, which takes place in the early 1200s, William Shakespeare mentions a cannon. Cannons were not invented until the 1300s.

• In his play *Julius Caesar*, which takes place in 44 B.C.E., Shakespeare refers to a clock that strikes the hour—a type of clock that wasn't developed in Western civilization until the late 1200s.

• In his play *Antony and Cleopatra*, which takes place in ancient Egypt, William Shakespeare mentions billiards, millennia before the game was invented.

• In his play *Henry IV—Part I*, which takes place in 1403, Shakespeare mentions turkeys—creatures that were not brought to Europe from Mexico by the Spaniards until 1519 and which did not reach England until 1524.

• In his play *Coriolanus*, William Shakespeare calls Delphi an island. Delphi, the site of Apollo's oracle, was an ancient Greek town on the southern slope of Mount Parnassus.

• In his play *The Winter's Tale*, Shakespeare writes that a ship is "driven by storm on the coast of Bohemia." Bohemia, a landlocked region that is now a part of the Czech Republic, does not have a coast. He also has the character Antigonus claim, "Our ship hath touched upon the deserts of Bohemia." Bohemia does not contain any deserts. It is a fertile plateau surrounded by mountains and forests.

• In his play *Hamlet*, Shakespeare mentions Elsinore's "beetling cliff." Elsinore, a seaport in Denmark now called Helsingör, does not have any cliffs.

Bad Ideas

THE UNSINKABLE TITANIC

The designers of the "unsinkable" R.M.S. *Titanic* divided the ship into sixteen watertight compartments, which could be individually sealed shut by the flip of an electronic switch. If any two of the compartments flooded, the ship would remain afloat. In the unlikely event that three compartments flooded, the ship would sink.

When the *Titanic* hit an iceberg on its maiden voyage just before midnight on April 14, 1912, the resulting 300-foot-long gash opened six of the sixteen compartments. Also, the ship's designers provided only sixteen lifeboats—the minimum number for a 15,000 ton vessel (the *Titanic* weighed 46,000 tons and carried more than 2,200 passengers and crew). At 2:20 A.M. on April 15, 1912, the *Titanic* sank. Only 705 people survived—less than one third of those aboard.

THE SPRUCE GOOSE

In 1942, during World War II, shipping tycoon Henry J. Kaiser and millionaire Howard Hughes became partners and received eighteen million dollars from the United States government to build a giant seaplane, the Hercules HK-1, larger than a modern-day 747 and capable of carrying sixty tons of cargo. They began building the world's biggest plane from wood impregnated with resin, but when the project exceeded the original ten-month projection, the government cut its funding.

Kaiser quit the partnership, but Hughes invested seven million dollars of his own money. Nicknamed the *Spruce Goose* (despite the fact that there was no spruce used), the plane was finished in 1946—a year after World War II ended. The *Spruce Goose* flew only once and not very well. On November 2, 1947, Hughes took off from Long Beach Harbor, flying one mile in one minute.

The *Spruce Goose* sat in a climate-controlled warehouse in Long Beach, California, until 1993, when it was moved to the Evergreen Aviation Museum in McMinnville, Oregon.

Old-Fashioned Ice Bags Are Still an Effective, Drug-Free Pain Remedy

A friend tells us the only relief she gets from migraine headaches is with her trusty ice bag. An ice bag will also chase away the pain of muscle strain, sprains, and toothaches. Just fill the bag with ice and set it on what hurts for instant relief. Heavy-duty bags are rubber-lined with fabric outside and have a leakproof cap. Two sizes. Will arrive in assorted patterns.

No.26603 Ice Bag 6" $8.95
No.26277 Ice Bag 11" $13.95
No.H1584 Both Sizes $19.95

THE BAT BOMB

During World War II, the Pentagon developed a one-ounce incendiary bomb that could be strapped to the chest of a bat and then dropped over Japanese cities, where the bat would chew through the straps, detonating the bomb. The bomb would flare for eight minutes with a twenty-two inch flame.

The Pentagon planned to use these bat bombs to set fire to Japan's rickety wood houses and buildings. After researching "Project X-Ray" for two years and recruiting two million bats from the American Southwest, the Army tested the bat bombs in New Mexico. During the testing, several bats escaped, setting fire to a large aircraft hangar and a general's staff car.

The Navy took over the project and decided to freeze the bats into hibernation before dropping them out of the bombers. In a test run in August 1944, the frozen bats were dropped out of the bombers, remained asleep, and penetrated into the earth. Project X-ray was suspended, having cost two million dollars.

THE EDSEL

In September 1957, after years of research and millions of dollars in investment costs, the Ford Motor Company introduced a new line of mid-size automobiles—the Edsel, named after Henry Ford's only son. The new cars featured push buttons mounted in the center of the steering wheel for gears and stylish vertical grilles rather than the typical horizontal grilles.

Ford spent ten million dollars on advertising to launch the car in eighteen models in four series. When the Edsel failed to sell, Ford spent another ten million dollars on advertising. Although the Edsel was promoted as the car of the future, it was only superficially different than cars already on the road.

By 1957, the economic boom of the early 1950s had slowed, and consumers were hesitant to buy an expensive car. As many as half of the Edsels purchased were lemons with problems including malfunctioning doors, faulty brakes and power steering, poor paint jobs, frozen transmissions, and push buttons that stuck in the steering wheel.

After three years, only 110,000 Edsels had been sold, and in 1960, Ford—having lost an estimated 350 million dollars—stopped producing the Edsel. The name Edsel has become synonymous with failure.

Get Back To The Basics With Our Hand Cranked Dough Maker

In this modern fast-paced world, high-tech doesn't automatically mean better. And judging from the number of requests we received for this hand crank dough maker we're not the only one's who feel that way. Unlike noisy, complicated bread machines, our dough maker quietly creates a better texture of dough and allows you to stop kneading the dough without ruining it. Easy to assemble and comes apart for quick storage. Makes 2 to 6 loaves of bread at a time. The stainless steel hook and 10 qt. bowl are dishwasher safe. Hand wash the cast aluminum crank with wooden handles. Complete instructions included along with bread recipes.

No.40101 Dough Maker $79.95
☛*(Requested by Ginny Johnson, Cedar Park, Texas)*

DISHWASHER

In the 1880s, wealthy socialite Josephine Cochrane, the wife of an Illinois politician living in Shelbyville, Illinois, decided to invent a dishwashing machine because she frequently hosted formal dinners, and she could no longer tolerate having her expensive china broken by irresponsible servants as they washed the dishes. Tired of replacing her broken china by mail, Cochrane used her woodshed as a workshop and attached a motorized sprinkler wheel on top of a large copper boiler. She then devised wire compartments to hold her china plates, saucers, and cups. She fastened the compartments in place around the sprinkler wheel. When she activated the motor, the sprinkler wheel spun, showering the dishes with hot soapy water from the boiler. Cochrane's friends, impressed with her contraption, placed orders for the "Cochrane Dishwasher" for themselves.

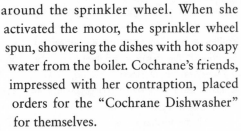

Before long, hotels and restaurants began ordering large-capacity dishwashers from Cochrane, prompting her to patent her design in 1886. In 1914, Cochrane's company introduced a smaller dishwasher for the typical home, but the model failed to sell because most homes did not have hot water tanks large enough to provide enough scalding water needed by the machine to clean a load of dishes. Second, most homes had hard water that necessitates elbow grease to get soap to suds sufficiently. More surprising, a poll revealed that while most American housewives dreaded laundering the family clothes, they actually considered dishwashing a pleasant chore that helped them unwind at the end of the day.

Undaunted, Cochrane's company began promoting the dishwasher as a machine that used scalding water to both clean and sanitize dishware, killing germs. Still, sales remained low—until the early 1950s when Cochrane's company merged with an Ohio manufacturer to make the KitchenAid dishwasher, and the American housewife, spurred by postwar prosperity, embraced a life of leisure over a life doing household chores.

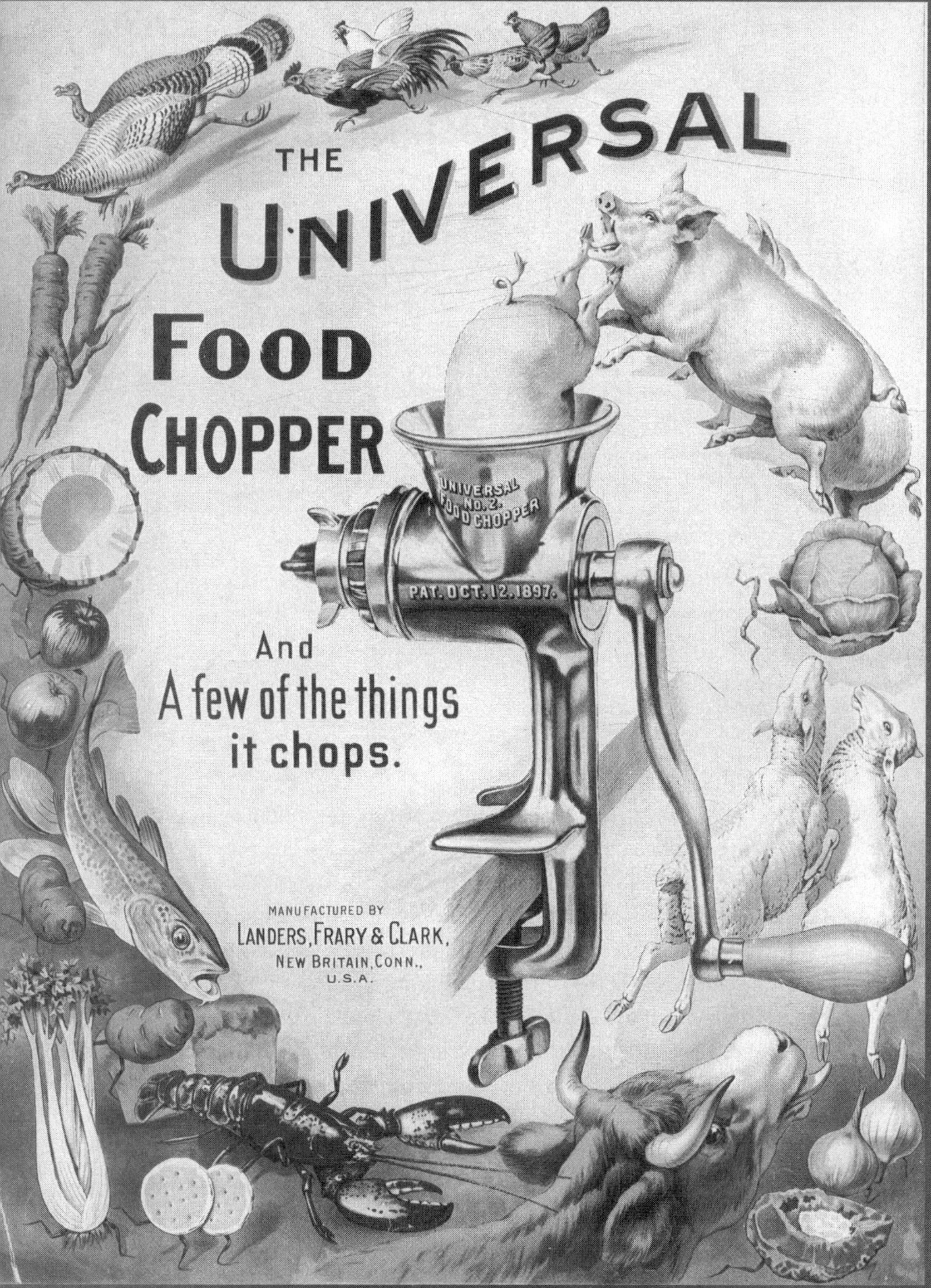

THE
UNIVERSAL
FOOD
CHOPPER

And
A few of the things
it chops.

UNIVERSAL
NO. 2.
FOOD CHOPPER

PAT. OCT. 12. 1897.

MANUFACTURED BY
LANDERS, FRARY & CLARK,
NEW BRITAIN, CONN.,
U.S.A.

Secret Formula

OLD-FASHIONED DISHWASHING LIQUID

WHAT YOU NEED

From the supermarket:
- 2 bars Ivory Soap
- Pam Cooking Spray

From the tap:
- 1 gallon water

WHAT TO DO

Spray a grater with a thin coat of cooking spray (to make cleanup afterward easier). Grate the bars of soap into flakes. Mix the soap flakes and water in a large pot. Bring the mixture to a boil over medium heat, stirring frequently until the soap flakes dissolve. Lower the heat and sim-mer for ten minutes, stirring occasionally. Remove from the heat and let cool. Using a funnel, pour the liquid soap into a clean container (like a clean, used dishwashing liquid bottle) and cover tightly. Makes about one gallon.

HOW YOU USE IT

If you'd like to see yourself in the dishes, pour one tablespoon of this sensational liquid soap into a sink filled with hot water and scrub those dishes until they sparkle like new. Don't use this solution in your dishwasher; this potent potion works with elbow grease only!

HAIR DRYER

In the early 1900s, manufacturers frequently promoted multiple uses for a newly devised electrical appliance in the hopes of increasing sales of the product. An early advertisement for a vacuum cleaner called the Pneumatic Cleaner showed a woman using a hose connected to the machine to dry her hair, assuring readers that the vacuum produced a "current of pure, fresh air from the exhaust." At the time, using the exhaust from a vacuum cleaner was the only way to blow-dry hair. The handheld electric hair dryer had yet to be invented because no one had developed a motor small enough to power it—until 1922, when the advent of the blender produced the first fractional horsepower motor.

In 1920, two companies in Racine, Wisconsin—the Racine Universal Motor Company and Hamilton Beach—essentially combined the vacuum cleaner with the blender to create the handheld hair dryer. The Racine Universal Motor Company introduced the "Race"; Hamilton Beach launched the "Cyclone."

While the first handheld hair dryers were bulky and frequently over-heated, manufacturers made improvements during the decade that followed, providing adjustable speeds and temperature settings. In 1951, Sears & Roebuck introduced a portable handheld dryer that attached to a pink plastic cap that fit over the woman's hair. In 1968, Leandro P. Rizzuto, founder of Continental Hair Products in New York City, developed the hot comb, and three years later, introduced the first handheld pistol-grip blow-dryer to the United States.

KITCHEN RANGE

In the 1790s, British statesman and inventor Count von Rumford, born Benjamin Thompson, designed the first practical cooking stove—a box built from bricks with holes in the top to hold pots.

In 1802, British iron founder George Bodley invented and patented a compact cast-iron, closed-top, even-heating cooking range, fueled by coal, with a modern flue. That same year, German inventor Frederick Albert Winson produced a makeshift gas cooking range. Unfortunately, more permanent gas range models tended to leak fumes and explode. Thirty years later, European manufacturers finally developed practical and safe gas ranges.

In 1855, German chemist Robert W. Bunsen invented the first practical gas burner, and the following decade, Americans who had gas piped into their homes to fuel gaslights began embracing the gas range.

In 1890, manufacturers introduced the first electric stoves. Unfortunately, these contraptions, equipped with crude thermostats, tended to incinerate meals and send electric bills through the roof. Luckily for consumers, most homes in America were not yet wired for electricity.

In 1910, gas became available in pressurized containers, enabling people living in rural areas to use gas ranges. Twenty years later, manufacturers introduced the modern electric range.

Ridiculous Theories

THE ATOMIC SOUL
Ancient Greek natural philosopher Democritus first proposed the theory that all matter is composed of atoms. He also theorized that atoms could not be split, that atoms were solid, that sharp atoms caused sour tastes, and that the human soul was made up of the smallest atoms in the universe.

THE DAY THE EARTH STOOD STILL
In 150 C.E., Greek astronomer Ptolemy claimed that the sun, moon, and planets rotate around the earth, which is motionless and located in the center of the universe. Ptolemy also insisted that the earth does not move because otherwise people, animals, and objects would be thrown into the air. He also believed that the stars were merely bright spots of light fixed within a concave dome that arched over the universe. His theories were accepted as fact for 1,500 years.

NO SPACE SUITS REQUIRED
Ancient Greek philosopher Aristotle insisted that the space between the moon and the earth was full of air.

THE TRUTH HURTS
In 1600, Pope Clement VIII sentenced Italian scientist Giordano Bruno to be burned alive at the stake for insisting that the earth is round, the universe is infinite, life exists on other planets, the sun does not revolve around the earth, and the earth is not the center of the universe.

THE PLANET VULCAN
In 1859, French mathematician Urbain Jean Joseph Le Verrier, who had accurately predicted the location of the planet Neptune in 1846, announced the discovery of another planet, Vulcan, without ever seeing it. Le Verrier pointed to irregularities in the orbit of the planet Mercury and the sighting of a possible planet between Mercury and Venus by an amateur astronomer. Although the Paris Observatory, which Le Verrier directed, could never confirm the existence of the planet, Le Verrier went to his grave convinced that Vulcan existed. The irregularities in Mercury's orbit were eventually explained by Einstein's theory of relativity; the sun's massive gravity affects Mercury's path through space.

THE HARMONIC EXPLOSION
In 1919, meteorologist Albert Porta predicted, "The conjunction of six planets on December 17 could generate a magnetic current that might cause the sun to explode and engulf the earth."

HERE'S NEW ECONOMY FOR YOU NOW_AND FOR YEARS TO COME!

Plymouth's Finest gives you 10% more Power—now 95 H.P. And you get a big "Thrift Bonus" in extra gas mileage and long engine life. The body is low-slung, long, wide and roomy. You get a wonderful new ride. Buy Wisely—Buy Quality—Buy the Car that Stands Up Best!

PLYMOUTH IS CHRYSLER CORPORATION'S NO. 1 CAR

Here's the finest car investment low price can buy! A brilliant, new car—styled to stay beautiful and engineered to stay new—*Plymouth's Finest!*

Plymouth's Finest is long, wide and roomy. And the smart, low-to-the-road design that gives it its sleek, dashing appearance also contributes wonderful new smoothness and steadiness to Plymouth's ride!

Plymouth's Finest is so powerful that you use only a fraction of its power in all normal driving. The big 95-h.p. engine purrs along with fewer revolutions per mile —saving gas and adding to engine life. This is thrifty driving at its finest!

Plymouth is famous as the best-engineered low-priced car. Vital engine parts are Superfinished against wear as in a modern aircraft engine. You get an Oil Bath Air Cleaner, Oil Filter, Coil Springs, Hypoid Rear Axle, 4-Ring Pistons—many fine features that identify Plymouth as *the low-priced car most like high-priced cars.*

See this fine car at your Plymouth deal-

*Buy Wisely_* BUY PLYMOUTH

er's—drive it! It's your wise low-priced car buy! All prices and specifications are subject to change without notice. Plymouth Division of Chrysler Corporation.

TUNE IN MAJOR BOWES' HOUR, C.B.S., THURSDAYS

Products of Chrysler Corporation

Army Tanks • Anti-Aircraft Guns
Aircraft Parts • Army Vehicles • Passenger Cars • Trucks • Marine and
Industrial Engines • Diesel Engines
Oilite Bearings • Airtemp Heating
and Air Conditioning.

MASSIVENESS and lowness distinguish the front end of Plymouth's Finest. The car is long, wide, roomy... with concealed running boards...new-styled interiors.

THE CAR THAT STANDS UP BEST!

Is There Really Such a Thing as a Radio Shack?

The Big Boys

Yes, radio shacks really do exist. A radio shack is a small ramshackle building used to boost radio signals.

RadioShack began in 1921 as a Boston-based mail-order company catering to ham radio operators and electronics buffs. The company issued its first catalog in 1940 and began marketing its products under the Realistic private label in 1954. But by the early 1960s, with nine stores in the Boston area, RadioShack was nearly bankrupt.

In 1963, Charles Tandy, who had expanded his family's small Fort Worth leather business into a publicly owned, nationwide chain of leathercraft and hobby stores, bought RadioShack. Tandy collected part of the 800,000 dollars owed the company and began expanding, stocking the stores with quick turnover items and pumping up to nine percent of sales revenue into advertising. As RadioShack expanded between 1961 and 1969, Tandy's sales grew from 16 million dollars to 180 million dollars. In 1968, Tandy had 172 RadioShack stores. By 1973, he had 2,294 stores. Three years later, the CB radio craze pushed RadioShack's sales up 125 percent as Tandy opened another 1,200 RadioShack stores.

With locations in virtually every mall and community in America, RadioShack could be called the 7-Eleven of consumer electronics and computers. The stores sell audio, video, security, and computer products, but their forte is high-margin, hard-to-find products, such as cables, collectors, jacks, batteries, and obscure electronic parts and accessories.

STRANGE FACTS
• In 1979, the year after Charles Tandy died, there were 5,530 McDonald's restaurants, 6,805 7-Eleven stores, and 7,353 RadioShack stores.
• In 1977, Tandy introduced the first mass-marketed personal computer, the TRS-80, (affectionately known as Trash-80), which, ironically, became the number-one personal computer on the market.
• One out of every three households in America purchases RadioShack products each year.

THESE

modern
phonograph
inventions
ARE YOURS

Only
IN A
PHILCO

"Music on a Beam of Light"

★ A permanent jewel reflects the music on a beam of light to a photo-electric cell. No needles to change. Surface noise and record wear reduced 10 to 1. Glorious new beauty and purity of tone. *Only Philco has it!*

Stroboscope
PITCH AND TEMPO CONTROL

★ An exclusive feature of the amazing new Philco Automatic Record Changer. Hear your records with *absolute fidelity of pitch.* And enjoy simpler, gentler, more reliable changing of records. *Only Philco has it!*

Tilt-Front CABINET

★ No lid to lift; no need to remove decorations. To play the phonograph, you merely tilt forward the grille, place your records and tilt it back again. *Only Philco has it!*

These are the marks of the *modern* phonograph. It is old-fashioned, now, to put up with surface noise and expensive record wear. These new delights, plus the exclusive Philco FM System and other radio inventions, which you enjoy in a Philco Photo-Electric Radio-Phonograph are yours *only in a Philco!*

Philco 1013, Illustrated. Easiest Terms.
See the 1942 Philco Phonographs and Radios at Your Nearest Dealer

159

PAPER CUP

In 1908, Hugh Moore started the American Water Supply Company of New England to market a vending machine that for one penny would dispense a cool drink of water in an individual, clean, disposable paper cup. Moore soon realized that his sanitary cups had greater sales potential than his water, particularly when Dr. Samuel Crumbine, a health official in Dodge City, Kansas, began crusading for a law to ban the public tin dipper.

Lacking the capital to manufacture enough paper cups to abolish the tin dipper, Moore and his associate Lawrence Luellen traveled to New York City with a few handmade samples. They eventually hooked up with an investment banker who invested 200,000 dollars in the venture, incorporated as the Public Cup Vendor Company in 1909. That same year, Kansas passed the first state law abolishing the public dipper, and Professor Alvin Davison of Lafayette College published a study reporting the germs of communicable diseases found on public dipping tins. As state after state outlawed public drinking tins, Moore and his associates created a paper cup dispenser to be distributed for free to businesses and schools who would then buy the paper cups. By 1910, the company changed its name to the Individual Drinking Cup Company, only to change it again in 1912 to Health Kups.

Inventor Hugh Moore's paper cup factory was located next door to the Dixie Doll Company in the same downtown loft building. The word Dixie printed on the company's door reminded Moore of the story he had heard as a boy about "dixies," the ten dollar bank notes printed with the French word *dix* in big letters across the face of the bill by a New Orleans bank renowned for its strong currency in the early 1800s. The "dixies," Moore decided, had the qualities he wanted people to associate with his paper cups, and in 1919, with permission from his neighbor, he changed the name of his company to Dixie Cups.

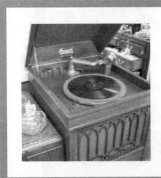  

In 1923, Dixie Cups produced a 2½ ounce Dixie Cup for ice cream, giving the ice cream industry a way to sell individual servings of ice cream and compete with bottled soft drinks and candy bars. The American Can Company purchased the Dixie Cup Company in 1957 and merged the company with Northern Paper. In 1982, the James River Corporation acquired Dixie Cups/Northern Paper for 455 million dollars.

STRANGE FACTS

• Etymologists believe that the sobriquet for the southern United States, *Dixie Land*, originated on the Mississippi River before the Civil War by riverboat men for whom a *dixie* was a New Orleans bank note printed with the word *dix,* French for "ten."

• The Dixie Cups, a popular singing trio comprised of sisters Nadine, Marta, and Lucile LeCupsa, sang the 1964 hit song, "Chapel of Love."

SUNBEAM MIXMASTER

In 1928, Swedish immigrant Ivar Jepson, a mechanical engineer who worked as head designer at Sunbeam, a subsidiary of the Chicago Flexible Shaft Company, invented the Mixmaster, the first mechanical mixer with two detachable beaters whose blades interlocked.

Unlike the single-beater milkshake mixer invented twenty years earlier by L. H. Hamilton, Chester Beach, and Fred Osius, the Mixmaster featured a motor encased in a sleek pivoting arm that extended out over the mixing bowl. In 1930, Sunbeam marketed the Mixmaster, and despite the Depression, the Mixmaster quickly became a huge seller, turning Sunbeam into a household word.

Jepson continually worked to improve the Mixmaster, enhancing the motor and controls and adding several attachments, enabling the Mixmaster to make juice, peel fruit, shell peas, press pasta, grind coffee, open tin cans, sharpen knives, and polish silverware.

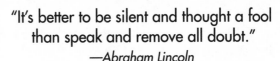

Presidential Know-How

"The man who reads nothing at all
is better educated than the man who
reads nothing but newspapers."
—*Thomas Jefferson*

"It's better to be silent and thought a fool
than speak and remove all doubt."
—*Abraham Lincoln*

"I know only two tunes: one of them is
'Yankee Doodle,' and the other isn't."
—*Ulysses S. Grant*

"A man who has never gone to school
may steal from a freight car;
but if he has a university education,
he may steal the whole railroad."
—*Theodore Roosevelt*

"Never murder a man who is committing suicide."
—*Woodrow Wilson*

"I don't know much about Americanism,
but it's a damned good word
with which to carry an election."
—*Warren G. Harding*

"When more and more people are
thrown out of work, unemployment results."
—*Calvin Coolidge*

"Blessed are the young,
for they shall inherit the national debt."
—*Herbert Hoover*

"The best way to give advice to your children
is to find out what they want
and then advise them to do it."
—*Harry Truman*

"Things are more like they are now
than they ever were before."
—*Dwight D. Eisenhower*

"Mothers all want their sons to
grow up to be president
but they don't want them to
become politicians in the process."
—*John F. Kennedy*

"I wouldn't want to wake up
next to a lady pipefitter."
—*Richard Nixon*

"If Lincoln were alive today,
he'd roll over in his grave."
—*Gerald Ford*

"Abortion is advocated only by persons who
have themselves been born."
—*Ronald Reagan*

"Half the time, when I see the evening news,
I wouldn't be for me either."
—*Bill Clinton*

TOASTER

The first electric toasters, invented in the early 1900s, were metal cages that held the slices of bread next to heating coils, without any way to control the temperature. The user had to keep an eye on the slice of bread to make sure the toast did not burn and then flip over the slice to toast the other side. While far from perfect, the early electric toaster enabled people to make a slice of toast without having to fire up the stove.

During World War I, master mechanic Charles Strite, tired of the burnt toast served in the company cafeteria in Stillwater, Minnesota, used springs and a variable timer to create the world's first pop-up toaster. After receiving a patent in 1919, Strite raised enough money from friends to produce one hundred pop-up toasters assembled by hand. The Childs restaurant chain placed an order for the first batch but returned every toaster to be mechanically adjusted, eager for Strite to perfect his invention.

In 1926, Strite introduced the Toastmaster, the first pop-up toaster for the home—complete with a dial to adjust to the desired degree of darkness. Unfortunately, the Toastmaster grew hotter after making each slice of toast. The first slice popped up underdone, and the sixth slice popped up burnt. Still, advertisements for the Toastmaster boasted, "This amazing new invention makes perfect toast every time! Without watching! Without turning! Without burning!"

STRANGE FACTS

• Ancient Egyptians toasted bread to remove moisture, impede molds and spores, and give it a longer shelf life.

• Before the invention of the toaster, people toasted bread on a prong held over a fire.

• In the nineteenth century, people used a product called the Toaster Over, a hollow tin box with wire cages on each of its four sides to hold slices of bread over the opening in a cast-iron coal-burning stove.

VACUUM CLEANER

At an exhibition at London's Empire Music Hall in 1898, aspiring inventor H. Cecil Booth watched an inventor demonstrate his new "dust-removing" machine. The contraption forced compressed air into a carpet in the futile hope of sending the dirt and dust flying back up into an attached metal box. Upon learning that no inventor had succeeded in devising a machine that sucked up dust and dirt, Booth realized that the solution lay in finding the proper material to use as a filtering bag to trap the dirt and dust particles while allowing air to pass through. He tested different kinds of fabrics by placing each one over his lips, lying on the floor, and sucking the carpet with his mouth—eventually happening upon a tightly woven cloth handkerchief that filtered the dust perfectly.

In 1901, Booth patented his suction cleaner—a machine as large as a contemporary refrigerator that had to be rolled on a dolly by one person while a second person used an attached flexible hose to vacuum up dirt and dust. The vacuum cleaner, extracting germ-carrying dust from carpets and upholstered furniture, vastly improved sanitation and health.

In 1907, James Murray Spangler, a janitor working in a department store in Canton, Ohio, experienced fierce allergic reactions to the dust stirred up by the mechanical sweeper he used. Desperate to keep his job and determined to end his plight, Spangler decided to invent a "dustless cleaning machine." He attached the motor from an old electric fan to a soapbox, sealed the cracks with adhesive tape, and attached a pillowcase as a dust bag. The following year, he received a patent for his invention and borrowed money from friends to found the Electric Suction Sweeper Company.

Susan Hoover, the wife of wealthy Ohio leather goods manufacturer William Hoover, bought one of Spangler's machines. That same year, William Hoover bought the rights to manufacture Spangler's suction sweeper, began making the first portable vacuum cleaners, and ran a two-page advertisement in the *Saturday Evening Post* offering readers a free ten-day home trial. Hoover received hundreds of letters from homemakers eager to receive the

Dumb Mistakes

COLUMBUS GETS LOST

Christopher Columbus miscalculated the circumference of the globe by 7,600 miles and inaccurately estimated the earth to be 25 percent smaller than it actually is. He also estimated Asia to be larger and the Atlantic Ocean to be smaller than they actually are. He also failed to predict the existence of a landmass between the two continents of Europe and Asia and, after four trips, remained convinced he had landed in Asia—not the New World. Unbeknownst to Columbus, he actually discovered the Bahamian island of San Salvador (which he believed to be an island of the Indies), Cuba (which he thought to be a part of China), and the Dominican Republic (which he insisted was the Far East). He named the islands the West Indies (because he incorrectly thought they were part of the Indies islands of Asia) and dubbed the natives Indians (wrongly convinced he was in India). Columbus named Costa Rica (meaning "rich coast") because he saw natives wearing gold necklaces and thought the land was rich with gold. In fact, Costa Rica has less gold than any country in Latin America. Columbus also claimed to have discovered the portal to the Garden of Eden.

THE VATICAN BANS GALILEO

In 1633, the Vatican summoned astronomer Galileo Galilei before the Inquisition and threatened to burn him at the stake for stating that the earth revolves around the sun in his 1632 book, *Dialogue Concerning the Two Chief World Systems*. Instead, Galileo retracted his discoveries and spent the remaining eight years of his life under house arrest. In 1992, 359 years later, Pope John Paul II, having conducted a thirteen-year investigation into the matter, formally stated that the Church was wrong to have condemned Galileo.

AMERICA IS PAVED WITH GOLD

The settlers at Jamestown, the first colony in the New World, mined gold and sent a shipload back to London, where assayers identified the glittering metal as iron pyrite, better known as "fool's gold."

new gadget. Having created a demand for the product, Hoover went about creating a supply line.

He contacted selected storeowners and offered to deliver the trial machines to them so respondents could come into the store and pick them up for their free trial. Hoover offered each storeowner a commission on every machine sold. Storeowners jumped at the offer, giving Hoover a network of dealers. He then sent out letters to all his respondents, telling them where

FONCK IGNORES A WORD TO THE WISE

In 1924, when Raymond Orteig offered a 25,000-dollar prize to the first person to fly from New York to Paris, French World War I pilot René Fonck had a 38,000-pound three-engine biplane built at a cost of 105,000 dollars. Fonck ignored pleas from the plane's renowned designer, aviation pioneer Igor Sikorsky, to stress test the plane, which weighed ten thousand pounds over its engineered maximum. When Fonck tried to take off for his journey from New York's Roosevelt Field, the landing gear bent, the rear landing wheel fell off, and the plane crashed through a fence and burst into flames.

STALIN FORGETS TO SET THE CLOCK BACK

In the spring of 1930, Soviet dictator Josef Stalin ordered that clocks in the Soviet Union be set ahead one hour for daylight savings time. In the fall, he forgot to order everyone to turn their clocks back again, but no one had the courage to tell the mercurial dictator he had erred. Sixty-one years later, in 1991, the Soviet government finally admitted the error and agreed to fix it. That spring, citizens of the Russian Federation did not set their clocks ahead one hour, but that fall they all set their clocks back one hour.

WRONG-WAY CORRIGAN MISSES CALIFORNIA

On July 16, 1938, pilot Douglas Corrigan took off in an airplane to fly solo nonstop from New York to Los Angeles. Twenty-six hours later, he landed in Dublin, Ireland. He explained that he had followed the wrong end of his compass needle, flying through fog and heavy cloud cover.

While many people believed Corrigan had intended to cross the Atlantic to emulate his hero Charles Lindbergh, Corrigan did not carry any water or maps of the Atlantic or enough food for the trans-Atlantic journey.

W. C. FIELDS FORGETS WHERE HE PUT HIS MONEY

Afraid of finding himself in a strange town without any money, comedian W. C. Fields opened a bank account in every town he passed through.

Unfortunately, he remembered only twenty-three out of an estimated seven hundred accounts—misplacing approximately 1.3 million dollars.

they could pick up their trial machine—turning the name Hoover into a household word and revolutionizing household cleaning.

STRANGE FACTS

• H. Cecil Booth vacuumed the carpets in Westminster Abbey for the 1901 coronation of King Edward VII.

• When naval reserve men quartered in London's Crystal Palace during World War I fell prey to a spotted fever epidemic, the British military hired Booth to use his vacuum machines to clean germ-laden dust from the premises. Booth used fifteen machines to remove twenty-six truckloads of dust.

WHISTLING TEAKETTLE

In 1921, Joseph Block, a retired cookware executive from New York, toured a teakettle factory in Westphalia, Germany. Seeing so many teakettles at once suddenly triggered a childhood memory in Block's mind. He remembered watching his father design a pressurized potato cooker that emitted a whistling sound when the cooking cycle finished. Block suggested that the teakettle manufacturer create a teakettle that whistled when the water boiled. The simple idea of combining a teakettle with a whistle intrigued the factory owner, who immediately produced thirty-six whistling teakettles, put them on sale at Wertheim's department store in Berlin, and sold out in less than three hours.

The next year, Block came out of retirement to debut his whistling teakettle in the United States at a Chicago housewares fair. He kept at least one kettle whistling throughout the weeklong show, prompting bewitched store buyers to place huge orders for the one-dollar item. Before long, Block was selling 35,000 whistling teakettles a month to department stores across the United States.

Do-It-Yourself
MINT TEA

WHAT YOU NEED
From the supermarket:
- 3 teaspoons Chinese green tea
- 1/4 cup chopped fresh mint
- 4 mint sprigs
- Sugar

From the tap:
- 4 cups water

WHAT TO DO
Combine the tea and chopped mint in a glazed ceramic teakettle. Boil the water and then pour it slowly into the teakettle. Cover the teakettle with a towel, and let the tea and mint steep for five minutes. Stir well, then pour the tea through a strainer into tall cups. (Moroccans use five-inch tall drinking glasses.) Garnish the tea with mint sprigs. Add sugar to taste. Makes four cups.

SAVES TIME
...MANY TIMES A DAY !!

SEALS... With a touch of the finger, Scotch Tape seals gift, lunch and other packages; envelope flaps; mothproof bags and boxes; labels to jars, bottles and shelves.

HOLDS... Scotch Tape holds snapshots in albums; clippings in scrapbooks; coins to letters; window signs and posters; bulletins and notices, windings to golf clubs.

MENDS... With full transparency, Scotch Tape mends torn file cards, vouchers, book pages, sheet music, blueprints, checks, ledger sheets, window shades, broken toys.

FASTENS... Scotch Tape quickly fastens shelf paper in place, recipes in cook books, decorations to walls, letters to packages, combines work sheets, reinforces index tabs, edges file cards.

Use Scotch Tape in home or office to do daily tasks the easy, modern way. Discover how it saves time and trouble—mending, sealing and holding.

Just a touch of the finger seals Scotch Tape tightly—no water required. Made of "Cellophane," it's transparent as glass.

At Stationery, Drug, Hardware, Department, and 5 & 10¢ Stores.

SCOTCH *Cellulose* TAPE
SEALS WITHOUT WATER • TRANSPARENT AS GLASS

25¢

Utility Dispenser with ½ x 36" roll. "Scotch Cellulose Tape."

FREE BOOKLET tells how to save time and trouble with Scotch Tape. Also how to create distinctive gift packages. Just write to—Scotch Tape, Dept. L91, 900 Fauquier Ave., Saint Paul, Minn.

Copr. 1941, Minnesota Mining & Mfg. Co.

MADE & PATENTED IN U.S.A. BY MINNESOTA MINING & MFG. CO. SAINT PAUL, MINNESOTA
SOLD IN FOREIGN COUNTRIES UNDER THE NAME "DUREX" CELLULOSE TAPE. FOREIGN MFRS.
& DISTRIBUTORS. FOR CANADA — CANADIAN DUREX ABRASIVES LTD. TORONTO. FOR ALL
OTHER COUNTRIES — ADDRESS DUREX ABRASIVES CORP., 62 WALL ST., NEW YORK, N.Y.

ZIPPER

On August 29, 1893, Whitcomb L. Judson, a mechanical engineer in Chicago, received a patent for the first "clasp-locker"—a series of clunky eyes and hooks that fastened together with a slider. Judson replaced the long, buttonhooked shoelaces on his boots and the boots of his business partner, Lewis Walker, with clasp-lockers.

Unable to interest any manufacturers in his new-fangled gadget, Judson and Walker displayed the invention at the 1893 Chicago World's Fair—where it was virtually ignored by the twenty-one million attendees.

Eventually, the United States Postal Service placed an order for twenty mailbags fastened with Judson's clasp-lockers, but the clasp-lockers jammed too often to make the bags useful. Judson died in 1909—before perfecting his invention or finding a practical use for it.

In 1913, Swedish-American engineer Gideon Sundback perfected Judson's invention by replacing the cumbersome hook-and-eye design with a more reliable and less bulky meshed-tooth slider fastener. During World War I, the United States Army ordered Sundback's invention for use on uniforms and equipment. Manufacturers began using the metal slide fasteners on boots, change purses, and money belts—and eventually on clothing. Since few people knew how to use the slide fasteners, clothing manufacturers included small instruction booklets on how to operate and maintain the contraption.

In 1922, the B. F. Goodrich Company gave the trademark Zipper to its new rubber galoshes with new "hookless fasteners." Goodrich reportedly coined the word "zipper," onomatopoeia for the sound the device made when he zipped up his boots. The catchy name made the zipper a household word and a common fastener on clothing. In 1935, fashion designer Elsa Schiaparelli introduced a line of clothing bursting with decorative colored zippers of various sizes, turning the zipper into a popular fashion statement.

Sparkling Eyes
attract admirers

Make your eyes gleam with light, dance with brightness! Use KURLASH, the wonderful eyelash curler that sweeps lashes upwards, makes eyes appear larger and lovelier. Requires no heat, cosmetics or practice. This dainty beauty aid is only $1.00.

P. S. KURLENE, the rich, oily-base cream makes lashes appear dark and luxuriant. Used with Kurlash, makes curl last longer. Ideal for daytime make-up, too. 50¢

KURLASH
The Only Complete Eye-Beauty Line
THE KURLASH COMPANY, INC.
ROCHESTER N. Y.   CANADA, TORONTO 3

Write John Heath, Dept. C-8, for generous trial tube of Kurlene (send 10c in coin or stamps). Receive Free chart analysis of your eyes and how to make the most of them.

Name
Address
Color: Eyes   Hair   Skin

Don't Know Much About Geography

• In 1517, when Spanish explorer Francisco Fernández de Córdoba arrived in what is now known as Mexico's Yucatán peninsula, he asked the Mayan Indians what they called their land. The Mayans replied "Yucatán," which means "What do you want?"

• In 1521, Portuguese explorer Ferdinand Magellan, having crossed the Pacific Ocean without encountering a storm, called it Mar Pacifico, meaning "peaceful sea." In reality, the Pacific Ocean is home to some of the most destructive storms, tidal waves, and typhoons on earth.

• In 1770, English explorer Captain James Cook landed in Australia and asked the aborigines what they called the large marsupials indigenous to the continent. He was told "kangaroo," which, unbeknownst to Cook, is an aboriginal word for "I don't know."

• In 1796, a city in Ohio was named after its founder, Moses Cleaveland, a surveyor for the Connecticut Land Company. In 1831, a newspaper misspelled the city's name as Cleveland. The city's name has been incorrectly spelled Cleveland ever since.

• The name Nome was wrongly copied from a British map of Alaska drawn around 1850. The original map maker had written "? Name" to mark the town.

• In the 1880s, two surveyors worked together to map the western border of South Dakota along the same meridian. One surveyor walked south, the second surveyor walked north. The surveyor walking south accidentally started out a mile west of the surveyor walking north, so the western border of South Dakota jumps one mile east-west where it hits the southern border of Montana.

Soothing Plug-In Vaporizer Is As Small As A Night-Light

Keep breathing passages clear while you sleep, with this ingenious little plug-in device from England. It's smaller than most night-lights, fits any standard wall outlet, and is far easier to move around and use than freestanding vaporizers. It slowly heats little compressed disks (5 disks included) of natural menthol, eucalyptus, and camphor to fill an average-size bedroom with chest-clearing vapors for 8-10 hours. For a good night's sleep anytime, use Blissful Sleep disks made with essential oils, like lavender and chamomile, to naturally lull you to sleep.

No.25258 Vaporizer $14.95
No.H1528 Twelve Menthol Refill Disks $11.90
No.32697 Twelve Blissful Sleep Disks $11.90

Waistband Stretcher
For Too-Snug Pants And Skirts

Stretch pants and skirts while still wet for up to five extra inches of breathing room. Waistbands fit comfortably until you wash them again. Made of durable, lightweight plastic. Fits waist sizes 21"-50".
No.30975 Waistband Stretcher $29.95

Did Sears Kill Roebuck?

The
Big
Boys

In 1886, Richard W. Sears, a 23-year-old railroad agent in North Redwood, Minnesota, bought a shipment of watches that a local jeweler was returning to the manufacturer, sold the watches to other station agents, and then ordered more. Six months later, Sears started the R. W. Sears Watch Company, moved to Chicago, and in 1887 hired watchmaker Alvah C. Roebuck. The next year, Sears issued his first catalogue, featuring only watches and jewelry. Sears sold the watch business in 1889 and two years later formed another mail-order business that became Sears, Roebuck & Co. in 1893.

The Sears, Roebuck & Co. Mail Order catalogue, filled with Richard Sears' fanciful advertising copy, provided farmers with a low-cost alternative to high-priced rural stores. Sales in 1895 topped 750 thousand dollars. Roebuck left the company in 1895 for unknown reasons, and Sears found two new partners: Aaron Nussbaum and Chicago clothing manufacturer Julius Rosenwald. In 1906, Sears, Roebuck & Co. went public and opened a forty-acre mail-order plant, then the largest business building in the world, built at a cost of five million dollars. When Rosenwald began editing Sears's flamboyant advertising copy, insisting it be factual, Sears left the company. Ros-

enwald became president, and in 1911, established a testing center to guarantee quality merchandise.

With the advent of the automobile, Sears, Roebuck & Co. opened its first retail store in 1925 in the Chicago mail-order plant so farmers could drive to town to buy merchandise. By 1933, Sears, Roebuck & Co. had four hundred stores. The company continued opening new stores during the Depression, and when the United States entered World War II in 1941, Sears, Roebuck & Co. had more than six hundred stores and a network of catalogue sales offices in small towns.

STRANGE FACTS
• Company founder Richard Sears was once called "a showman of P. T. Barnum's caliber." Barnum was famous for the saying, "There's a sucker born every minute."
• The 1911 Sears, Roebuck & Co. catalogue offered blood purifiers, liver and kidney remedies, and "pink pills for pale people."
• A former chief of the Moscow bureau of the Associated Press claimed: "Two innocent articles of American life—the Sears, Roebuck & Co. catalogue and the phonograph record—are the most powerful pieces of foreign propaganda in Russia. The catalogue comes first."
• During one twelve-month period in the late 1920s, a new Sears, Roebuck & Co. store opened on the average of one every other business day.
• Sears, once the largest mail-order company in the world, brought a wide range of clothes, tools, and machinery to the American frontier. The company's repu-

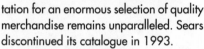

tation for an enormous selection of quality merchandise remains unparalleled. Sears discontinued its catalogue in 1993.

• In 1931, Sears, Roebuck & Co. launched Allstate Insurance, named after its brand-name tire.

• Sears brand-name products (most notably Kenmore, Craftsman, and DieHard) helped firmly establish Sears as an American institution.

• A Kenmore appliance can be found in one out of every two American homes.

• In 1969, Sears, Roebuck & Co. began building the 110-story Sears Tower in downtown Chicago. When it opened in 1973, the 1,454-foot-tall building was the world's tallest building.

• In 1990, K-mart surpassed Sears as the number-one retail store in the United States, only to be overtaken two years later by Wal-Mart.

• As of 2002, Sears employed 289,000 people. That's more than 55 times the population of North Redwood, Minnesota, the town where company founder Richard Sears started selling watches.

THE-TOASTER-WITH-THE-TESTER

THE ONLY TOASTER WITH THE TESTER INSPECTION DEVICE

TOAST POPS UP HERE

SUIT YOURSELF! REMOVE A SLICE ANY TIME

$14.95

DIAL CONTROL FOR "LIGHT" OR "DARK"

LOW CURRENT COST, TOASTS 6 SLICES FOR LESS THAN ½¢ FLASHING MONITOR LIGHT INDICATOR

HANDSOME CHROMIUM...

ATTRACTIVE BAKELITE TRIM

SMOKELESS TABLE BROILER and HOT PLATE - No smoke ...no odor...no effort! Smart, modern, saving!...$10.95.

IRON-THAT-WAGS-ITS-TAIL ...Non-klink cord with swivel action that follows your strokes!...$9.95.

TWIN-O-MATIC...The Waffle Baker that has Twins! It makes two four-section waffles at once!...$16.00.

LONG-LAST...The Percolator of a Lifetime! Modern design, unbreakable, the first cost is the last!...$9.95.

See these and other electrical conveniences of Manning-Bowman quality at better stores. Toasters from $2.75. Irons from $3.50. Waffle bakers from $3.95. Percolators from $6.95. Write for folders. Manning, Bowman & Co., Meriden, Conn.

Manning
MEANS BEST
Bowman

5

HOME & HEARTH

Candles, Potpourri, and Crafts

T he warm glow of candles. The floral scent of potpourri. The comfort of a hand-sewn quilt. The elegance of marbled paper. The integrity of home-woven fabrics. The local country store sold a wide miscellany of items created by local craftspeople—brooms, stools, homemade papers, pottery, knickknacks, even gift-wrapping paper. These local craftspeople usually bartered at the country store, providing their wares in exchange for store credit. The storekeeper also traveled to nearby cities to purchase goods, ordered them from catalogs, and had them delivered to the store by train. These handcrafted items enhanced the home, brought warmth and beauty, and helped families savor their love for one another.

Candle Making

WHAT YOU NEED

From the supermarket:
- Crisco All-Vegetable Shortening or Pam Original Cooking Spray

From a hobby center or candle supply store:
- Several pounds general-purpose paraffin wax (with a melting point between 135 and 145 degrees Fahrenheit)
- Candle mold (Craft stores sell a large variety of metal, rubber, and plastic candle molds. Or use a clean, empty yogurt container, Jell-O mold, cottage cheese container, cup, bowl, drinking glass, or tin can without a lip.)
- Mold sealer (or florist's putty or plumber's putty)
- Three feet of wick (Use flat or square braided wicks for molded and dipped candles. Use wire core wicks for container candles or for inserting a wick into a candle. Use 24-ply wick for taper candles, 30-ply wick for candles with diameters between two and four inches, and 36-ply wick for candles with diameters larger than four inches.)
- Candle dye or Crayola crayons (Other crayons contain plastic; Crayola crayons are pure paraffin wax, stearic acid, and pigment.)
- Candle or candy thermometer
- Scent (if desired)
- Knitting needle (or thin dowel)

From a camping store:
- Metal pot holder (or pliers)

From the kitchen:
- Newspaper

- Cookie tin or aluminum pan
- Double boiler (or old pot, clean empty coffee can, and metal trivet)
- Wooden spoon
- White paper
- Knife
- Oven mitt
- Plastic or metal pan
- Pie tin

From the workshop:
- Hammer
- Chisel
- Scissors
- Pencil
- Weight (lead, small brick, or heavy ceramic tile)

From the tap:
- Water

WHAT TO DO

Cover your work area with newspaper.

Rub a thin coat of Crisco All-Vegetable Shortening on the inside of the candle mold, or spray a small amount of Pam Original Cooking Spray into the mold.

Place the mold on a cookie tin or aluminum pan just in case the mold leaks or topples over accidentally.

Fill the plastic or metal pan with enough water to come up to the level of the wax in the mold to use later as a water bath.

If using a store-bought candle mold, insert the wick through the hole in the bottom of the mold, pull it through the hole until one inch remains, and secure the wick in place with the small retaining screw provided with the mold. Wind the end of the wick under the head of the screw and tighten. Roll a small piece of mold sealer into a ball and press it down on the screw head, filling the wick hole.

If using a homemade mold, hang a wire core wick from a pencil (or after the candle hardens, drill a hole through the candle, fill with hot wax, and insert the wick).

Lay the dowel (provided with the mold) across the top of the mold. Pull the free end of the wick taut and wrap it round the dowel.

Using a hammer and chisel, break the

block of wax into small chunks. Put enough wax in the top of the double boiler (or in the coffee can) to fill the mold.

Fill the bottom section of the double boiler (or the pot) halfway with water and bring to a boil. If using a pot, place a trivet in the bottom of the pot to prevent the coffee can from sitting on the bottom.

Using this double-boiler method, the wax will not exceed a temperature above the boiling point of water—as long as you do not boil away all the water.

When the wax reaches 185 degrees Fahrenheit on the candle thermometer, add a few shavings of candle dye or a small piece of Crayola crayon. Using a wooden spoon, stir until the dye or crayon dissolves. Too much dye may cause the candle to burn poorly. To get an accurate idea of what color the finished candle will be, place a few small drops of the hot wax on a piece of white paper.

When the temperature of the wax reaches 195 degrees Fahrenheit, remove the wax from the heat and add scent (one teaspoon of essential oil per pound of wax, or $1/8$ of a block of scent). Too much scent may ruin the finished candle (and some plastic molds).

Tilt the mold on a slight angle to avoid creating air bubbles and, wearing an oven mitt, slowly and smoothly pour the wax to within $1/2$ inch of the top of the mold. Always wear an oven mitt when handling molds filled with hot wax because the molds get very hot. Save a cupful of wax for

later. Gently tap the sides of the mold with a spoon, and wait one minute for any trapped air bubbles to rise to the surface.

Place the mold in the water bath, making sure no water runs into the mold. If necessary, set a weight across the top of the mold, not touching the wax.

When a thin film forms across the top of the wax, remove the mold from the water bath and set on a level table. Since wax hardens from the outside toward the center, shrinking as it cools, a well will form around the wick. After forty-five minutes, insert the knitting needle (or thin wooden dowel) in three different places one inch from the wick to admit air into the void formed by the hardening wax. Reheat the cup of wax you set

aside earlier to 195 degrees Fahrenheit and refill the well, being careful not to pour above the original wax level. Over-filling the mold at this point will make removing the candle difficult and ruin the finish. For large candles, you may need to poke and refill the well a second time after another forty-five minutes passes.

Let the candle set in the mold overnight to cure fully. When both the mold and the wax are cool to the touch, remove the mold sealer, retaining screw, and dowel. Hold the mold upside-down and let the candle slide out. The top of the candle is the part that faced the bottom of the mold.

If the candle does not slide out of the mold, place the mold in the refrigerator for twenty minutes, then try again. As a last resort, hold the mold under hot running water until the candle slides out (softening the wax and usually marring the finish). Never attempt to pry or scrape the wax out of the mold. This may irreparably damage the mold, making future

candles difficult to remove and creating scratch marks in them.

Trim the seam line and the bottom of the candle with a knife. If the base of the candle is uneven, place a pie tin atop a pot of boiling water. Holding the candle by the wick, let it touch the heated pie tin until the base is flat and level. Cut the exposed wick to a length of ¹/₂ inch.

Clean the mold with hot, soapy water, then rinse it with clean, hot water. Dry the mold thoroughly, then store it upside-down to prevent dust and dirt from settling inside the mold.

CANDLE VARIATIONS

Here are some variations to the basic candle-making process.

LAYER CANDLES

Prepare the mold and when the wax reaches a temperature of 195 degrees Fahrenheit, pour a one-inch layer of colored wax into the mold. Place the mold in the water bath for a few minutes, remove the moment the

wax forms a firm, warm film across the surface, heat a second pot of wax, stir in a different color, and pour a second one-inch layer of wax into the mold. Place the mold in the water bath for a few minutes, remove, and continue this process until you fill the mold to the desired level.

Pour a combination of thick and thin layers, or pour a multicolored stack of very thin layers. To make sure the layers adhere to each other, pour each additional layer before the previous layer has cooled.

TILTED LAYER CANDLES

Tilt the mold on a block of wood and pour the first layer of wax. Before pouring the second layer, tilt the mold in a different direction. Continue this process until you are ready to pour the last layer, which should be level to make the base of the candle flat.

CHUNK CANDLES

Oil a cookie sheet with Crisco All-Vegetable Shortening or Pam Original Cooking Spray, melt the wax to 195 degrees Fahrenheit, and pour onto the cookie sheet to create chunks of whatever thickness you desire. Let cool until fairly hard, then use a knife to slice the wax into squares (without removing them from the pan). Let cool completely, cut through the

original slice marks, turn over the pan, and pop out the chunks. Repeat to make chunks of several different colors.

Prepare a mold and fill it with different chunks. Melt a pound of wax (without adding any color) and bring the temperature to 180 degrees Fahrenheit, and pour the wax into the mold, covering the chunks.

SAND CANDLES

Fill a large rectangular plastic container, wooden box, or cardboard box (lined with plastic wrap) with sand (collected from the beach or purchased from a hardware or garden supply store). Mix enough water into the sand until a small handful of the sand squeezed together retains its shape in your open palm without falling apart. Too much water will make the muddy sand stick to your hand.

Press a can, block of wood, bowl, small ball, or glass jar into the sand and pack the sand around it. Remove the object slowly, leaving an impression intact in the sand to be used as your candle mold.

To make legs on the candle, wrap a piece of tape around a wooden dowel ½ inch from an end, and insert that end of the dowel into the sand in three spots (up to the end of the tape) to make holes of equal depth.

Carefully melt an inch or two of the wax (with a minimum melting point of 145 degrees Fahrenheit) in a seamless container (to avoid leaking flammable wax) over direct low heat. Once the wax melts, add the rest of the wax, and increase the heat and bring the wax to a temperature between 275 and 300 degrees Fahrenheit. Observe proper safety precautions to

avoid serious burns from the wax, and make certain the temperature does not exceed 300 degrees Fahrenheit (combustion occurs at temperatures above 400 degrees Fahrenheit). Remember, wax is a flammable petroleum product. The wax will heat up quickly. Do not be alarmed if the wax begins to smoke, crack, and pop. Smoking is normal; cracking and popping results from small amounts of water in the wax and will cease once the water evaporates.

Do not add color to the wax. These high temperatures will distort it. Wearing an oven mitt, hold a spoon over the middle of the hole in the sand mold, and slowly pour the hot wax over the bowl of the spoon so the wax does not erode the sand mold or splatter onto your hand. The wax will bubble and hiss as it contacts the wet sand. Fill the hole to the top with wax. Wax will seep into the sand, lowering the level of the wax roughly one inch.

Let the wax cool until a thick film forms on the surface. Use a knitting needle to poke a wick hole into the middle of the candle (without punching through the bottom), and insert a wire core wick into the hole, letting it extend above the surface of the sand. When the wax hardens, remove the candle from the sand and lightly brush away the excess sand. In a double boiler, melt some wax to a temperature of 210 degrees Fahrenheit, add color, let the wax cool to 170 degrees Fahrenheit, and pour into the well of the sand candle, filling to the top of the shell. Let cool.

MOTTLED CANDLES
Create small crystals in the wax by preparing the mold without lubrication, bringing the melted wax to 160 degrees Fahrenheit, and mixing

in three tablespoons mottling oil (or mineral oil) for every pound of wax. (For more mottling, add more oil; for less mottling, add less oil and cool the candle faster.) Immediately after stirring the oil into the wax, pour the wax into the mold to the desired level and cover with a paper bag or cardboard box so the wax cools slowly. Do not place the mold in a water bath.

ICE CANDLES

Fill a prepared mold with ice cubes or crushed ice, then pour wax heated to 195 degrees Fahrenheit over the ice, filling the mold. When the candle is removed, the melted ice will leave decorative pockets of air in the candle.

SWIRLING ABSTRACT CANDLES

Melt a few ounces of colored wax, bring the temperature down to 165 degrees Fahrenheit, and pour a small amount of the wax into the bottom of a prepared mold. Tilt and turn the mold so small rivulets of wax create an interesting design on the inside wall of the mold, then pour the excess wax back into the container. Let cool. Repeat with a second colored wax.

Heat a large container of wax to 170 degrees Fahrenheit, color if desired, and pour a small amount into the bottom of the mold. Slowly pour the wax back into the container, turning the mold so the wax coats the entire inside surface of the mold. Repeat several times until a thin wax shell covers the abstract designs. If the designs begin to melt, hold the mold in the water bath for a minute. Wait two minutes for the wax shell to cool. Then fill the mold with hot wax and let cool.

Troubleshooting

- **BUBBLES AT THE BASE OF THE CANDLE:** The water level in the water bath was not even with or was above the level of wax in the mold, the wax was poured too quickly, or the mold was not tapped to let air bubbles escape.
- **CANDLE SMOKES:** The wick is too large, the melting point of wax was too low, the well was not completely filled, or the candle is burning in a draft.
- **FRACTURES:** The candle was cooled too rapidly, the water bath was too cold, the candle cooled in a draft of cold air, the well was filled with wax heated above 195 degrees Fahrenheit, the well was filled after the candle hardened completely, or the candle was placed in a refrigerator or freezer for too long.
- **FROST MARKS:** The wax was too cool or too hot when poured, the mold was too cold when wax was poured into it, or the mold was not cleaned and contained wax particles from a previous use.
- **LAYER SEPARATION** (in layer candles): The wax was too cool when poured, or individual layers cooled for too long before the next layer was poured.
- **MOTTLING:** The wax cooled too slowly, causing large crystals to form.
- **PIT MARKS:** The wax was too hot when poured, the mold did not sit in the water bath for enough time, the inside of the mold was coated with too much lubricant, the mold was not tipped when the wax was poured, or the wax was poured into the mold too rapidly.

HURRICANE CANDLES

Pour a small amount of hot colored wax into the bottom of a prepared mold. Slowly pour the wax back into the container, turning the mold so the wax coats the entire inside surface of the mold. Repeat several times until a 1/2-inch wax shell covers the wall of the mold. Place in the water bath to let the shell cool completely. Fill the mold with wax heated to 170 degrees Fahrenheit and let cool.

GLOW-THROUGH CANDLES

Make a regular block candle from clear wax and, after it cools completely, remove it from the mold. Holding the candle by the wick, dip it into colored wax heated to 190 degrees Fahrenheit, twirling the candle to melt off any scale and rough edges for a few seconds. Let cool for one minute, then smoothly dip again for a few seconds. Repeat until a thick coat of colored wax covers the candle.

You can make a multicolored glow-through candle by dipping the entire candle into yellow wax four times, dipping the lower two-thirds of the candle into red wax three times (creating an orange layer), and then dipping the bottom one-third of the candle into blue wax three times (creating a purple layer).

ALUMINUM FOIL CANDLES

Make an impression in a box of sand, place a sheet of aluminum foil into it, and mold the foil to the shape, creating your candle mold. When the candle hardens, peel off the foil.

TAPER CANDLES

Melt the wax without any color in a container twelve inches tall. Fold a long wick in half and tie a washer or nut to both ends of the wick. Keep the temperature of the wax within 10 degrees Fahrenheit of the melting point of the wax. Holding the wick at the fold and keeping the two ends separated, dip the wick

Hot Warnings

- Never leave melting wax unattended on a stove.
- Always use a candle thermometer.
- Never heat wax beyond its flash point (above 400 degrees Fahrenheit for paraffin), otherwise the hot wax will combust, causing a fire.
- Keep wax away from open flames.
- Keep a pot lid, a box of baking soda, and a dry-chemical fire extinguisher within easy reach when heating wax. Should the wax catch fire due to overheating, turn off the heat, and smother the fire with the pot lid, baking soda, or fire extinguisher.

- Never put water on a wax fire. It causes the wax fire to spread.
- Fumes from overheated wax can cause severe illness, so in the event of an accident, immediately evacuate and ventilate the area.
- Always use metal pot holders or pliers when handling hot pots or cans.
- Turn pot handles so they are not sticking out from the stovetop.
- If hot wax splashes on your skin, apply cold water immediately, then peel off the wax.
- Never pour wax down the drain. It will clog the pipes.

into the wax for a brief moment and raise it back out. Then dip the wick into a bucket of water for a few seconds, remove, and dry thoroughly with a hand towel. Repeat until the candles attain the proper thickness. Use colored wax for the last five dips. When the candles are complete, clip the wicks to the appropriate length and trim the bottoms with a knife.

BEESWAX TAPERS

Place the wick along the edge of a sheet of colored beeswax and roll the sheet around the wick.

FINISHING TOUCHES

• To make your own wick, mix one tablespoon salt, three tablespoons borax, and two cups water. Soak a cotton string in the solution for twenty-four hours. Let dry thoroughly, then coat the string with paraffin wax.

• Before placing a wick in a mold or candle, coat the wick with wax to eliminate air trapped between the fibers.

• Wax can be colored with dye or pigments. Pigments go into suspension, meaning small particles float in the liquid wax, giving the appearance of color, but settle to the bottom of the mold, making one end of the candle darker than the other. Pigment particles also clog the wick. Oil-soluble dyes, on the other hand, go into solution, meaning they actually become part of the wax, yielding candles with uniform color.

• Liquid candle scents yield better results than scent blocks.

• To remove blemishes from a candle, polish with a damp paper towel or a piece of nylon cut from a pair of panty hose.

• The lit wick of a candle melts the surrounding wax. The porous wick absorbs the molten wax, which travels up the wick, feeding the flame with fuel.

• If a lit candle creates a minimal pool of wax and smokes excessively, the wick (absorbing too little molten wax) is too thick. If the wax pool formed by a lit candle drowns the wick or flows over the sides of the candle, the wick (absorbing too much molten wax) is too thin.

• A dripless candle is an ordinary candle made with a wick properly sized to consume all the wax.

• To make a thick wick, twist two thin wicks together (or braid three thin wicks together) and coat with hot wax.

• Candles colored with dyes sometime fade over time if exposed to direct sunlight or fluorescent lighting.

• Rolling candles in a sheet of wax paper before placing them in a drawer or storage box protects them from getting scuffed.

• Prevent wax from sticking to candle holders by giving the insides of candle-holders a thin coat of Vaseline Petroleum Jelly.

• Remove candle wax from a table or countertop by blowing warm air with a blow-dryer an inch above the drips, then wipe away the wax with a paper towel.

• Remove candle wax from a tablecloth or carpeting by using an old credit card to scrape off as much wax as possible. Then place a paper towel over the wax and press gently with a warm iron. The heat from the iron melts the wax, and the paper towel absorbs it.

Do-It-Yourself Recipe
BREAD-GLUE DOUGH

WHAT YOU NEED

From the supermarket:
- 3 slices Wonder Bread
- 2 tablespoons Elmer's Glue-All
- Food coloring
- Wax paper
- Toothpicks

From the drugstore:
- 1/2 teaspoon glycerin

From the kitchen:
- Soup bowl

From the craft store:
- Styrofoam block
- Paintbrush
- Tempura paint

From the tap:
- Water

WHAT TO DO

Cut the crust from the bread, discard, and tear the bread into small pieces.

Place the pieces of bread in the bowl, and drizzle with glue and glycerin. Knead the ingredients together until the mixture feels like dough. Tear the dough into four equal portions. Color each portion of dough a different color by adding food coloring one drop at a time, kneading the dough after each drop until you achieve the desired hue.

Cover your work surface with wax paper. Mold the dough into various shapes as if working with clay. If the dough begins to dry, add a little water. Place the molded pieces on toothpicks stuck in a Styrofoam block. Let dry for one week. Paint the finished pieces with tempura paint. To give the bread-dough sculpture a smooth, porcelainesque finish, mix equal parts of Elmer's Glue-All and water, and apply several coats with a paintbrush.

187

How Woolworth Nickel-and-Dimed America

Convinced that a store that sold only merchandise priced less than five cents would be an instant success, twenty-year-old Frank Winfield Woolworth, a grocery store clerk born in Rodman, New York, opened The Great Five Cent Store in Utica, New York, in 1879. The store failed. Undaunted, Woolworth moved to Lancaster, Pennsylvania, in the heart of Amish country, and opened the world's first five-and-dime at 21 North Queens Street. This time, the store succeeded.

In 1886, Frank Woolworth moved his headquarters to New York City and began acquiring other dime-store chains. In 1905, with ten million dollars in annual sales and 120 stores, the company incorporated as the F. W. Woolworth Company, with Frank Woolworth as president. In 1912, Woolworth merged with five rival chains and went public with 596 stores, making 52 million dollars in sales the first year. When Woolworth died in 1919, the chain had 1,081 stores and 119 million dollars in annual sales.

For the next fifty years, Woolworth continued to grow by acquiring other chains and expanding its selection of merchandise. In 1974, Woolworth introduced Foot Locker, the athletic-shoe chain, opening Lady Foot Locker in 1982 and Kids Foot Locker in 1987.

In 1993, declining sales forced Woolworth to close four hundred stores in the United States, sell 122 Canadian Woolco stores to Wal-Mart, and close some 300 underperforming shoe stores.

In 1996, institutional investor Greenway Partners tried to get Woolworth to split up into two companies—one consisting of the profitable Foot Locker and other sporting equipment stores and the second comprised of Woolworth and the other floundering stores. The split never happened.

In 1997, the Woolworth company closed the remaining four hundred of its F. W. Woolworth five-and-dime stores and changed its name to Venator.

STRANGE FACTS

• In 1919, Frank W. Woolworth built the sixty-story Woolworth Building in New York City, paying 13.5 million dollars in cash. At the time, it was the world's tallest building, towering 792 feet high.

• In February 1960, four black college students broke the segregation barrier by taking seats at F. W. Woolworth's downtown lunch counter in Greenboro, North Carolina. The peaceful civil disobedience sit-in against the Jim Crow custom spread nationwide and became a movement to end legal segregation. Today, the Smithsonian Institution features the four original chrome-and-vinyl stools from the Woolworth lunch counter.

• In the 1969 movie *If It's Tuesday, This Must Be Belgium*, starring Suzanne Pleshette, when one of the American tourists on an eighteen-day bus tour of Europe remarks how wonderful it is to see such unusual sights, the camera cuts to a shot of a Woolworth's store.

• In 1990, Woolworth became the first United States retailer to open a store in East Germany. Woolworth actually "reopened" a store in Halle, Germany, that it had operated before World War II.

• In 1995, Woolworth had more than 94,000 employees. That's nearly double the population of Lancaster, Pennsylvania, the city where the first Woolworth store opened.

• In 1995, Woolworth had sales of over 8.2 billion dollars worldwide. That's more than the total of all nickels and dimes in circulation.

Do-It-Yourself Recipe

HERBED VINEGARS

WHAT YOU NEED

From the supermarket:

- 1 cup white wine vinegar
- 1 teaspoon fennel leaves
- 1 garlic clove
- Two-inch sprig of parsley

From the kitchen:

- Sterilized glass jar with lid

WHAT TO DO

Place the sprig of parsley, fennel leaves, and garlic clove in the glass jar.

Heat the vinegar in a saucepan, without boiling it. Pour the vinegar into the jar. Let the vinegar cool, then seal the lid of the jar tightly, and store in a cool, dark place to steep for three weeks up to a year. Use the vinegar in salad dressings and marinades. Makes one cup.

VARIATIONS

Try these other flavorful combinations:

- Combine one teaspoon borage leaves, one-half teaspoon dill, and one sliced shallot with one cup white wine vinegar.
- Combine two sprigs of sage, one sprig of parsley, and one sliced shallot with one cup white wine vinegar.
- Combine one-half teaspoon dill, one nasturtium flower with leaves, and one garlic clove with one cup cider vinegar.
- Combine one tablespoon rose petals and one tablespoon violet petals with one cup rice wine vinegar.

Rock City Birdhouses

During the Depression in the 1930s, Garnet Carter and his wife Frieda decided to turn the rock formations on their land on Lookout Mountain, six miles from downtown Chattanooga, Tennessee, into a tourist attraction called Rock City.

To promote Rock City, Carter had the roofs of hundreds of barns along major roadways painted with the concise slogan "See Rock City," creating one of the most famous advertising campaigns of all time with just a ladder, paintbrush, and a few hundred buckets of paint.

Carter also designed mailboxes painted with his slogan, but when the United States

Postal Service rejected the design, he turned his mailboxes into birdhouses.

Marbled Paper

WHAT YOU NEED

From the supermarket:
- 2 tablespoons white vinegar
- Six sticks of different colored chalk
- Six paper cups
- 6 tablespoons of corn oil
- Half sheets of white paper
- Paper towels

From the kitchen:
- Newspaper
- Baking pan
- Mortar and pestle
- Spoon

From the tap:
- Water

WHAT TO DO

Cover the kitchen counter with newspaper. Fill the baking pan with water, add the vinegar, and place the pan in the middle of the newspaper.

Using the mortar and pestle, crush a piece of colored chalk to a fine powder, then pour into a paper cup. Repeat for all six pieces of chalk, using a different cup for each piece. Add a tablespoon of oil to each cup, stirring thoroughly with the spoon. Pour the contents of each paper cup into the pan of water. The chalky colored oil will form large pools on the water's surface.

Gently lay a piece of paper on the water's surface for a moment, lift off, then set to dry on a sheet of newspaper for twenty-four hours. When the marbled paper dries, gently wipe off any surface chalk grains with a paper towel.

STRANGE FACTS

- Marbling paper was practiced in Japan and China as early as the twelfth century. According to a Japanese legend, the gods gave knowledge of the marbling process to a man named Jiyemon Hiroba as a reward for his devotion to the Katsuga Shrine.
- For centuries, paper-marbling masters worked in secrecy to maintain a shroud of mystery to prevent others from mastering the craft and going into business for themselves.

Paper Making

WHAT YOU NEED

From the supermarket:
- 3 tablespoons cornstarch

From the hardware store:
- Metal screening (8 by 10 inches)

From the kitchen:
- Newspaper
- Electric blender
- Wooden spoon

- Metal baking pan (larger than 8 by 10 inches)
- Clean, empty, large glass jar with lid
- Measuring cup
- Scissors
- Markers, crayons, paints, pencils, or pens

From the tap:
- Hot water

WHAT TO DO

Cut sheets of newspaper into long, thin strips (or feed the newspaper through a paper shredder). Pack them into the measuring cup until you have 1½ cups of shredded newspaper.

Put the shredded newspaper into the jar and fill it three quarters full of hot tap water. Screw on the lid and let stand for three hours, shaking the jar occasionally and beating and stirring the paper with the wooden spoon. As the paper absorbs the water, add more hot tap water.

When the mixture becomes pasty and creamy, pour it into the blender. Dissolve the cornstarch in ½ cup hot tap water, pour into the blender, and blend. Pour the mixture into the baking pan.

Place the metal screen on top of the mixture in the baking pan, then gently push it down into the pan until the mixture covers it.

Bring the screen up, place it on a sheet of newspaper, and press the mixture on the screen flat with the palm of your hand to squeeze away the water.

Let the screen-backed paper mixture dry in the sun for several hours. When the paper is thoroughly dry, peel it from the screen backing and trim the edges with scissors.

The recycled newspaper has the texture of a gray egg carton and can be decorated with markers, crayons, paints, pencils, or pens.

STRANGE FACTS

- Newspaper pulp—a blend of sulfite pulp and ground cellulose fibers—when formed into a sheet over a screen, dries into paper again. The cornstarch—a sizing material—is added to the mixture to give the paper a smooth surface and prevent too much ink absorption. Any discarded paper—paper bags, computer punch cards, junk mail—can be made into pulp.
- The first paper, invented in China in 105 C.E. by Ts'ai Lun, the Emperor Ho-Ti's minister of public works, was made from the inner bark of the mulberry tree, fishnets, old rags, and waste hemp.
- For hundreds of years, paper was made by hand from the pulp of rags. Rag pulp is still used today to make most high-quality bond paper.
- Toilet paper and facial tissues are made from wood pulp treated with plant resins to make it absorbent.
- Before the advent of paper, most documents were written on parchment (made from the skin of sheep or goats) or vellum (made from the skin of calves). A single book three hundred pages long would require the skins of an estimated eighteen sheep.
- Money is made out of cotton, not paper.
- The watermark was discovered by accident. In 1282, a small piece of wire caught in the paper press being used at the Fabrino Paper Mill made a line in the finished paper that could be seen by holding the paper up to the light. The papermakers realized a design made from wire would create a decorative watermark, which could also be used on banknotes to thwart counterfeiters.
- Paper can be made inexpensively from hemp. However, in 1937, cotton growers, fearing competition from hemp growers, lobbied against marijuana (the dried leaves of the hemp plant) to make hemp illegal. In 1999, Governor Jesse "The Body" Ventura signed legislation making hemp farming legal in Minnesota.

Papier—Mâché

Mix one cup Gold Medal Flour with two-thirds cup water in a medium-size bowl to a thick-glue consistency. To thicken, add more flour. Cut newspaper strips approximately one to two inches in width. Dip each strip into the paste, gently pull it between your fingers to remove excess paste, and apply it to any object (an empty bottle, carton, or canister). Continue until the base is completely covered. Let dry, then decorate with poster paint. After the paint dries, coat with shellac.

Potpourri

Potpourri—a medley of moist or dry flower petals, herbs, twigs, roots, woods, and spices—gives a home warm, welcoming scents and adds a beautiful decorative accent. You can make potpourri using two basic methods. The dry method creates more decorative potpourri (the petals retain their colors and shape) that is easier to make. The moist method yields bleached-out potpourri with a more pungent and enduring scent that is more time-consuming to make.

INGREDIENTS

Classic recipes for potpourri include five basic groups of ingredients: flower petals, herbs, spices, fixative (to hold the scent so it lasts longer), and essential oils. (See "Scented Materials" on page 196.)

You can make potpourri from just about any type of dried flower petals including roses, carnations, and violets. Pick the flowers early on a dry day, before the heat of the day. Select budding or newly opened blooms, picking the flowers right after they have opened but after the dew or other moisture has dried off them. Do not pick too many at one time so you can deal with them before they wilt. Do not pick full-blown flowers; they will never dry. Sort through the flowers and discard any damaged ones.

You can collect plants all year round from gardens or woods. (To store, dry the materials with one of the methods below, pack the dried material in screw-top jars in alternating layers of petals and a thin layer of orris root, and store in a dark place.)

Since flowers and leaves shrink when dried, collect four times the amount of plant material needed for the final potpourri mix. If you lack plant material, ask your local florist for discarded flowers.

DRYING FLOWERS

There are two ways to dry flowers. You can hang them to dry, or you can spread them out on flat screens. Most flowers and herbs can be hang-dried. Individual leaves and blossoms, decorative rose petals and flower heads, and roots (thoroughly washed) are best dried flat. When using the moist method to make potpourri, dry the plant material on flat screens. Dry fruit-rinds in a microwave oven.

HANG DRYING

String a line of rope or twine tautly across the ceiling of a dry, warm, airy room. (Strung flowers make excellent decorations.)

Remove most of the leaves from the flower stems to improve air circulation, reduce the risk of mildew, and expedite the drying process.

Remove the thorns from roses with a sharp pair of scissors to avoid pricking yourself.

Cut the stems to different lengths.

Bunch together a group of six stems, staggering the flower heads so they do not touch each other.

Tie the bunch together tightly with a loop of nylon cut from a leg of a pair of clean, used panty hose. As the stems dry and shrink, the nylon loop will contract, holding the bunch together.

Hang the bunch upside-down from your drying line, making sure the flowers do not touch anything. Do not hang the flowers in direct sunlight, which will fade the colors. The faster the plant material dries, the more color the flowers, leaves, and stems will retain.

FLAT DRYING

Clip off one flower head at a time and quickly pluck off the petals and spread them face-up across sheets of newspaper, non-metallic screens (such as a window screen), or a sheet of muslin stretched across two pieces of wood in a warm, dark room. (Colors will fade in direct sunlight.)

Make sure layers of single petals are stacked no more than two petals deep, and place small decorative blooms so they do not touch one another.

Stir the plant materials once a day.

If the petals are to be used in dry potpourri, let them partially dry for a couple of days until they feel rubbery like leather.

Potpourri Ingredients

The following scented materials can be used to make potpourri.

SCENTED MATERIALS

Flowers

Astilbe	Hydrangea	Pinks
Bachelor's button	Knautia	Pot marigold
Bower vine	Knotweed	Queen Anne's lace
Carnation	Lady's mantle	Rose
Cinquefoil	Larkspur	Shasta daisy
Cosmos	Loosestrife	Sneezewort
Crocosmia	Love-in-a-mist	Violet
Dalmation toadflax	Masterwort	
Daylily	Montbretia	

Aromatic Garden Foliage

Bergamot	Jerusalem sage	Red salvia
Burnet	Juniper	Scented geranium
Curly-leaved wood sage	Lad's love	St. John's wort
Daisybush	Myrtle	Sweet flag
Dropwort	Ostrich fern	Sweet gale
Eucalyptus	Pittosporu	

Berries and Small Fruit

Cotoneaster berries	Hawthorn berries	Sloe berries
Crab apples	Mixed dried berries	
European mountain ash hips	Rose hips	

Citrus Fruits

Grapefruit peel	Lemon and lemon peel	Orange and orange peel
Kumquat	Lime and lime peel	Ruby grapefruit peel

HERBS

Subtly Scented Herbs

Dark opal basil	Meadowsweet	Spearmint
Elecampane	Peppermint	Variegated rosemary
French tarragon	Purple sage	Yarrow
Lemon balm	Queen of the meadow	
Lemon thyme	Queen of the prairie	
Meadow sage	Rosemary	

Strongly Scented Herbs

Artemisia	French lavender	Russian sage
Blue vervain	Horsemint	Scented white geranium
Clary sage	Lavender (white, pink, mauve)	Variegated sage
Crete dittany	Marshmallow	White sage

SPICES, SEEDS, WOODS, CONIFERS, AND ROOTS

Alder cones	Cinnamon sticks	Nutmeg
Allspice	Elecampane root	Pine needles
Angelica root	Geranium root	Pine buds
Balm-of-Gilead buds	Golden clematis seed heads	Pussy willow catkins
Barberry bark	Herb bennet	Quassia chips
Caraway seeds	Hops	Small pine cones
Cardamom seeds	Juniper berries	Spruce
Cedar wood shavings	Large pine cones	Star anise
Cedar needles	Logwood chips	Sweet flag root
Cinnamon bark	Mace	Sweet cicely roots

AROMATIC FIXATIVES

Angelica seeds	Cumin seeds	Orris root powder
Chamomile flowers	Frankincense	Sweet cicely seeds
Cinnamon powder	Gum benzoin	Tonka beans
Cloves	Nutmeg	Vanilla beans
Coriander	Oakmoss	

ESSENTIAL OILS

Angelica	Hyacinth	Star anise
Balsam	Iris Florentine	Storax
Birch	Jasmine	Sweet cicely
Carnation	Jonquil	Sweet flag
Cardamom	Labdanum	Sweet pea
Cassia	Lilac	Vervain
Cedarwood	Lily-of-the-valley	Vetiver
Cinnamon	Musk	Violet
Clove	Myrrh	Wallflow
Cumin	Nutmeg	Ylang-ylang
Elecampane	Orange blossom	
Fennel	Patchouli	
Frankincense	Roman chamomile	
Geranium	Rose	
Ginger	Roseroot	
Heliotrope	Rosewood	
Honeysuckle	Sandalwood	

Ooh-La-La!

The word *potpourri* is French for "rotten pot."

DRY METHOD OF POTPOURRI MAKING

WHAT YOU NEED

From the supermarket:
- 2 teaspoons ground cinnamon
- $1/2$ teaspoon grated nutmeg

From the health food store or perfume supply house:
- 1 ounce orris root powder
- 6 drops ylang-ylang essential oil

From the kitchen:
- Small bowl
- Mixing bowl
- Wooden spoon
- Large glass jar with lid

From the garden:
- 1 quart fragrant flower petals
- 2 ounces mixed sweet herbs
- 1 ounce lavender
- $1/2$ teaspoon whole cloves
- $1/4$ vanilla bean
- Decorative dried flower heads

WHAT TO DO

In a small bowl, mix the spices (cinnamon powder and grated nutmeg) and the fixative (orris root powder) with a small wooden spoon.

Add six drops essential oil (ylang-ylang) and blend thoroughly, rubbing the mixture between two fingers so the spices absorb all the oil.

In a mixing bowl, use the wooden spoon to mix together the flower petals, herbs, lavender, cloves, and vanilla bean. Store any decorative dried flower heads in a dry place until later.

Pour the contents of the first bowl (spices, fixative, and oil) into the mixing bowl (containing the flower petals and herbs). Using the wooden spoon, mix well to distribute the spices, fixative, and oil evenly.

Store the mixture in a tightly sealed glass jar—not a plastic container (that lets the scent escape) or a metal canister (that taints the scent). Set the jar in a dark room for a minimum of six weeks, allowing the fragrance to mature. Shake the container once a day during the first week.

After the potpourri has matured, pour it into a decorative open bowl. Top with the dried flower heads previously set aside.

Store the remaining potpourri in a glass jar, tin canister, or Ziploc Storage Bag for future use.

POTPOURRI RECIPES

To concoct simple, sure-fire potpourri, combine three to five types of flowers (generally including rose petals and lavender), two or three herbs and spices, and one or two oils. For delicate mixtures, use only floral scents. For tangier mixtures, add herbs or spices, using strongly scented ingredients prudently. Too much cedar, mint, peppermint oil, or eucalyptus oil will overpower potpourri.

FINISHING TOUCHES

You can fill bowls, jars, baskets, sachets, or pillows with potpourri. Place potpourri in a decorative glass jar, and tuck a piece of lace into the top

MOIST METHOD OF POTPOURRI MAKING

WHAT YOU NEED

From the supermarket:
- Kosher salt
- Brown sugar

From the liquor store:
- Brandy

From the kitchen:
- Wooden spoon
- Wide-mouth glass or glazed ceramic jar with tightly sealing lid
- Metal spoon
- Mixing bowl
- Small bowl
- One unopened can of soup
- A circle of cardboard cut to fit inside the perimeter of the jar

From the garden:
- Rose petals

WHAT TO DO

Place a $^1/_2$-inch layer of partially dried flower petals (rose) on the bottom of a wide-mouth, glass or glazed ceramic jar.

Cover the layer of petals with a $^1/_4$-inch layer of kosher salt.

Use the cardboard circle to press down the first layer and compress the petals by pushing it down with the unopened can of soup until the layer of combined petals and salt is $^1/_2$-inch deep. Add a second layer of petals and salt, then compress.

Sprinkle a pinch of brown sugar and a few drops of brandy on top of this layer.

Alternate layers of petals and salt, stopping to compress each double layer, and adding brown sugar and brandy after every two double layers, until the container is two-thirds full.

Seal the lid on the jar and let sit in a dark place for two months to mature. Every three days for the first two weeks, open the jar and either drain it or break up the crusty layer that forms on top and mix it in with the petal and salt mixture.

After a total of two months, open the jar and crumb the cured "cake" into a mixing bowl.

Using a wooden spoon, mix the spices, herbs, fixative, and essential oils required by the recipe. (See "Potpourri Recipes" on page 198.) Add this mixture little by little to the bowl of crumbs, mixing with a wooden spoon, until you achieve a level of potency you consider fragrant (remembering that the fragrance will strengthen when the potpourri matures).

Return the scented mixture to the jar, compress tightly, cover securely, and let cure for another two months.

After two months elapse, pour the potpourri into a decorative bowl or a lidded, perforated potpourri dish.

of the container, or place it over the rim and hold in place with a piece of ribbon. You can also make potpourri gift baskets or bags containing homemade potpourri wrapped in netting and tied with a ribbon, a potpourri simmering pot, and a bottle of the essential oils to refresh the potpourri when desired.

Note: If you discover insects in your potpourri, place the potpourri in the freezer overnight to kill the insects and their eggs.

Pumpkin Carving

WHAT YOU NEED

From the supermarket:
- Pumpkin
- X-Acto knife or special pumpkin-carving tool

From the kitchen:
- Newspaper
- Crayola crayon or felt-tip marker
- Sturdy, sharp knife
- Soup spoon
- Paper towel
- Vegetable peeler

- Votive candle or small battery-powered light
- Matches

WHAT TO DO

Choose a fresh, smooth, evenly colored pumpkin in a shape that inspires your creativity.

Cover your worktable with newspaper.

Using a crayon or marker, draw a circle or octagon on top of the pumpkin around the stem.

With a sharp knife, carefully cut along the outline, angling the blade inwards toward the stem.

Remove the lid (using the stem as a handle) and scrape off the seeds and pulp from the underside.

Using a soup spoon, scoop out the seeds and pulp from inside the pumpkin—until the walls of the pumpkin are roughly one inch thick.

Wash your hands and wipe the outside of the pumpkin with a paper towel.

Using a crayon or marker, draw your design (a scary face, a bat, a spider, a ghost, a black cat, stars, or whatever your imagination desires) on one side of the pumpkin.

Leave It to Wax Paper

Preserve autumn leaves by placing the leaves between two sheets of Reynolds Cut-Rite Wax Paper, then place the wax paper between two sheets of brown paper. Press with a warm iron to seal, then trim the paper around the leaves.

Using a small knife, X-Acto knife, or pumpkin-carving tool, slowly and carefully cut along the lines, cutting through the wall of the pumpkin skin.

Slowly push the cutout pieces from inside the hollow pumpkin and discard.

You can also create a fancy effect by removing only the tough orange skin from some areas. Cut halfway into the pumpkin skin along the outline of your design. Then slowly and carefully remove only the outer skin with a vegetable peeler, X-Acto knife, or pumpkin-carving tool.

Place a votive candle or battery-powered light inside the bottom of the hollow pumpkin to create an eerie glow.

STRANGE FACTS

• During the Halloween season, craft stores and supermarkets often sell special pumpkin-carving tools.

• If you accidentally cut off a critical piece of pumpkin, pin it back in place with a toothpick.

• Most Americans carve jack-o'-lanterns from Connecticut Field pumpkins, direct descendants of the original pumpkins grown by Native American Indians.

• In his 1883 poem "When the Frost Is on the Punkin," James Whitcomb Riley wrote:

"O, it sets my heart a-clickin' like the tickin' of a clock,

"When the frost is on the punkin and the fodder's in the shock."

Flower Power

To preserve flowers, mix one part 20 Mule Team Borax and two parts Albers Corn Meal. Fill the bottom inch of an empty airtight Tupperware canister with the mixture. Place the flower on the mixture, then gently cover the flower with more mixture, being careful not to crush the flower or distort the petals. For flowers with a lot of overlapping petals, such as roses and carnations, sprinkle mixture directly into the blossoms before placing them into the box. Seal the canister and store at room temperature in a dry place for seven to ten days. When the flowers are dried, pour off the mixture and dust the flowers with a soft artist's brush. Borax removes the moisture from blossoms and leaves, preventing the wilting that would normally result.

Do-It-Yourself Recipe

PUMPKIN ICE CREAM

WHAT YOU NEED

From the supermarket:

- 1 pumpkin
- 1 cup condensed milk
- 8 tablespoons honey
- 1 cup brown sugar
- 20 marshmallows

WHAT TO DO

Wash the pumpkin, cut it in half, and remove the strings and seeds. Lay the pumpkin halves shell-side-up in a pan and bake in an oven at 325 degrees Fahrenheit for one hour or until tender and falling apart. Scrape the pulp from the shell and blend well.

Blend the milk and honey together with an electric mixer. Gradually add two cups cooked pumpkin, brown sugar, and marshmallows. Blend for two minutes. Pour into a tray and place in the freezer until the mixture reaches a soft and mushy consistency. Meanwhile, chill the mixing bowl. Pour the mixture back into the mixing bowl and blend again with the electric mixer until smooth. Pour the mixture back into the freezer trays and refreeze. Makes four cups.

Do-It-Yourself Recipe

PUMPKIN PIE

WHAT YOU NEED

From the supermarket:

- 1 pumpkin
- 1 unbaked 9-inch pie shell with fluted standing rim
- Crisco All-Vegetable Shortening
- 2 eggs
- 1/2 cup brown sugar
- 2 tablespoons molasses
- 1/2 teaspoon salt
- 1 teaspoon ginger
- 2 teaspoons cinnamon
- 1/4 teaspoon nutmeg
- 1 1/2 cups light cream

WHAT TO DO

Wash the pumpkin, cut it in half, and remove the strings and seeds. Lay the pumpkin halves shell-side-up in a pan and bake in an oven at 325 degrees Fahrenheit for one hour or until tender and falling apart. Scrape the pulp from the shell and blend well.

Preheat the oven to 450 degrees Fahrenheit. Brush the pie shell with a light coat of vegetable shortening. In a large bowl, beat the eggs, then stir in the brown sugar, molasses, salt, ginger, cinnamon, and nutmeg. Beat until well blended. Add two cups cooked pumpkin and the cream. Mix well. Pour the mixture into the prepared pie shell and bake for ten minutes on the lower shelf of the preheated oven. After ten minutes, reduce the oven temperature to 350 degrees Fahrenheit and bake for another thirty minutes or until a knife inserted into the center of the pie emerges clean. Let cool. Makes one delicious pumpkin pie.

• In the 1904 children's book *The Marvelous Land of Oz,* the first sequel to *The Wonderful Wizard of Oz,* author L. Frank Baum introduces Jack Pumpkinhead, a man made from sticks with a jack-o'-lantern head and brought to life by a magical powder.

• The *Jack-O-Lantern,* the campus humor magazine founded in 1908 at Dartmouth University, boasts such famous alumni as Dr. Seuss, Buck Henry, Chris Miller, and Robert Reich.

• In the 1950 Walt Disney animated movie *Cinderella,* Cinderella's fairy godmother turns a Rouge Vif D'Etampes pumpkin—developed in France during the late nineteenth century—into a coach. When French writer Charles Perrault told the Cinderella story in his book, *Tales of Mother Goose,* published in 1697, the Rouge Vif D'Etampes pumpkin did not yet exist.

• In 1990, E. and R. Gancarz of Wrightstown, New Jersey, grew the largest recorded pumpkin in history, weighing 816 pounds, 8 ounces.

• On October 8, 1997, a large pumpkin mysteriously appeared sitting atop the pointy tip of the famous bell tower at Cornell University. No one came forth to take credit for the prank, and no one could figure out how the pranksters had managed to get the pumpkin, estimated to weigh sixty pounds, pinned atop the 173-foot tower—where it sat undisturbed for several weeks.

• Every Halloween in the comic strip *Peanuts,* by Charles Schulz, Linus waits up all night in a pumpkin patch for the arrival of the Great Pumpkin. In the animated television special *It's the Great Pumpkin, Charlie Brown,* Snoopy rises from the pumpkin patch, and Linus, seeing only the beagle's silhouette, faints—convinced he has seen the Great Pumpkin.

• Every November the town of Lewes, Delaware, hosts the annual "World Championship Punkin' Chunkin'" contest, in which participants compete using home-made catapults to see who can hurl a pumpkin the farthest distance.

The Family Bible

• **BATHROOM BIBLE.** A bible published in 1971 in the United States modernized I Samuel 24:3 from "And Saul went in to cover his feet" to "Saul went into a cave to go to the bathroom."

• **BREECHES BIBLE.** A 1560 version of the Bible, published in Geneva, Italy, translated Genesis 3:7 to read that Adam and Eve "sewed fig leaves together and made themselves breeches." Breeches are knee-length trousers that did not exist in biblical times.

• **BUG BIBLE.** A 1551 version of the Bible mistranslated the verse "Thou shalt not be afraid for the terror by night" (Psalm 91:5) as "Thou shalt not be afraid of any buggies at night."

• **ESKIMO BIBLE.** A version of the Bible in an Eskimo dialect included one misplaced letter so the verse "nation shall rise up against nation" (Mark 13:8) became "a pair of snowshoes shall rise up against a pair of snowshoes."

• **FOOL'S BIBLE.** A 1653 version of the Bible printed in England accidentally substituted the word *a* for *no* so Psalm 14:1 reads, "The fool hath said in his heart there is a God." The printer was fined £3,000.

• **SIN BIBLE.** In 1716, the first Bible printed in Ireland included a typographical error that made the line "Sin no more" (John 5:14) read "Sin on more."

• **TREACLE BIBLE.** A 1568 version of the Bible mistranslated the line "Is there no balm in Gilead?" from Jeremiah 8:22 as "Is there no treacle in Gilead?" Treacle, a medicinal compound once used as an antidote for poison, did not exist during biblical times.

• **WICKED BIBLE.** In 1631, London printers Robert Barker and Martin Lucas published an authorized edition of the Bible that inadvertently printed one of the Ten Commandments as "Thou shalt commit adultery" (Exodus 20:13). King Charles I fined Barker and Lucas £300 and recalled all one thousand copies of their Bible, which became known as the "Wicked Bible."

Does the "K" in K-mart Stand for "Kwality"?

In 1897, Sebastian S. Kresge and John McCrory opened five-and-dime stores in Detroit and Memphis. When the partners split up two years later, Kresge got the Detroit stores, and McCrory took the Memphis stores. By the time Kresge incorporated as the S. S. Kresge Company in 1912, his company had become the second largest dime store chain in the United States, with eighty-five stores and more than ten million dollars in annual sales.

In 1962, the advent of discount stores prompted Kresge President Harry B. Cunningham to open the first K-mart discount department store at 29600 Ford Road in Garden City, Michigan. He opened seventeen more K-mart stores that same year. In K-mart's first year, sales surpassed 483 million dollars. When company founder Sebastian S. Kresge died at the age of ninety-nine in 1966, he owned 915 stores, including 162 K-mart stores, and had more than one billion dollars in annual sales.

Preserving Newspaper Clippings

Dissolve one tablespoon Phillips' Milk of Magnesia (or one tablet) in one quart Canada Dry Club Soda. Let the mixture stand overnight. The next day, stir the mixture well, then soak your clipping in the solution for one hour. Blot the newspaper clipping between two sheets of paper towels and place on a screen to dry. The antacids in Milk of Magnesia neutralize the acids in newsprint, preserving the clipping.

K-mart expanded aggressively in the 1970s, opening 271 stores in 1976 alone. The following year, with 1,206 K-mart stores generating 95 percent of Kresge's sales, S. S. Kresge Company changed its name to K-mart Corporation. In 1990, K-mart surpassed Sears in sales to become the number-one retail store in the United States, but both companies were soon overtaken by Wal-Mart.

STRANGE FACTS

• The "K" in K-mart stands for the K in company founder Sebastian Kresge's last name.

• In 1962, the year the first K-mart opened, the first Wal-Mart opened in Rogers, Arkansas, and the first Target opened in Roseville, Minnesota.

• Every week K-mart advertises with 72 million circulars inserted in 1,500 newspapers nationwide, reaching more people than *The New York Times, The Wall Street Journal, USA Today, Los Angeles Times,* *The Washington Post, Chicago Tribune, The New York Daily News, The Boston Globe, The Philadelphia Inquirer, Reader's Digest,* and *TV Guide* combined.

• In 1987, Martha Stewart became K-mart's Entertainment and Lifestyle Spokesperson and Consultant.

• Every year, 180 million people shop at K-mart. That's 5.7 customers every second.

• Eighty percent of the United States population is within a fifteen-minute drive of a K-mart store.

• K-mart has 1,650 pharmacies, making it the third largest pharmacy chain in the United States.

• K-mart develops more than 25 million rolls of film each year, making K-mart the world's number-one photo processor.

• K-mart stores sell 83,000 tons of potting soil each year.

• In 2003, K-mart had more than 170,000 employees. That's five times the population of Garden City, Michigan, where the first K-mart store opened.

WRAPPING PAPER

Here are three great ways to make your own unique wrapping paper:

• Spray hair spray on the comic section from the Sunday paper to seal in the ink and give the paper a shiny gloss.

• Add five drops food coloring to one cup water, making one cup for each one of the four colors. Stack several sheets of white tissue paper on top of each other, fold them in half, in half again, and in half again. Dip each one of the four corners into a different color solution without soaking the paper. Let the tissue dry on newspaper, unfold, and then iron flat.

• Old roap maps make excellent decorative wrapping paper, particularly poignant for wrapping a bon voyage gift, a graduation gift, or a wedding gift. Accompany the gift with a homemade greeting card with the appropriate message, such as "Happy trails," "May the road rise up to meet you," "Always take the road less traveled," or "Be sure to enjoy the scenery on the highway of life."

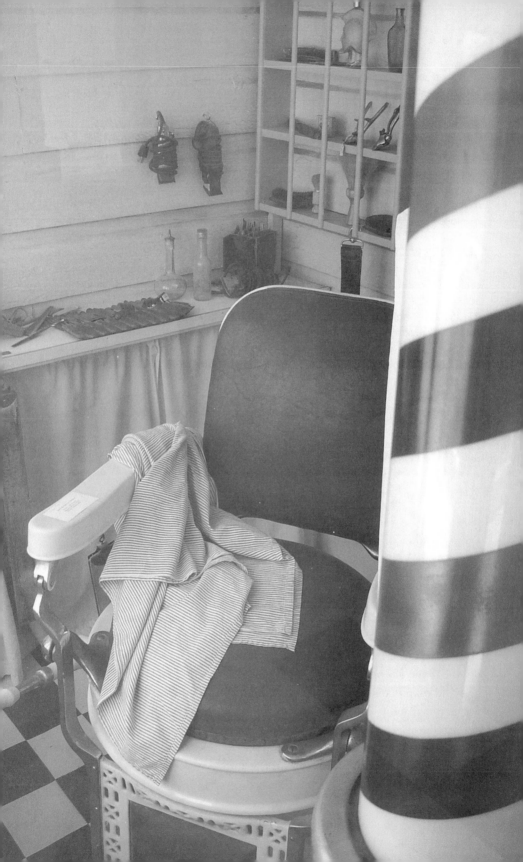

6

The CORNER BARBERSHOP

Soaps, Perfumes, and Close Shaves

Proper grooming and personal hygiene require soaps, deodorants, shaving creams and razors, perfumes and colognes. Luckily, anyone can make soaps and perfumes at home. Soap can be made by running water through wood ashes to extract the lye, collecting the grease from cooking, boiling the lye with the fat in a kettle until it thickens like gravy, and then pouring the mixture into molds to cure. Perfumes can be concocted by mixing essential oils with alcohol. Of course, making soaps and developing perfumes are time-consuming tasks that require a bit of patience and know-how. Country stores wisely stocked these items so customers could buy wrapped bars of finished soap and labeled bottles of perfume fashioned by experts—producing a better bathed clientele.

Secret Formula

BUBBLE BATH

WHAT YOU NEED

From the supermarket:
- 1 cup Dr. Bronner's peppermint oil soap
- 2 cups liquid detergent (Ivory, Palmolive, or Dove)

From the drugstore:
- 1/4 cup glycerin

WHAT TO DO

Using a funnel, mix the ingredients in a one-quart plastic bottle or container. Blend well. Makes twenty-six ounces.

HOW TO USE IT

For an enchanting and soothing bath filled with bubbles galore, add approximately 2 ounces of this silky smooth bubble bath under the running water of your bathtub faucet as the tub fills with water. Then sit back, relax, and let the long-lasting bubbles do their magic to soothe your tired skin and restore your entire being.

Secret Formula

CONDITIONING HAIR CREAM

WHAT YOU NEED

From the supermarket:
- 1 tablespoon sunflower oil

From the drugstore:
- 1/2 ounce beeswax
- 1/4 cup castor oil
- 1/4 cup anhydrous lanolin

From the health food store:
- 2 teaspoons essential oil of bergamot

WHAT TO DO

In the top of a double boiler, slowly melt the beeswax. In a small saucepan, heat the castor oil, anhydrous lanolin, and sunflower oil—stirring well to blend. Add the melted beeswax to the oils and stir well to blend. Add the essential oil of bergamot and stir to blend. Pour the mixture into a clean jar and let cool. Makes one cup.

HOW TO USE IT

Everybody looks at your hair! Particularly when it's a gosh-darn mess-and-a-half! But just rub a dab of this wonderful all-natural hair cream between your palms, then run your hands through your hair, and comb to give your natural beauty new allure. It keeps you finished and glamorous in any setting—wind, monsoon, sun, or stars!

Heard Around the Barbershop

• In his painting "George Washington Crossing the Delaware," artist Emanuel Leutz depicts a United States flag that was not adopted by Congress until a year after Washington crossed the Delaware. Leutz also portrays the Durham boats Washington and his troops used as being approximately twenty feet long when they were actually forty to sixty feet long. He also incorrectly shows the soldiers holding their guns with the barrels pointed upward to catch the falling sleet.

• In 1902, when the volcano Mount Pelée threatened to erupt on the island Martinique, the mayor of Saint-Pierre refused to allow the residents of the town to evacuate because important elections were about to take place. On May 8 the volcano erupted, destroying the town and killing approximately 38,000 people in two minutes.

• In 1938, the citizens of Milton, Washington, elected a mule Republican precinct committeeman. The Democratic mayor had put the mule, named Boston Curtis, on the ballot, signing the filing notice as legal witness, to prove that many voters cast their vote carelessly. The mule won by a fifty-one-vote plurality.

• Japanese soldier Hiroo Onodo, stationed on the island of Lubang in the Philippines in 1944, refused to believe World War II had ended. He dismissed dropped leaflets as propaganda, attempts by his family to contact him as impersonations, and stacks of Japanese newspapers left for him in the jungle as clever forgeries.

In 1974, Onodo discovered a Japanese backpacker, Norio Suzuki, camping in the jungle and, convinced that he was an authentic Japanese, admitted that only a direct order from his commanding officer would convince him to leave the island. On March 9, Major Yoshimi Taniguchi arrived in Lubang and formally ordered Onoda to cease fighting.

• In 1992, South Carolina's Greenville County Department of Social Services sent a letter to a dead person that read: "Your food stamps will be stopped effective March, 1992, because we received notice that you passed away. May God bless you. You may reapply if there is a change in your circumstances."

Secret Formula

CASTILE SHAMPOO

WHAT YOU NEED
From the health food store:
- 1 bar Castile soap
- 8 drops essential oil of lavender
- 1 tablespoon isopropyl alcohol

From the tap:
- 4 cups water

WHAT TO DO
Spray a grater with a thin coat of cooking spray (to make cleanup afterwards easier). Grate the bar of soap into four ounces of flakes. Place the soap flakes in a bowl, bring the water to a boil, and carefully pour the water over the soap flakes. Stir until the soap dissolves. Dissolve the essential oil of lavender in the alcohol, then add to the soap mixture, stirring well. Let cool, and store in clean, empty bottles (such as old shampoo bottles). Makes one quart.

HOW TO USE IT
This all-natural shampoo won't make an abundance of lather, but it sure will get your hair squeaky-clean in a jiffy! And if getting your hair squeaky-clean is your number-one priority in life, then this shampoo is just what the doctor—er, better make that hairdresser—ordered!

EVEN IF I'M "ALL IN" AT BEDTIME I NEVER NEGLECT MY **ACTIVE-LATHER FACIAL** WITH LUX SOAP

PAT **LUX SOAP'S** CREAMY LATHER LIGHTLY INTO YOUR SKIN. RINSE WITH WARM WATER, THEN COOL

CLAUDETTE COLBERT

PARAMOUNT STAR

THEN PAT TO DRY. SEE HOW MUCH **SMOOTHER** YOUR SKIN FEELS—HOW FRESH IT LOOKS

Take Hollywood's tip— try ACTIVE-LATHER FACIALS for 30 days

HAVE YOU FOUND the right care for *your* skin? Claudette Colbert tells you how to take an ACTIVE-LATHER FACIAL with Lux Toilet Soap. Here's a gentle, *thorough* care that will give your skin protection it needs to stay lovely. Lux Toilet Soap has ACTIVE lather that removes dust, dirt and stale cosmetics *thoroughly* from the skin —does a *perfect* job. Try Hollywood's ACTIVE-LATHER FACIALS for 30 days. You'll find they really *work*—help keep skin smooth, attractive.

YOU want skin that's lovely to look at—soft to touch. Don't risk unattractive Cosmetic Skin: little blemishes, coarsened pores. Use cosmetics all you like, but take regular ACTIVE-LATHER FACIALS with Lux Toilet Soap.

LUX
TOILET SOAP

9 out of 10 Hollywood Screen Stars use Lux Toilet Soap

213

Soap Making

WHAT YOU NEED

From the supermarket:
- 72 ounces olive oil
- 6 ounces coconut oil
- 6 ounces palm oil
- 12-ounce can Red Devil Lye (or pure powdered or crystal sodium hydroxide without any additives)
- Oblong, flexible Tupperware container with square sides, or a glass cake pan lined with plastic wrap (nothing aluminum as lye eats it) or soap molds
- Crayola crayons or color dye

From the hardware store:
- Rubber gloves
- Goggles
- Impermeable apron

From the health food store or perfume supply house:
- Essential oils

From a chemical supply store:
- Litmus paper

From the kitchen:
- Freezer paper
- Large stainless steel pot
- Scale
- Two-quart Pyrex glass bowl
- Plastic or glass mixing bowl

- Large plastic or wooden spoon
- Candy thermometer (from 60 degrees to 400 degrees Fahrenheit)
- Handheld stick blender
- Spatula
- Cardboard
- Towels

From the tap:
- Water

From this book:
- Saponification Chart for Lye (see Chart on page 216)

WHAT TO DO

Cover your working area with newspaper. Lay a single layer of cellophane on the bottom of a box, a galvanized tub, a wooden box with a cloth laid in the bottom of it, or any square edged, flexible, food-grade plastic container, or small soap molds like a clean, used margarine tub. Lay two pieces of trimmed freezer paper perpendicular to each other and both hanging over the sides of the mold, and tape them down.

Weigh the stainless steel pot and record the weight. Add the olive oil, coconut oil, and palm oil by weight (not fluid ounces) in the large stainless steel pot.

Calculate the amount of water needed. First add the weight of the fats. (72 ounces olive oil + 6 ounces coconut oil + 6 ounces palm oil = 84 ounces total fats.) Add 0.38 parts water to every one part fat by weight. (84 ounces total fats x .38 = 31.92 ounces water.)

Use the Saponification Chart to calculate the amount of lye needed to change each oil or fat into soap. Here's how this recipe is calculated:

72 ounces olive oil x 0.134 = 9.648 ounces lye
6 ounces coconut oil x 0.19 = 1.14 ounces lye
6 ounces palm oil x .141 = 0.846 ounces lye
Total lye needed: 11.634 ounces lye

Using the purest water possible (such as rain water, distilled water, or de-mineralized water), pour the exact amount of water needed into a two-quart Pyrex bowl. (Lye eats aluminum and instantly and permanently removes the shine from Formica.)

Wearing rubber gloves, goggles, and an impermeable apron, and working outdoors (in case of spills and for proper ventilation to avoid dangerous fumes), measure out the lye into an enameled, plastic, or glass bowl and pour into the water. Never pour the water into the lye. Doing so can cause the mixture to explode and blow very corrosive lye water and crystals everywhere. The colder the water, the better. If lye splashes your skin, immediately rinse with cold water. (Vinegar or lemon juice will neutralize the lye solution.) Stir immediately with a wooden or plastic spoon and dissolve the lye in the water (to prevent the lye from settling to the bottom and solidifying). The lye and the water will generate a lot of heat. If the water starts boiling, stop stirring

Caution

Lye is a highly caustic alkali that can cause burns to skin and eyes. Always wear proper gloves and goggles when working with lye and handle carefully.

Saponification Chart for Lye

Saponification is the chemical reaction that causes a fat to fuse with an alkali to form soap. This charts shows how many ounces of lye are needed to saponify an ounce of each kind of fat.

FAT	OUNCES OF LYE
Beef Tallow	0.140
Chicken Fat	0.138
Lard	0.138

VEGETABLE OIL	
Almond Oil (Sweet)	0.136
Apricot Kernel Oil	0.135
Avocado Oil	0.133
Brazil Nut Oil	0.175
Beeswax (White)	0.069
Borage Oil	0.136
Canola Oil	0.124
Castor Oil	0.128
Cocoa Butter	0.137
Coconut Oil	0.190
Cod Liver Oil	0.132
Corn Oil	0.136
Cottonseed Oil	0.138
Crisco All-Vegetable Shortening	0.136
Flaxseed Oil	0.135
Grapeseed Oil	0.126
Hazelnut Oil	0.136
Hemp Seed Oil	0.137
Java Cotton Oil	0.137

Jojoba Oil	0.069
Karite Butter	0.128
Kukui Nut Oil	0.135
Lanolin	0.074
Macadamia Oil	0.139
Mink Oil	0.140
Mustard Seed Oil	0.124
Neem Oil	0.136
Olive Oil	0.134
Olive Pomace Oil	0.156
Palm Butter	0.156
Palm Kernel Oil	0.156
Palm Oil	0.141
Peanut Oil	0.137
Poppyseed Oil	0.138
Pumpkinseed Oil	0.135
Rice Bran Oil	0.129
Safflower Oil	0.136
Sesame Seed Oil	0.133
Shea Butter	0.128
Soybean Oil	0.134
Sunflower Seed Oil	0.134
Vegetable Tallow	0.138
Walnut Oil	0.136
Wheat Germ Oil	0.132

until the bubbling stops. After a minute of stirring, the water will clear. Using a thermometer, let the lye water cool to 110 degrees Fahrenheit.

In the stainless steel pot, heat the oils to 140 degrees Fahrenheit (130 degrees Fahrenheit when working with beef tallow, or 85 degrees Fahrenheit for lard). The hotter the oil, the faster the chemical reaction between the lye and the fat (but the easier the soap separates into layers during the mixing stage).

IF YOUR ROMANCE ISN'T "CLICKING"

LOOK AT YOUR SKIN AND SEE IF IT'S DRY, LIFELESS, OLD-LOOKING!

TO HELP KEEP YOUR COMPLEXION ALLURINGLY SMOOTH, USE THIS SOAP MADE WITH OLIVE OIL!

LOOK, SIS! I REALLY DON'T BLAME DON FOR LOSING INTEREST! A MAN ADORES SMOOTH, LOVELY SKIN AND YOU'VE LET YOURS GET SO DRY, LIFELESS AND OLD-LOOKING! YOU KNOW I TOLD YOU SOME TIME AGO THAT YOU OUGHT TO TRY PALMOLIVE SOAP!

BECAUSE PALMOLIVE IS MADE WITH OLIVE AND PALM OILS, NATURE'S FINEST BEAUTY AIDS. THAT'S WHY ITS LATHER IS SO DIFFERENT, SO GOOD FOR DRY, LIFELESS SKIN! PALMOLIVE CLEANSES SO THOROUGHLY YET SO GENTLY THAT IT LEAVES SKIN SOFT AND SMOOTH ... COMPLEXIONS RADIANT!

BUT WHY IS PALMOLIVE SO DIFFERENT?

WELL, YOU OUGHT TO KNOW WHAT YOU'RE TALKING ABOUT, SIS—BECAUSE YOUR COMPLEXION IS SIMPLY GORGEOUS! SO I GUESS I'D BETTER START USING PALMOLIVE RIGHT AWAY!

PALMOLIVE

MADE WITH Olive Oil TO KEEP SKIN SOFT AND SMOOTH

If the temperature of the oils reaches 140 degrees Fahrenheit before the lye cools to 110 degrees Fahrenheit, speed the cooling of the lye by setting the Pyrex cup in a pan of cold water (a few inches deep). Set the lye-tainted thermometer and spoon in the sink to await washing. Once the oil and lye both reach their desired temperatures, stir the oil in only one direction and very slowly pour the lye water into it as you continue stirring.

Use a handheld stick blender (designated solely for soap making to keep lye residue away from food preparation utensils) to mix the soap until it "traces" (the point at which you can gently draw a line on the top of it with a spoon). To do this, blend until the mixture reaches the consistency of molasses or cooked pudding, which should happen within twenty minutes. The mixture is

Dirty Ideas

Make sure that whatever fat or oil you use is clean and free of impurities. To purify rancid and dirty fat, place four parts water to one part fat in a pot, and boil for a few minutes. Let cool. After the fat solidifies, run hot water around the outside of the pot briefly, and remove the fat from the pot in one piece. Using a knife, carefully scrape the foreign particles from the bottom of the chunk of fat. Repeat the entire process if necessary.

Soap That Floats

To make soap that floats, simply hold the stick blender closer to the surface to whip more air into the mixture, or add one tablespoon baking soda to your soap mixture after adding the lye. The sodium bicarbonate reacts with the fatty acids, releasing carbon dioxide (and a small amount of caustic material) into the mixture.

ready when drips from a spoon stay on the surface of the mixture like piped frosting. To avoid mixing air into the soap, blend the soap in a tall container, holding the whirring blender far below the surface for most of the stirring. If the soap separates and looks like curdled milk, add a little water as you mix. If you wish to slow down the saponification process to avoid mixing the soap too thick, when the soap begins to get smooth and glossy, turn off the stick blender and use a wooden spoon to blend in the additives.

When the soap is thick enough to "trace," add colorings, scents, and other ingredients. At this stage, adding superfatting oils (such as avocado oil, cocoa butter, or essential oils for scenting) makes soap softer. Add 1 ounce per pound of total fat.

Color the soap by adding clays, mineral pigments, or pieces of Crayola crayon. If using crayon, melt it into the soap after it has traced. If necessary, melt the crayon in four ounces of traced soap heated to 150 degrees Fahrenheit.

When the soap gets slightly thicker, use a large spoon to ladle the soap into the mold. Unplug the stick blender, and use a spatula to scrape all the

Making Tallow

Collect fat from trimming beef cuts until you have twelve pounds (or buy twelve pounds beef fat from a butcher). Cover the bottom of a large heavy kettle with an inch of water and add a heaping tablespoon of salt. Cut up the fat and put it in the kettle. Cook over very low heat for three to four hours, or until most of the fat has been rendered. Place a fine meshed strainer into a large pan, and ladle the fat through the strainer. Discard unmelted fat. Let cool at room temperature, then refrigerate. The fat will set in three layers. The solid top layer is the tallow. Place an empty container on a food scale and record its weight. Then spoon the tallow into the container, until you have the amount of tallow you need.

soap off the blender and out of the pan into the mold. Pour the soap one inch deep if you intend to cut the soap bar face up, or pour $2^{1}/_{2}$ inches deep if you plan to cut the bars laying on edge. Smooth the surface of the soap with a spatula and cover with a sheet of cellophane. Cover the mold with a cardboard cover, and then place several old towels on top (to retain the heat and prevent the soap from cooling too quickly).

When the soap begins to harden (sometime between one hour and three days), use a thin knife to cut the soft soap into bar-sized sections (without letting the cut soap melt back together again).

Once the bars harden to the point that they maintain their shape (sometime between three and ten days), remove the soap from the mold, and break it into bars following the cut marks. If your lye/fat ratio was correct, any trace amount of lye will dissipate into the soap during the final stage of the saponification process. Place the soap bars on edge in a warm, dry place, and let sit undisturbed for two or more weeks to dry out and cure.

With water, wash off any soda ash (white powder) that has formed on the soap and use litmus paper to test the lye content of your finished soap. (Soda ash results from the carbon dioxide in the air interacting with the lye in the soap.) Within the first 36 to 72 hours, the pH should measure below 10. The closer the pH of the finished soap is to 7, the better. If the pH measures above 10, let the soap sit for a week or two, so it continues to saponify, transforming the lye and lowering the pH. Ideally, the soap should have a pH of 7, but amateur soap makers can expect to achieve a pH around 9.

Bubble Science

Coconut oil in soap yields big, fluffy bubbles. Olive oil in soap yields fine, silky bubbles. To achieve the desired bubbles, make one of these oils at least 25 percent of your total fat.

Let the soap dry out, round off the bar's sharp edges with a potato peeler, place your soap in a plastic bag, and store in a cool, dry place until ready for use.

STRANGE FACTS

• Nearly 4,000 years ago, the Mesopotamians and Phoenicians used wood ashes and water to clean themselves, and then applied oil to their bodies to prevent their skin from becoming irritated. Eventually, they made soap from ashes, various plants, and natural oils and animal fats.

• Archaeologists excavated a fully equipped soap factory in the ruins of Pompeii, the Roman resort town destroyed by a volcano in 79 C.E.

• Prior to the introduction of modern hygiene in the nineteenth century, the human body was often infected with parasites that caused the Black Death plague, typhus epidemics, cholera, and many other illnesses.

• Body odor is not caused by perspiration, but rather by bacteria on the skin's surface breaking down the perspiration. Left uncleansed, the skin becomes a breeding ground for germs.

• Fats for soap making include animal fats, such as tallow (fat from beef) and lard (fat from pork), and oils and hydrogenated fats (derived from plants). Beef tallow makes the hardest soap, and lard makes a medium hardness soap.

• The average American uses 30.5 pounds of soap and detergents every year.

Separation Anxiety

If the removed bars of soap have liquid on the bottom and grease on top, or the soap contains substantial pockets of liquid and emits a strong odor, the soap separated and needs to be reclaimed. (Minuscule pockets of lye water in the soap that leave the knife moist when cut will be safely absorbed when the soap cures.) To reclaim the soap, shave it up and place the shavings in a large stainless steel pan, cover, and heat in an oven between 200 and 225 degrees Fahrenheit, stirring occasionally with a large spoon. If necessary, add a small amount of water. Within an hour or two, when the soap turns to a blended jelly, stir gently (to avoid whipping in air), and pour into the mold, smoothen the surface, and let cool.

SOAP RECIPES

ALL-VEGETABLE SOAP
(with olive and coconut oil)

- 30 ounces Crisco All-Vegetable Shortening
- 25 ounces olive oil
- 24 ounces coconut oil
- 30 ounces cold water
- 12 ounces lye crystals
- 1.5 to 4 ounces essential oil

Let oils cool to between 95 and 120 degrees Fahrenheit before adding lye solution.

ALL-VEGETABLE SOAP
(with soybean and coconut oil)

- 43 ounces Crisco All-Vegetable Shortening
- 21 ounces soybean oil
- 18 ounces coconut oil
- 31 ounces cold water
- 12 ounces lye crystals

Let oils cool to 100 degrees Fahrenheit before adding lye solution.

OLIVE-OIL CASTILE SOAP

- 50 ounces olive oil
- 16 ounces palm oil
- 16 ounces coconut oil
- 31 ounces cold water
- 12 ounces lye crystals

Let oils cool to between 110 and 115 degrees Fahrenheit before adding lye solution.

OLIVE OIL SOAP

- 53 ounces olive oil
- 28 ounces Crisco All-Vegetable Shortening
- 9 ounces castor oil
- 34 ounces cold water
- 12 ounces lye crystals
- 2 tablespoons salt (dissolved in 1 cup hot water and added to lye solution)

Let the oils cool to 140 degrees Fahrenheit before adding lye solution.

CANOLA AND OLIVE OIL SOAP

- 35 ounces canola oil
- 35 ounces olive oil
- 16 ounces coconut oil
- 32.5 ounces cold water
- 12 ounces lye crystals

Let oils cool to 100 degrees Fahrenheit before adding lye solution.

COCOA BUTTER SOAP

- 35 ounces soybean oil
- 16 ounces olive oil
- 16 ounces coconut oil
- 8 ounces palm oil
- 8 ounces cocoa butter (food
grade—available at health food stores)
- 31.5 ounces cold water
- 12 ounces lye crystals
- 2 ounces essential oil of almond

Let oils cool to 100 degrees Fahrenheit before adding lye solution.

BUBBLY VEGETABLE SOAP

- 24 ounces coconut oil
- 24 ounces olive oil
- 16 ounces canola oil
- 16 ounces palm oil
- 34.5 ounces cold water
- 12 ounces lye crystals

Let oils cool to 110 degrees Fahrenheit before adding lye solution.

BASIC ANIMAL FAT SOAP

- 40 ounces beef tallow or pork lard
- 20 ounces olive oil
- 20 ounces coconut oil
- 12 ounces lye crystals
- 30.5 ounces cold water

Let oils cool to 115 degrees Fahrenheit before adding lye solution.

OATMEAL AND HONEY SOAP

- 60 ounces lard
- 12 ounces olive oil
- 8 ounces coconut oil
- 4 ounces cocoa butter
- 2 ounces beeswax
- 32 ounces cold water
- 12 ounces lye crystals

Let oils cool to 100 degrees Fahrenheit before adding lye solution.
At trace stage add:
- 1/4 cup honey
- 1 cup rolled oats (pulverized in a blender)

DIAL

In 1948, just after World War II, scientists at the Armour Soap Company began analyzing the cause of perspiration odor to develop an effective deodorant soap. Armour chemists determined that perspiration odor resulted when bacteria decompose the perspiration. Realizing that perspiration odor could be eliminated by controlling the bacteria, Armour scientists went to work developing an odorless, non-irritating bactericide that would remain effective when combined with soap.

Hexachlorophene, a chemical offered to soap manufacturers a few years earlier, seemed to fit the bill. Armour scientists made up sample bars of soap with a 2 percent concentration of hexachlorophene, and laboratory technicians systematically used the sample bars of soap to wash under one arm each morning, while using ordinary soap to wash under the other. Convinced they had developed an effective deodorant soap, the company hired outside research laboratories. All confirmed the soap stopped perspiration odor before it could start. Armour named the chemical AT-7. Meanwhile, Armour scientists conducted experiments to find the right perfume for the soap—eventually selecting a light clover fragrance made up of some fourteen different oils.

Armour executives decided to test-market the soap in 1948. Dial was introduced at a price of twenty-five cents a bar—or twice the price of competing brands. Sales were so brisk that before the thirteen-week test period was over, the company was preparing to introduce the product in Chicago, followed by New York, Washington, and Philadelphia. National advertising began in 1949, and by 1953 (the year Dial introduced its advertising slogan, "Aren't you glad you use Dial? Don't you wish everybody did?") Dial was the number-one soap in dollar volume. Armour eventually changed its name to The Dial Corporation.

STRANGE FACTS

• An Armour employee suggested the name Dial because the soap offers around-the-clock protection. The Armour advertising department developed the design of the clock's dial and the slogan: "Keep Fresh Around the Clock," later changed to "Round the Clock Protection."
• The bright yellow monument wall at the entrance to the Dial Corporation building in Scottsdale, Arizona, looks like a bar of Dial soap.
• A bar of Dial soap can be found in one out of three American homes.

IVORY

Ivory is a Castile soap, named after the kingdom of Castile in north-central Spain where this simple but expensive soap with a hard consistency was first produced. When Harley Procter decided to develop a creamy white soap to compete with imported Castile soaps, he asked his cousin, chemist James Gamble, to formulate the product. One day after the soap went into production, a factory worker (who remains anonymous) forgot to switch off the master mixing machine when he went to lunch and too much air was whipped into a batch of soap. Consumers, delighted by the floating soap, demanded more, and from then on, Procter and Gamble gave all white soap an extra-long whipping.

LIFEBUOY

In 1885 in England, grocer William Hesketh Lever and his brother James formed Lever Brothers and introduced Sunlight, the world's first packaged, brand-name laundry soap, with ads that asked, "Why does a woman look old sooner than a man?" The answer—"wash-day evil," which could only be remedied by using Sunlight Soap—made the new soap a best seller. In 1895, Lever Brothers created Lifebuoy soap and sold it as an antiseptic soap, later changing its name to Lifebuoy Health Soap. Lever Brothers first coined the term "B.O." for body odor as part of their marketing campaign for the soap. Lever Brothers was soon selling soap across Europe, Australia, South Africa, and the United States.

To acquire vegetable oil to make soap, Lever Brothers established plantations and trading companies around the world, including the United Africa Company, Africa's largest enterprise for twenty years following its founding in 1929. During World War I, Lever Brothers used its vegetable oil to make margarine, merging in 1930 with the Margarine Union—composed of rival Dutch butter makers Jurgens and Van den Berghs—forming Unilever PLC in London and Unilever NV in Rotterdam.

Unilever acquired Thomas J. Lipton Company in 1937, Pepsodent in 1944, Birds Eye Foods of the United Kingdom in 1957, Good Humor in 1961, Ragu in 1986, Chesebrough-Pond's in 1987, Calvin Klein Cosmetics in 1989, and Faberge/Elizabeth Arden in 1989.

All the News That Fits

• In 1897, the *New York Journal* published novelist Mark Twain's obituary. On June 2, 1897, Twain sent a note to the London correspondent of the newspaper stating: "The report of my death was an exaggeration."

• On April 15, 1912, the headline on the front page of the *New York Evening Sun* incorrectly announced: "All Saved from *Titanic* After Collision." The newspaper reported that the *S.S. Carpathia* and *S.S. Parisian* had rescued the *Titanic* and were towing the liner to Halifax. Reporters had misinterpreted garbled telegraph messages about the start of a rescue mission. The *Titanic* sank on April 15, and the *Carpathia* rescued 705 passengers. More than 1,500 passengers were killed.

• In 1915, the *Washington Post* reported that President Woodrow Wilson attended the theater with his fiancée, Edith Galt, but was more occupied entertaining her than watching the play. A typographical error in the story made a pivotal sentence read: "The President spent most of his time entering Mrs. Galt."

• On January 13, 1920, the *New York Times* editorialized that rocket scientist Robert H. Goddard, who had proposed trying to reach the moon by rocket, "does not know the relation of action to reaction, and of the need to have something better than a vacuum against which to react—to say that would be absurd. Of course he only seems to lack the knowledge ladled out daily in high schools . . . ." On July 17, 1969, three days before Apollo 11 landed on the moon, the *New York Times* retracted the statement. Unfortunately, Goodard was unable to accept any apologies. He had been dead since 1945.

What I've Learned

"If you think nobody cares if you're alive,
try missing a couple of car payments."
—Flip Wilson

"Common sense is not so common."
—Voltaire

"Experience is the name everyone gives
to their mistakes."
—Oscar Wilde

"The secret of life is honesty and fair dealing.
If you can fake that, you've got it made."
—Groucho Marx

"Everybody talks about the weather,
but nobody does anything about it."
—Mark Twain

"It's a small world, but I wouldn't
want to have to paint it."
—Steven Wright

"Having a baby is like taking your lower lip
and forcing it over your head."
—Carol Burnett

"It's amazing that the amount of news
that happens in the world every day
always just exactly fits the newspaper."
—Jerry Seinfeld

"Let a smile be your umbrella,
and you'll end up with a face full of rain."
—*George Carlin*

"The secret of staying young is to live honestly,
eat slowly, and lie about your age."
—*Lucille Ball*

"Too much of a good thing is wonderful."
—*Mae West*

"The future will be better tomorrow."
—*Dan Quayle*

"The only really happy folk are
married women and single men."
—*H. L. Mencken*

"There is no cure for birth or death save to enjoy the interval."
—*George Santayana*

"People who throw kisses are hopelessly lazy."
—*Bob Hope*

"The two most beautiful words in the English language are:
'check enclosed.'"
—*Dorothy Parker*

"Bisexuality immediately doubles your chances
for a date on Saturday night."
—*Woody Allen*

"The grass is always greener over the septic tank."
—*Erma Bombeck*

"If life was fair, Elvis would be alive
and all the impersonators would be dead."
—*Johnny Carson*

Wal-Mart: The Un-Country Store

The Big Boys

With money he saved while serving in the United States Army during World War II, Sam Walton, a graduate in economics from the University of Missouri, leased a Ben Franklin franchised dime store in Newport, Arkansas. In 1950, the store landlord, whose son was due home from the Army and wanted to run the store, refused to renew Walton's lease.

Walton relocated to Bentonville, Arkansas, and opened a Ben Franklin self-service hardware store franchise called Walton's Five & Dime. By 1962, Walton owned fifteen Ben Franklin stores under the name Walton's Five & Dime. When Ben Franklin executives rejected his idea to open discount stores in small towns, Walton, with his brother James "Bud" Walton, opened his own discount store, the first Wal-Mart Discount City at 2110 West Walnut Street in Rogers, Arkansas.

The first Wal-Mart sold one million dollars of merchandise in its first year. In 1970, the family-owned company went public with eighteen stores and sales of 44 million dollars. Two years later, Wal-Mart had forty-one stores and 72 million dollars in sales. The company established its first highly automated distribution center, cutting shipping costs and time, and implemented a computerized inventory system that sped up checkout and reordering. In 1976, Wal-Mart phased out its Ben Franklin stores, and by 1979, there were 276 Wal-Mart stores in eleven states—mostly in towns with populations of less than 25,000—with sales exceeding 1.2 billion dollars.

When a Wal-Mart store opens in a small town, its low prices seem to knock many local merchants out of business. The company opens its stores in small towns that the big chains ignore—within a day's drive of a Wal-Mart distribution center—and then saturates that market area with stores. With its everyday low prices, Wal-Mart brings bright, clean stores and decent merchandise to far-flung towns. Instead of opening stores in big cities, Wal-Mart builds its stores in a ring around the city and waits for the city to grow out.

In 1992, Wal-Mart overtook Sears and K-mart as the number-one retail store in the United States.

STRANGE FACTS

• Company Founder Sam Walton liked the name of the California discount store Fed-Mart so much, he copied the idea, combining the first syllable of his last name and the word *mart*.

• Wal-Mart founder Sam Walton met his wife, Helen Robson, in a bowling alley.

• Sam Walton used his fleet of small airplanes to scout real estate, check out traffic flows, and assess city and town growth. "Once we had a spot picked out," recalled Walton, "we'd land, go find out who owned the property, and try to negotiate the deal right then."

• In 1962, the year the first Wal-Mart

opened, the first K-mart opened in Garden City, Michigan, and the first Target opened in Roseville, Michigan.

• Wal-Mart sells 1.13 pairs of underwear for every man, woman, and child in America.

• A Barbie doll is sold in a Wal-Mart store every three seconds. In fact, 33 percent of all Barbie Dolls sold in the United States are sold at Wal-Mart.

• Thirty-four shopping bags are used in Wal-Mart stores in one year for every man, woman, and child in the United States.

• In 1996, the average American spent 360 dollars in Wal-Mart. That's more than the average person in Mozambique earns in three years.

• Approximately sixty million customers visit a Wal-Mart each week. That's equal to the population of France.

• Every year, Wal-Mart sells enough fishing line in the United States to circle the globe twenty-four times.

• Wal-Mart sells 227,592,400 clothespins each year—enough to give every citizen of New York City thirty clothespins.

• In a 1992 essay in the *Dallas Morning News*, Steve Bishop, a Church of Christ minister who grew up in Hearne, Texas (population 5,400), and served a church there for seven years, wrote: "Wal-Mart killed Hearne, Texas—twice . . . . The first death was the end of a downtown that held much more than stores, it held memories, values, and people who stayed long enough to make a difference in our lives. Wal-Mart's arrival ended all that. The second killing occurred in December 1990, when Wal-Mart closed its doors in Hearne. It closed because it couldn't turn a profit. Wal-Mart leaves an empty building as testimony to the '80s' greed, and it leaves a downtown of vacated shops as testimony to our rush to save a little money—maybe not a very different kind of greed."

• Communities in Maine, Massachusetts, and New Hampshire have voted to keep Wal-Mart out.

• A state-of-the-art corporate satellite system gives Wal-Mart round-the-clock inventory control so that the products customers want are nearly always in stock. At Wal-Mart's headquarters in Bentonville, Arkansas, a computer center the size of a football field tracks inventory, credit, and sales via a Hughes satellite.

• Wal-Mart stores compete against each other for the "Store of the Year" award, and friendly rivalries between department managers often result in sales contests with funny "prizes" for the loser, such as riding a tricycle around the store.

• In 1996, Wal-Mart banned an album by Grammy-winner Sheryl Crow from its stores because the song "Love is a Good Thing" contained lyrics suggesting the retailer sells guns to children, who then kill other children. This marked the first time that a major retailer banned a song in which it was the target of a lyric. Crow grew up in the heart of Wal-Mart country in Kennett, Missouri, and is an alumna of the same university as Wal-Mart founder, Sam Walton.

• In 1996, Wal-Mart sold more than 1.8 billion coffee filters. That's enough to make one pot of coffee every day for the next fifty million years.

• As of 1996, Wal-Mart employed more than 675,000 people. That's 27 times the population of Rogers, Arkansas, the city where Wal-Mart first opened.

• In 1970, Wal-Mart went public at $16.50 per share. Since then, the stock has split ten times.

• Before his death in 1992, Sam Walton was America's richest person, his family's wealth estimated at 23 billion dollars. "Mr. Sam," as he was known to Wal-Mart "associates," drove a 1988 Ford pickup truck.

Perfume Making

WHAT YOU NEED

From the supermarket:
- Spring water

From the drugstore:
- Eyedropper
- Funnel
- Clean, sterilized, glass bottle
- Coffee filter

From a liquor store:
- 190-proof grain alcohol

From a health food store or perfume supply house:
- Essential oils

WHAT TO DO

Select the major fragrance family from which you would like to make your perfume (See "Fragrance Families" Chart on page 231).

Perfume contains essential oils that fall into four categories: base notes (scents that last longest on your skin), middle notes (scents that linger second longest), top notes (scents that evaporate first), and a bridge (an oil that joins the top, middle, and base notes together). Based on the fragrance family you desire, select the fragrance notes for your perfume. (See "Fragrance Families and Fragrance Notes Chart" on page 232.")

Choose a total of at least twenty-four drops of essential oils divided between base, middle, and top notes—using a 1:2:3 ratio (base: middle:top). Once you gain more experience making perfume, experiment by changing this ratio. Using an eyedropper to count the drops, combine the oils in a clean, sterilized, glass bottle. Start with the base notes, then middle, then top. Add two or three drops of the bridge oil. Swirl after adding each ingredient. Be sure to write down your formula so you can recall how you made the perfume should you want to make it again.

Fragrance Families

- **CITRUS:** Citrus notes (such as bergamot, lemon, mandarin, orange, and petitgrain) frequently combined with feminine scents (flowers, fruits and woods)
- **FLORAL:** A blend of different floral notes that can be combined with any other family
- **WOOD:** A blend of musks and precious woods complemented by exotic essences
- **GREEN:** Natural scents frequently blended with fruity and floral notes
- **SPICY:** A woody, mossy, and flowery blend, occasionally with a hint of leather or fruits

Last, add 2.5 tablespoons alcohol, seal the bottle tight to prevent the alcohol from evaporating. (Perfumes contain 10 to 20 percent essential oils dissolved in alcohol; colognes contain 3 to 5 percent essential oils dissolved in 80 to 90 percent alcohol, with balance consisting of water; toilet water has between 2 percent essential oils dissolved in 60 to 80 percent alcohol, with balance consisting of water.) Shake the bottle gently. Store in a cool, dark place, and for the next four days, shake the bottle twice a day.

Let sit for four weeks to mature. Add two tablespoons spring water, stir, and then pour through a coffee filter, and store in a tightly sealed bottle.

Fragrance Families and Fragrance Notes

	CITRUS	FLORAL	WOOD	GREEN	SPICY
BASE NOTES	none	galbanum jasmine labdanum myrrh neroli oakmoss orris sandalwood vanilla vetiver ylang-ylang	cedarwood cypress frankincense	patchouli	elemi
MIDDLE NOTES	none	jasmine mimosa neroli osmanthus rose tuberose ylang-ylang	frankincense	chamomile elemi geranium lemongrass litsea melissa myrtle palmarosa rosemary tagetes yarrow	cardamon elemi ginger
TOP NOTES	bergamot lemon lime mandarin orange petigrain	lavender neroli	none	lavender petigrain	none
BRIDGE		lavender vanilla			

CHANEL NO. 5

When asked by reporters what she wore to bed, Marilyn Monroe smiled coyly and replied, "Chanel No. 5." Parisian fashion designer Coco Chanel introduced Chanel No. 5, her first perfume, in 1921. Chanel explained that when she asked Ernest Beaux to create her first fragrance, he developed several perfumes. She chose the bottle numbered "5," and introduced her new fragrance to the world on the fifth day of the fifth month and named the perfume No. 5. Beaux also developed the use of aldehydes for synthetic Chanel No. 5, the first aldehydic fragrance.

Secret Formula
HOMEMADE "CHANEL NO. 6"

WHAT YOU NEED
From the health food store or perfume supply house:
- 10 drops Grasse jasmine fragrance oil
- 5 drops rose fragrance oil
- 5 drops essential oil of ylang-ylang
- 5 drops essential oil of iris
- 3 drops essential oil of amber
- 3 drops essential oil of patchouli

From the kitchen:
- Blue, amber, or green glass bottle
- Funnel

From the liquor store:
- ³/₄ teaspoon 100-proof vodka

WHAT TO DO
Boil a ¹/₂-ounce blue, amber, or green glass bottle in pot of water for ten minutes, then dry thoroughly. If using an old perfume bottle, wash well in hot, soapy water, rinse with isopropyl alcohol, and let dry thoroughly. Using a funnel, fill the sterilized bottle with ³/₄ teaspoon 100-proof vodka and add the scented oils in the order given above. Seal with a stopper, cork, or screw top. Label and date the bottle. Store in a cool, dark place to avoid damage from heat and light. Makes one teaspoon.

HOW TO USE IT
Put a dab of this elegant fragrance on your favorite pulse points—wrists, ear lobes, throat, the bend in your elbow, behind your knees, and along your neckline—and you'll be snagging that man before he ever knows what hit him!

OLD SPICE

Old Spice, the world's best-selling men's fragrance, was originally a perfume for women. The Shulton Company, founded in 1934 by William Lightfoot Shultz, created Early American Old Spice in 1937, and soon after, started making products for men, featuring the famous colonial sailing ship on the bottle. In keeping with the aftershave's nautical theme, the Old Spice bottle, originally made from pottery, was made to look like buoys out at sea. During World War II, American soldiers, needing to protect their skin from infection after shaving on the battlefield, were issued Old Spice Aftershave. When they returned home, many former GIs continued using Old Spice. The famous Old Spice bottle, now made of glass, retains its original shape, as a beacon of consistency in an ever-changing world. In 1990, Procter & Gamble bought Old Spice products from the Shulton Company.

Secret Formula
ALLSPICE AFTERSHAVE

WHAT YOU NEED

From the drugstore:
- 1/2 tablespoon boric acid
- 1/4 cup glycerin
- 1 cup isopropyl alcohol
- 1 cup witch hazel

From the health food store:
- 5 drops essential oil of allspice
- 5 drops essential oil of sandalwood

From the tap:
- 1 cup water

WHAT TO DO

In a large mixing bowl, combine the boric acid and glycerin, mixing well to remove all lumps. Stirring constantly, add the alcohol and witch hazel. Let stand one hour. Pour the solution into a clean one-quart jar through a funnel lined with a clean coffee filter. Add the water and the essential oils. Store in a tightly capped bottle. Makes 3 1/4 cups.

HOW TO USE IT

A dash of this invigorating musk provides today's manly man with the masculine scent of manhood guaranteed to make any woman swoon into his strong arms with awe and admiration that only a manly man's manhood deserves.

BARBASOL

In 1920, Frank B. Shields, a former chemistry instructor at the Massachusetts Institute of Technology, who had founded the Napco Corporation in Indianapolis to make vegetable glue, developed the formula for Barbasol, one of the first brushless shaving creams on the market.

Barbasol is a combination of the Roman word *barba* (meaning beard, and the origin of the word *barber*) and the English word *solution*, denoting the shaving cream is the same solution used by barbers. The stripes on the can evoke the familiarity of barbershop-pole stripes.

The white cream in a tube providing a quick, smooth shave immediately won the allegiance of thousands, eliminating the drudgery of having to lather up shaving soap in a mug with a shaving brush and then rubbing it onto the face. The Barbasol factory and offices were both located in a small second-floor room in downtown Indianapolis. The tubes were filled, clipped, and packaged by hand. At the most, only thirty or forty gross made up an entire day's production schedule. By December 1920, Barbasol had outgrown the Napco Corporation and the Barbasol Company was created.

Barbasol was widely advertised on early radio by musical performers—most memorably Harry "Singin' Sam" Frankel—and by the catchy jingle: "Barbasol, Barbasol . . . No brush, no lather, no rub-in . . . Wet your razor, then begin."

In 1962, Pfizer—the pharmaceutical company founded in 1849 in Brooklyn by Charles Pfizer and his cousin, confectioner Charles Erhart, to manufacture camphor, citric acid, and santonin—acquired the Barbasol line of shaving products, extending and updating the popular old brand.

STRANGE FACTS

• Company founder Frank Shields developed Barbasol especially for men with tough beards and tender skins because he shared those problems.

• During the 1920s, Knute Rockne, Florenz Ziegfeld, and other celebrities of the day endorsed Barbasol.

• The Depression had practically no effect upon the Barbasol Company because shaving cream was not a luxury.

• In the 1936 Indianapolis 500, Barbasol sponsored the Barbasol Special #12, painted to look like a tube of Barbasol Brushless Shaving Cream.

• A 1937 advertisement for Barbasol read, "Barbasol does to your face what it takes to make the ladies want to touch it."

GILLETTE

In 1895, while shaving with a straight razor at home in Brookline, Massachusetts, King C. Gillette, traveling salesman and author of the 1894 book *The Human Drift*, decided to develop a disposable razor blade. For the next six years, Gillette sought investors and toolmakers to develop the technology to manufacture paper-thin steel blades. Finally, in 1901, Massachusetts Institute of Technology professor William Nickerson teamed up with Gillette to perfect the safety razor, and with the financial support of some wealthy friends, the two men formed the American Safety Razor Company. In 1903, Gillette sold 51 sets of safety razors and 168 disposable razors. Americans bought a total of 90,844 sets in 1904, and two years later, sales reached 300,000 razors and over half a million blades. Gillette retired as president of the company in 1931, ironically the same year that Jacob Schick invented the electric razor.

STRANGE FACTS

• During World War I, the United States government bought 3.5 million Service Set shaving kits from Gillette for the armed forces, totaling over 36 million blades.

• In the 1920s, Gillette distributed free razors through boxes of Wrigley's gum and its "Shave and Save" plan at banks.

• The strength of early lasers was measured in Gillettes, the number of blue razor blades a given beam could puncture.

• According to archaeologists, men shaved their faces as far back as the Stone Age—20,000 years ago. Prehistoric men shaved with clamshells, sharks' teeth, sharpened pieces of flint, and knives.

• Ancient Egyptians shaved their faces and heads before hand-to-hand combat so the enemy had less to grab.

• The longest beard, according to *Guinness Book of Records,* measured 17.5 feet long and was presented to the Smithsonian Institution in 1967.

• A typical shave will cut about 20,000 to 25,000 facial hairs.

• Shaving in the shower wastes an average of 10 to 35 gallons of water. To conserve water, fill the sink basin with an inch of water and vigorously rinse your razor often in the water after every second or third stroke.

• Among the 90 percent of American males who shave, roughly 30 percent use electric razors.

• Seventy percent of women rate clean-shaven men as sexy.

How Target Hit the Bull's-Eye

In 1902, former banker George Dayton opened a dry-goods store in Minneapolis on a spot where he had found the most foot traffic. Offering return privileges and liberal credit, his store grew to a twelve-story, full-line department store. In 1956, Dayton's built the world's first fully enclosed shopping mall in Edina, a wealthy Minneapolis suburb, and, in 1962, seeing a need for an upscale discount store, Dayton's opened the first Target store at 7000 York Avenue South in Roseville, Minnesota, a suburb of St. Paul.

Target became the first low-margin discount store to sell name-brand, quality, low-priced merchandise in an attractive store, upgrading the image of the discount store to a pleasant shopping experience—with courteous salespeople who treat customers like guests.

With eleven million dollars in sales by the end of 1962, Dayton began slowly opening more Target stores, generating 100 million dollars in sales by 1969. That same year, the company bought family-owned Hudson's, the largest retailer of men's clothing in America, forming Dayton Hudson Corporation. The company continued opening Target stores, and in 1975, Target became the company's top moneymaker, giving Dayton-Hudson enough money to buy Mervyn's department stores in 1977 and Marshall Field's department stores in 1990.

STRANGE FACTS

• Target is known by the nickname Targét (pronounced Tar-JHAY, as if it were a highbrow French word).

• In 1928, Hudson's built a new building in downtown Detroit that became the second largest retail store building in the United States, eventually growing to twenty-five stories with forty-nine acres of floor space.

• In 1962, the year the first Target store opened, the first K-mart opened in Garden City, Michigan, and the first Wal-Mart opened in Rogers, Arkansas.

• Target stores have a combined total floor space of more than 67 million square feet. That's big enough to hold more than 5,500 Boeing 747s.

• Each Target store stocks up to 750,000 pieces of merchandise. That means everyone in the United States could walk into a Target store at the same time and leave with at least one item.

• More than 400 million guests visited Target stores in 1994. That's more people than attend all the games in the National Football League, the National Hockey League, and the National Basketball Association over three years.

• As of 1995, Target employed approximately 141,000 people. That's four times the population of Roseville, Minnesota, the city where the first Target opened.

• The average American spends sixty-three dollars a year at Target.

The Big Boys

KITCHEN & PANTRY

7

Cooking, Cleaning, and Kooky Concoctions

The country store carried virtually every imaginable item homemakers would need to stock the kitchen and clean the house—rolling pins, pots, pans, cake molds, muffin tins, wooden spoons, whisks, egg beaters, maple syrup, beer, ladles, trivets, coffee urns, brooms, canned goods, cheeses, butter, eggs, jars of homemade jellies, and barrels of crackers and oatmeal. If you couldn't find what you needed, the storekeeper would gladly order the item from a catalog or purchase it during his next trip to the big city. Here you'll discover many products that are as familiar today as they were a century ago, and you'll also learn how to make maple syrup, brew your own beer, and concoct your own household cleansers.

BARNUM'S ANIMALS

In the late nineteenth century, Americans imported "Animals" or "Circus Crackers" (animal-shaped cookies) from England. As demand for the animal crackers grew, local American bakeries began making versions of the treats.

In 1898, Adophus Green consolidated several American baking companies into the National Biscuit Company (which eventually became known as Nabisco). The National Biscuit Company quickly began creating easily identifiable packaging for its products, and in 1902, the company gave its "Animal Biscuits" a new name—"Barnum's Animals," in honor of renowned showman P. T. Barnum (1810–1891), who called his circus "The Greatest Show on Earth." For Christmas, the company redesigned the package as a circus wagon cage with a string handle, so the box could be hung as a Christmas tree ornament. Barnum's Animals, selling for five cents a box, were an instant hit and immediately became a year-round favorite.

STRANGE FACTS

- During its first year of business in 1898, Nabisco's sales accounted for 70 percent of the cracker and cookie business in America.
- In 1899, Nabisco created a new light and flaky soda cracker sold in a package specially designed to preserve its crispness under the brand name Uneeda Biscuit, advertised with the Uneeda Biscuit slicker boy. In 1900, Nabisco sold over 100 million boxes of Uneeda biscuits—roughly six packages for every family in America.
- Nabisco's symbol, an oval topped by a double-barred cross, was used as a pressmark by Venetian printers Nicolas Jensen and Johannes de Colonia as early as 1480. In medieval times, the mark symbolized the triumph of the spiritual world over the material world.
- The box of Barnum's Animals was the first product designed with a string handle. To pro-

duce boxes of Barnum's Animals, Nabisco uses eight thousand miles of string every year.

• Barnum's Animals provide 10 percent of the United States recommended daily value of calcium.

• The Nabisco bakery produces more than 300,000 animal crackers every hour.

• Since 1902, Nabisco has produced thirty-seven different varieties of animal crackers.

• Barnum's Animals currently feature a menagerie of seventeen different animal-shaped crackers: bears, bison, camels, cougars, elephants, giraffes, gorillas, hippopotamuses, hyenas, kangaroos, lions, monkeys, rhinoceroses, seals, sheep, tigers, and zebras.

• The average box of Barnum's Animals contains twenty-two animal crackers.

• Nabisco sells more than forty million boxes of Barnum's Animals each year.

HOMEMADE "FIG NEWTONS"

WHAT YOU NEED

From the supermarket:

- $1/2$ cup chopped figs
- $1/2$ cup chopped raisins
- Juice of half a lemon (or two tablespoons ReaLemon lemon juice)
- $1/4$ cup sugar
- $1 1/4$ cups whole grain pastry flour
- 1 cup oat bran
- $1/4$ cup packed brown sugar
- $1/4$ teaspoon salt
- $1/2$ cup butter

From the tap:

- $1/2$ cup water, plus a few tablespoons of water

WHAT TO DO

Combine the figs, raisins, lemon juice, sugar, and water in a saucepan, bring to a boil, then reduce heat and simmer until thick. Remove from heat and let cool.

Preheat the oven to 400 degrees Fahrenheit. Grease baking sheets.

In a large bowl, mix the flour, oat bran, brown sugar, and salt. Cut the butter in small slices, add to the mixture, and blend well. Slowly add three or four tablespoons of water, one tablespoon at a time, stirring until the mixture forms a ball.

Turn the dough ball onto a floured surface, split into two equal portions, and use a rolling pin and knife to create two rectangles of dough, each three inches wide and twenty-four inches long. Spoon the fig filling down the center of each rectangle of dough. Fold the width ends of the rectangle over the fig filling, and pinch the ends together in the center. Slice into $1 1/2$-inch-long squares, and place on the prepared baking sheets.

Bake at 400 degrees Fahrenheit for ten minutes or until lightly browned. Let cool on a rack for two minutes, then place the cookies on the rack to cool completely. Makes twenty-six.

- In 1917, English poet Christopher Morley wrote:

    "Animal crackers, and cocoa to drink,

    That is the finest of suppers, I think.

    When I'm grown up and can have what I please,

    I think I shall always insist upon these."

- In the 1930 Marx Brothers movie *Animal Crackers*, Groucho Marx, starring as Captain Jeffrey T. Spaulding, says, "One morning I shot an elephant in my pajamas. How he got into my pajamas, I'll never know."
- In the 1935 movie *Curly Top*, Shirley Temple sings "Animal Crackers in My Soup," possibly the world's most famous reference to animal crackers.

Beer Making

WHAT YOU NEED

From a homebrew supply store:
- Fermentor (food-grade plastic bucket or glass carboy)
- Airlock
- 3 to 4 pounds pale malt extract syrup, unhopped
- 2 pounds amber dry malt extract
- 12 AAU bittering hops (1 ounce of 12 percent AA Nugget, or 1.5 ounces of 8 percent AA Perle)
- 5 AAU finishing hops (1 ounce of 5 percent Cascade, or 1.25 ounces of 4 percent Liberty)
- 2 packets dried ale yeast
- 48 twelve-ounce bottles
- Bottle capper
- Bottle caps
- Racking cane
- Siphon
- Bottle filler
- Copper finings (optional)
- Hydrometer

From the kitchen:
- One 20-quart brew pot
- Large stirring spoon (plastic or metal)
- Tablespoon
- Measuring cup (preferably Pyrex glass)
- Glass jar (at least 12 ounces) with lid
- Thermometer (optional)
- Bottle brush
- Large saucepan
- Measuring spoons
- Tall glass
- Strainer

From the supermarket:
- Alkaline dishwashing liquid, like Ivory or Palmolive
- Clorox
- Saran Wrap
- 2/3 cup cane sugar
- Knox gelatin (optional)

WHAT TO DO

Keep a logbook to record your ingredients, procedure, costs, original and final gravity (so you can calculate the alcohol content of your finished beer), and the number of bottles you fill.

Clean all equipment with a mild, unscented dishwashing detergent and rinse well. Make a sanitizing solution by filling the fermentor bucket with five gallons of water and adding five tablespoons of Clorox bleach (or one tablespoon per gallon). Soak the tablespoon, measuring cup, jar, lid, airlock, and thermometer in this solution for twenty minutes. Afterwards, discard the solution.

Homebrewing Kits

A homebrewing kit usually contains malt extract, yeast, hops (unless hops have already been added to the extract), glucose or dextrose, a fermentor (usually with a stick-on thermometer), bottle brush, caps, and hand capper. Some kits also include a crushed specialty grain, hydrometer, sterilizer, funnel, and spoon.

Boil one gallon of water for ten minutes, cover, and let cool to room temperature. Pour the cooled water into the fermentor bucket to rinse any excess sanitizing solution from the objects. Place the small spoon and thermometer in the jar and cover it with Saran Wrap. Cover the fermentor with the lid.

Test the yeast by adding one teaspoon of malt extract or table sugar to one-quarter cup water, and bring it to a boil. Let cool, then pour it into the sanitized jar, add one tablespoon yeast, and stir. Cover and place in a warm place out of direct sunlight. After thirty minutes, the liquid should be foaming or churning. If the yeast just seems to lie on the bottom of the jar, it is most likely dead. If necessary, repeat the test with good yeast.

Boil two gallons of water, pour into the fermentor, and let cool. Boil another three gallons of water. (If your beer kit includes a crushed specialty grain, place the crushed grains into the supplied muslin grain bag (or the sanitized foot of a pair of panty hose), tie the bag closed, drop in a large brew pot filled with one and half gallons of water, and heat, allowing the grains to steep for fifteen minutes until the water begins to boil. Remove the muslin grain bag, and use the liquid as part of the three gallons of water.)

While waiting for the brew water to boil, rehydrate two packets of dried ale yeast. To do so, pour one cup of warm (95–105 degrees Fahrenheit), pre-boiled water into the jar and stir in the yeast. Cover with Saran Wrap and let sit for fifteen minutes.

Place the can or bottle of malt extract syrup in a sink of hot water to warm the liquid, making it easier to pour. When the three gallons of water on the stove come to a boil, turn off the heat, and stir in the malt extract, blending it thoroughly (so the ingredients do not stick to the bottom of the pot). Turn on the heat again and resume a rolling boil. Add the bittering hops and begin timing the hour-long boil. Stir the solution (now called "wort") frequently during the boil to avoid scorching. Brew the malt for a minimum of one hour to force protein, which can cause hazy beer, to come out of solution.

As the wort boils, foam will form on the surface until the wort passes through the "hot break" stage. Stir frequently to prevent the wort from boiling over. If the wort begins to boil over, turn down the heat.

After 45 minutes, if you are using hopped malt extract, add finishing hops. Boil for another fifteen minutes (for a total of one hour).

If desired, add copper finings during the boil to attract proteins and precipitate them out, making the beer more stable and improving the shelf life.

Hop To It

Hops are measured in AAUs (alpha-acid units), the result of multiplying the percentage of alpha-acid in the hops by the weight of the hops you intend to use. For instance, two ounces of a 6 percent alpha-acid hops equals 12 AAUs. To determine how much of a particular hops you need, divide the required AAU by the alpha-acid percentage listed on the package of hops. For instance, 12 AAUs divided by 8 (Perle hop's alpha-acid rating) equals 1 1/2 ounces.

Cool the wort quickly to "yeast pitching" temperature (between 65 and 90 degrees Fahrenheit) by immersing the covered pot in a cold water bath. ("Yeast pitching" simply means adding yeast to the wort to start fermentation.) To expedite the cooling process, stir the cold water and wort every five minutes (with different spoons to avoid contaminating the wort). The temperature of the wort must be between 65 and 90 degrees Fahrenheit, otherwise when you add the yeast, high temperatures will kill the yeast or produce off-tastes, and low temperatures will cause the yeast to proliferate too quickly, fermenting the beer too rapidly and causing it to foam excessively.

Pour the rehydrated yeast solution into the fermentation bucket and stir.

Dump the cooled wort into the fermentation bucket (through a strainer to remove the hops), causing the liquid to splash and churn, aerating the wort.

Drain some of the wort into a tall glass, insert the hydrometer, twirl to remove any bubbles, and record the Specific Gravity (SG) measurement. Discard this wort to avoid contaminating the wort in the fermentor.

Seal the lid securely on the fermentor and set in a cool, dark place (ideally between 65 and 70 degrees Fahrenheit) out of direct sunlight, insert the airlock, and leave undisturbed for two weeks. After twenty-four hours, the airlock will begin to bubble steadily for two to four days, then the bubbling will decrease as the yeast consumes the malt sugars.

Using mild unscented detergents, clean the brew pot and other equipment, and rinse well.

After two weeks, take SG readings. When two readings two days apart yield the same result, fermentation is complete. Wait a couple of days to let the yeast settle and the beer to clear.

If you wish to use finings to help clear the yeast (by making the yeast drop out of solution), mix one-half ounce Knox gelatin in a cup of hot water, let cool, drain two cups of beer from the fermentor, mix with the gelatin solution, then pour back into the fermentor and stir. Let sit for one day to let the beer clear.

How To Siphon

Never start a siphon by sucking on it, otherwise bacteria from your mouth will contaminate and sour the beer. Sanitize all parts of the siphon and leave the siphon full of sanitizer.

Place the racking cane in your beer, hold the end of the siphon lower than the fermentor (to prevent the sanitizer from flowing into your beer), release the clamp or valve, and let the sanitizer drain into a jar. This simple action will suck the beer into the siphon so you can transfer it into bottles without the risk of contamination.

Place a sanitized cap on each bottle, and crimp it using the bottle capper.

To determine the alcohol content of your beer, subtract the final SG reading ("final gravity") from the SG reading you took before fermentation began ("original gravity") and multiply the result by .134. For instance, a beer with an original gravity of 1064 and a final gravity of 1025, contains 5.226 percent alcohol.

Thoroughly clean the bottles (using a bottle brush if necessary) with an alkaline dishwashing liquid, like Ivory or Palmolive (not detergent, which

Bottle Cappers

Here's how to use the three most popular types of bottle cappers:

- **HAND CAPPER:** To use this wooden handle with a metal fitting on the bottom, place a cap on the bottle, put the capper over the top, then hit it with a hammer to crimp the cap. Hand cappers tend to break bottles and create a poor seal.
- **LEVER CAPPER:** Gently push down two levers to crimp the cap over the top of the bottle, creating a tight seal but sometimes breaking the bottle.

- **BENCH CAPPER:** Place the bottle in the base, put a cap on the bottle, and pull down the attached lever to crimp the cap, forming a tight seal.

leaves a residue that destroys the head on a beer). Rinse well, then sanitize the bottles. Old-fashioned bottles that have a crown seal and are made of thick glass are less prone to breaking during bottling than contemporary bottles made of thin glass.

Soak the bottle caps in sanitizing solution (one tablespoon Clorox bleach per gallon of water), then rinse well with sterilized water (boiled and cooled).

To add carbonation to the beer (if desired), mix two-thirds cup cane sugar in two cups water, bring to a boil, cover, and let cool.

Gently pour the carbonation solution into the fermentor and slowly stir. Let the sediment settle for thirty minutes, then fill the bottles using the bottle filler attachment on your siphon.

Store the capped bottles out of the light in room temperature (between 64 and 72 degrees Fahrenheit for ales; between 50 and 59 degrees Fahrenheit for lagers). Let sit for two weeks to allow the beer to carbonate. A thin layer of yeast will form in the bottom of the bottles. The bottled beer will keep for approximately six months.

Chill before serving. To pour the beer without getting yeast in your glass, tip the bottle slowly.

If you dislike the taste of your beer, let the bottled beer mature for at least six months.

Budweiser

The
Big
Boys

In 1852, George Schneider founded the Bavarian Brewery in St. Louis, Missouri. When he went bankrupt eight years later in 1860, Eberhard Anheuser, a German immigrant and soap manufacturer who had loaned the Bavarian Brewery over ninety thousand dollars, assumed control of the company. Anheuser was soon joined by his son-in-law, Adolphus Busch, who used refrigerated railroad cars to enlarge distribution and put teams of Clydesdale horses to work, transforming the brewery's carts into working advertisements. In 1876, Busch helped restaurateur Carl Conrad create a light beer like those brewed in the Bohemian town of Budweis, naming the beer Budweiser. Budweiser's popularity over darker beers helped the brewery grow rapidly.

When Adolphus Busch died in 1913, his son, August Busch, took over the Bavarian Brewery, renamed Anheuser-Busch, Inc., in 1919. During Prohibition, August Busch kept the company in business by selling yeast, refrigeration units, truck bodies, syrup, and soft drinks. When Prohibition was repealed, Busch resumed the brewing operation, delivering a case of Budweiser to President Franklin Roosevelt in a carriage drawn by Clydesdale horses, which have since become the company's symbol.

STRANGE FACTS
• Budweiser was not the first "King of Beers." St. Louis A.B.C. Bohemian beer was billed as "King of All Bottle Beers," Michelob was called "King of Draught Beer," and both Regal Beer and Imperial Beer were both touted as "King of Beers."
• In October 1983, when Anheuser-Busch brought a Cleveland florist to court for using the Budweiser slogan "This Bud's for You," Federal Judge Ann Aldrich ruled in favor of the florist, claiming it would be absurd for anyone to confuse flowers with beer.
• Anheuser-Busch owns the St. Louis Cardinals, Campbell Taggart, Eagle Snacks, and ten theme parks, including Adventure Island, Baseball City Sports Complex, Busch Gardens, Cypress Gardens, Sea World, Sesame Place, and Water Country U.S.A.
• Anheuser-Busch operates thirteen breweries in the United States, and the company's beer is exported to sixty-five countries.
• Anheuser-Busch is the world's largest brewer and the self-proclaimed "King of Beers" in the United States (with the number-one spot and 44 percent of the beer market).

STRANGE FACTS

- Just four ingredients—barley, hops, yeast and water—combine to produce beer. Sugar is extracted from the barley, hops are added for bitterness, then yeast converts most of the sugars into alcohol.
- No one knows exactly when people started brewing beer, but the earliest record of beer can be found on a Mesopotamian tablet (circa 7000 B.C.E.) inscribed with a cuneiform recipe for the "wine of the grain." Anthropologists believe Mesopotamians and Egyptians first developed the process of malting (making barley more suitable for brewing by germinating the barley grains, developing

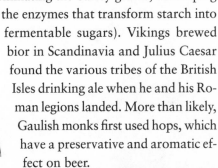

Homemade Hops Extract

Mix the hops, three tablespoons malt in two quarts of water in a saucepan, and slowly bring to a boil, stirring occasionally. (The malt helps extract the bitterness and aroma from the hops.)

Boil them for one hour.

Strain the liquid through a sieve or gauze.

the enzymes that transform starch into fermentable sugars). Vikings brewed bior in Scandinavia and Julius Caesar found the various tribes of the British Isles drinking ale when he and his Roman legions landed. More than likely, Gaulish monks first used hops, which have a preservative and aromatic effect on beer.

- The word "beer" is believed to come from the Celtic word beor, used to describe the malt brew produced in the monasteries of North Gaul.
- During the Inca empire in Cuzco, Peru, beer made from maize was a luxury served by the state on ceremonial occasions.
- The Pilgrims landed at Plymouth Rock in December 1620, because, in the words of a diarist aboard the Mayflower, "We could not now take time for further search or consideration,

our victuals being much spent, especially our beere."

• George Washington, Thomas Jefferson, and William Penn brewed beer on their estates.

• Beer is 92 percent water.

• Beer is the most popular alcoholic beverage in America, consumed regularly by more than 80 million Americans.

• Beer accounts for nearly 87 percent of all alcoholic beverages consumed in the United States. The average American drinks approximately 23 gallons of beer every year.

• According to New York's Simmons Market Research Bureau, 55.1 percent of all beer drinkers surveyed in 1985 were college educated, while 38.9 percent of all beer drinkers were high school dropouts.

• Most brewing kits sold at homebrew shops and supermarkets include liquid or powdered malt extract to which hops have been added to save you from the laborious task of mashing your own malt.

• Never use a plastic rubbish bin for beer making. The toxins in the plastic will leech into the beer.

• Adding small quantities of grain or hops can enhance the final taste, color, aroma, bitterness, and character of beer.

• To make malt, moistened barley grains are kept warm, prompting them

Malts and Grains Used to Make Beer

You can experiment with different malts and grains in beer making to create different flavors, aromas, and tastes.

COMMON MALTED BARLEY

- Amber malt
- Black malt
- Chocolate malt
- Crystal malt
- Lager malt
- Mild ale malt
- Munich malt
- Pale malt
- Victory malt
- Vienna malt

OTHER MALTED GRAINS

- Acid malt
- Brown malt
- Caramalt malt
- Caramunich malt
- Carapils malt
- Caravienne malt
- Malted wheat
- Malted oats
- White wheat malt

OTHER GRAINS

- Flaked wheat
- Flaked maize and maize grits
- Flaked rice and rice grits
- Flaked barley
- Oatmeal and rolled oats
- Roasted barley
- Rye
- Torrefied wheat
- Unmalted wheat

to germinate and produce an enzyme. As the barley begins to sprout, it is heated to kill the seed and stop germination, leaving the enzyme unscathed. The resulting "malt" is infused with water between 60 and 70 degrees Fahrenheit and held at this temperature for up to two hours to allow the enzyme to convert the starch to fermentable sugars.

• Beer made without hops is sickly sweet. The bitterness from hops, the female flower cone of the *Humulus lupulus* or *Humulus americanus* plant, balances the sweetness.

• Yeast, a microorganism that consumes sugar and produces alcohol and carbon dioxide, can be either top-fermenting or bottom-fermenting. Top-fermenting yeast rises to the top of the brew, producing an ale—a beer with a fruity bouquet and thicker body. Bottom-fermenting yeast produce a lager—a light beer with a less malty body.

• Adding dextrose or glucose to the wort creates more alcohol content without adding any taste or body. Cane sugar tends to produce a cider taste, brown sugar adds color or flavor, and lactose (or milk sugar) makes beer sweeter. Honey, molasses, and golden syrup add those specific tastes.

Miller Beer

After revolutionary upheavals ravaged Europe in 1848, hundreds of thousands of Germans immigrated to America, bringing with them a love of golden lager beer and the knowledge to brew it. In 1855, a young German immigrant, Frederick Miller, formerly the brew-master at Hohenzollern Castle in Germany, purchased the small, five-year-old Plank Road Brewery west of Milwaukee. Miller produced three hundred barrels of high-quality lager beer—which he aptly called Miller Beer—in his first year, storing the brew in a network of caverns in the hillside behind the brewery.

In 1903, when Miller's son, Carl, sought a new name for the light-colored pilsner, his wife's uncle, Ernst Miller, chanced upon a building down in New Orleans called High Life Cigars. The Miller Brewing Company paid 25,000 dollars for the factory and the right to use the name. In 1906, the company adopted "The Champagne of Bottled Beer" slogan to describe Miller High Life.

By Frederick Miller's death in 1888, the brewery was producing eighty thousand barrels of beer annually. By 1954, under the leadership of Frederick C. Miller, the founder's grandson, Miller Brewing Company was the ninth largest brewery in the world, shipping two million barrels each year.

When Philip Morris, the worldwide tobacco and consumer-packaged goods company, acquired the company in 1970, Miller was the nation's seventh largest brewer, producing 5.1 million barrels of beer that year. Philip Morris marketed Miller High Life with the popular "Miller Time" advertising campaign, and by the 1990s, Miller was brewing more than forty million barrels per year, making it the second largest brewery in the United States, behind Anheuser-Busch.

STRANGE FACTS

• Miller Brewing, founded twenty-one years before the first Budweiser was brewed in 1876, is the world's third largest beer producer (after Anheuser-Busch and Heineken).

• In 1855, Frederick Miller established a beautifully landscaped twenty-acre beer garden in Milwaukee that attracted weekend crowds for bowling, dancing, fine lunches and old-fashioned "gemutlichkeit." The garden caught fire on July 4, 1891, and was ultimately torn down in 1909.

• In 1850, Frederick Charles Best and his brother dug tunnels in the hills behind the Plank Road Brewery to store beer in the days before refrigeration. When Frederick Miller bought the brewery five years later, he expanded the tunnels to a total of six hundred feet—enough to store 12,000 barrels of beer. With the advent of refrigeration, the brewery abandoned the caves until 1952, when a portion of the caves opened to tourists through the Miller Caves Museum.

• When company president Carl Miller took his adolescent daughter Loretta on a visit to the brewery, he sat her at the end of the bar in the dining room. Loretta held her hand up dramatically, inadvertently providing Miller with the inspiration for the High Life "Girl in the Moon." Carl's brother, Fred, sketched the High Life girl, using a photograph of Loretta.

• Between 1907 and 1911, the "Girl in the Moon" graced metal beer-serving trays used in beer gardens, hotels, bars and restaurants. The trays and other "Girl in the Moon" promotional materials now are collector's items.

• Hollywood actor Arthur Franz portrayed Miller Brewing Company founder Frederick Miller in a 48-minute commercial film, *With This Ring*, produced in 1955. The movie, filmed in Hollywood, Milwaukee and Sigmaringen, Germany, followed the story of a fictitious "brewer's ring" allegedly passed on from generation to generation over the 100-year history of the Miller Brewing Company.

• In 1994, the Miller Brewing Company sold over four billion dollars worth of beer.

• Miller also makes Lowenbrau, Meister Brau, Milwaukee's Best, Molson, Red Dog, and Sharp's.

• Miller operates breweries in Milwaukee, Wisconsin; Eden, North Carolina; Albany, Georgia; Fort Worth, Texas; Trenton, Ohio; and Irwindale, California.

Say PICTSWEET

for prize flavor

America's Choicest PEAS AND CORN

TENDER, garden-green peas . . . big or little . . . picked and sealed at their sweetest, most flavorsome best. Enjoy their new and tempting goodness tonight!

3 GRAND STYLES OF CORN
Golden-sweet . . . all with that fresh-off-the-cob flavor. Rich cream style . . . tender whole kernel . . . and vacuum packed. You'll want to try every style . . . and often!

PICTSWEET
AMERICA'S PREMIUM PEAS and CORN

CAMPBELL'S SOUPS

In 1869, fruit merchant Joseph Campbell, who made his mark selling soup from a horse-drawn wagon, teamed up with icebox manufacturer Abraham Anderson to start the Joseph A. Campbell Preserve Company in Camden, New Jersey, to produce canned tomatoes, vegetables, jellies, soups, condiments, and mincemeat. Anderson left the business in 1876 to start a rival company. In 1897, the Campbell Company's general manager, Arthur Dorrance, re-

luctantly hired his 24-year-old nephew, Dr. John T. Dorrance, a chemist who had trained in Europe. The younger Dorrance was so determined to join Campbell that he agreed to buy his own laboratory equipment and accept a token salary of just $7.50 per week. The enthusiastic young chemist invented condensed soup. By eliminating the water in canned soup, he lowered the costs for packaging, shipping, and storage, enabling the company to offer a 10.5 ounce can of Campbell's condensed soup for a dime, versus more than thirty cents for a typical 32-ounce can of soup. In 1922, the Campbell Company formally adopted "Soup" as its middle name.

STRANGE FACTS

• The classic red-and-white Campbell's soup can labels, immortalized by Andy Warhol in his classic Pop Art silk screens, were adopted in 1898, after a company executive named Herberton Williams attended the traditional football game between Cornell University and the University of Pennsylvania. The dazzling new red-and-white uniforms of the Cornell University football team inspired Williams.

• The circular seal on the Campbell's Soup can pictures a medal won at the Paris Exposition of 1900.

• In 1904, Philadelphia illustrator Grace Wiederseim drew the cherubic Campbell's Soup Kids, modeling the chubby-faced kids after herself. Like the Campbell Soup Kids, Wiederseim had a round face, wide eyes, and a turned-up nose. Over the years, the Campbell Soup Kids grew taller and lost a little baby fat. The Campbell's Soup Kids were introduced in a series of trolley-car advertisements, as a way to appeal to working mothers.

We're ready to give our answers quick
On readin' and writin' and 'rithmetic;
And it helps a lot, we have a hunch,
If we have Campbell's Soup for lunch!

GOOD HOT SOUP *makes* A SCHOOLDAY LUNCH!

Lunch at Home

CAMPBELL'S VEGETABLE SOUP, with its 15 vegetables and bracing beef stock, is almost a meal in itself. A grand help on busy days! The children like it, and it's good for them, because it's easily digested and supplies needful vitamins and minerals. Here's a simple, satisfying lunch—

Campbell's Vegetable Soup
Cracker and Cheese Sandwiches
Sliced Egg Salad
Mixed Fresh Fruit   Milk

Lunch at School

CAMPBELL'S TOMATO SOUP, made of luscious tomatoes and fine table butter, is a youngsters' favorite . . . Dietitians urge hot food, such as soup, for children's lunches. Follow this advice and include a vacuum bottle of Campbell's Tomato Soup in the lunch box. Here's an easily fixed lunch the children will be sure to enjoy—

Campbell's Tomato Soup
Peanut Butter and Bacon Sandwiches
Apple and Cookies

• The original label on a can of Campbell's canned tomatoes portrayed two men hauling a tomato the size of an icebox.
• In the 1900s, Campbell's first magazine advertisement boasted twenty-one varieties of soup, each selling for a dime.
• In the 1930s, Campbell began sponsoring radio shows, introducing the familiar "M'm! M'm! Good!" jingle.
• In the 1950s, the Campbell's Soup Kids first appeared in television com-

255

mercials. Forty years later, the Campbell's Soup Kids were seen dancing to rap songs.

• In 1916, a cookbook entitled *Helps for the Hostess* originated the idea to use condensed soup in recipes. After World War II, Campbell's home economists cooked up recipes for dishes like "Green Bean Bake" and "Glorified Chicken."

• Today, Americans use more than 440 million cans of Campbell's Soup each year to cook with soup.

• Combined, Americans consume approximately 2.5 billion bowls of Campbell's three most popular soups—Tomato Soup, Cream of Mushroom, and Chicken Noodle—each year.

• Ronald Reagan, Johnny Carson, Jimmy Stewart, Orson Welles, Helen Hayes, Donna Reed, Robin Leach, George Burns, Gracie Allen, and John Goodman have served as spokespeople for various Campbell products.

• Besides "M'm! M'm! Good!," other Campbell taglines that have infected America's collective consciousness include "Wow! I could've had a V8!," "Uh-oh, SpaghettiOs," and "Pepperidge Farm Remembers."

• Campbell's Soups, the best-selling soups in the United States, are available in practically every country in the world.

CLABBER GIRL

In 1848, German immigrants in Terre Haute, Indiana, founded the company Hulman & Company. In 1879, Herman Hulman began experimenting with chemical leaveners, formulating new baking powders distributed under the names "Crystal" and "Dauntless." In 1887, Hulman introduced an improved baking powder named "Milk," followed in 1899 by yet another refined baking powder named "Clabber."

At the time, most homemakers leavened breads and biscuits by mixing soured, or clabbered, milk (often called "clabber"), and baking soda to start a chemical reaction that released carbon dioxide gas into the dough or batter, causing it to rise. This method produced inconsistent results because bakers could not accurately measure the sourness of milk and consequently could not judge how much baking soda to add to produce the proper reaction. While baking powder provided more consistent results, homemakers hesitated to embrace a chemical product. To help baking powder gain acceptance, Hulman chose the name "Clabber" for his product, making Clabber baking powder one of the most popular products among homemakers.

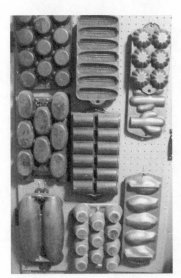

In 1923, new labeling laws prohibited manufacturers from giving a product a misleading name, forcing Hulman to change the name of Clabber Baking Powder, which did not contain any "clabber." Determined to save the Clabber name because it was so popular, Hulman wanted to keep the brand-name recognition. Forced to comply with the new federal labeling laws, yet determined to maintain the brand name recognition, Hulman changed the name "Clabber" to "Clabber Girl."

Hulman & Company remains a privately owned business, distributing its baking powders nationally and to several other countries.

CRACKERS

Crackers naturally evolved from bread. The Bible records that when the ancient Hebrews fled Egypt, they did not have time to let their bread rise and consequently took unleavened bread called matzah, essentially a large cracker, on their journey. In 1792, John Pearson of Newburyport, Massachusetts, combined flour and water to bake pilot bread, a large cracker with a long shelf life that stacked easily in barrels aboard sailing ships and soon became a staple of seafaring journeys. Pilot bread became known as hardtack or sea biscuit.

In 1801, baker Josiah Bent of Milton, Massachusetts, accidentally overcooked some biscuits in his brick oven. The crackling sound prompted him to name the tasty wafers "crackers," which he began selling in barrels to naval provisioners. In 1828, brothers Timothy and Charles Cross of Montpelier, Vermont, made the first common cracker in the United States. Charles mixed

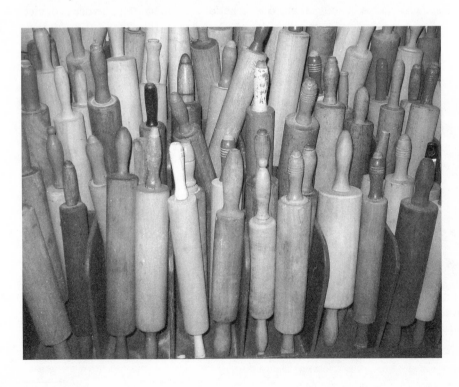

and shaped the dough by hand, used a wooden peel to place the flattened balls of dough into an oven, and distributed the crackers using a one-horse wagon. Most families in Vermont bought one barrel containing roughly twelve hundred Vermont Common Crackers to last the year.

Cracker barrels became a mainstay of the country store. In the nineteenth century, most country stores bought crackers by the barrel, and customers who gathered in the country store to play checkers around the cast-iron stove and partake in the art of conversation, often snacked from the cracker barrel. In fact, the term "cracker-barrel" soon referred to the informal and direct discussion or homespun philosophy characteristic of talkers in country stores.

John Pearson's factory continued making pilot bread, and in 1898, his company became the National Biscuit Company, which later bought Josiah Bent's company and became known as Nabisco.

Today, popular crackers include water crackers (made from flour and water), common crackers, and soda crackers (better known as saltines). In 1934, Nabisco introduced a butter cracker called the Ritz, which became an instant success. Today Nabisco makes sixteen billion Ritz crackers every year.

Do-It-Yourself Recipe
SODA CRACKERS

WHAT YOU NEED

From the supermarket:
- 4 cups flour
- 1 tablespoon baking powder
- ¼ cup Crisco All-Vegetable Shortening
- 1⅓ cups milk
- Salt

WHAT TO DO

Mix together the flour, baking powder, and shortening. Add the milk, and knead to form a ball of dough. Divide the ball into four equal portions for rolling. With a rolling pin, roll the dough paper-thin on a floured surface. With a knife, cut the dough into two-inch squares. Place on an ungreased cookie sheet. Prick with a fork four times and sprinkle with salt to taste. Bake at 325 degrees Fahrenheit for twenty minutes or until golden. Turn once if necessary. Let cool on a rack.

Cracker Barrel® Old Country Store

While working at the family gas station in Lebanon, Tennessee, in the late 1960s, Dan Evins reckoned a way to help meet the needs of families driving along the new interstate highway system. He decided to build an old-fashioned, homey restaurant that served up genuine home-style cooking—made with quality ingredients and based on old country recipes. To make weary travelers feel at home, he decided to recreate the warm, cozy, nostalgic atmosphere of an old-fashioned country store filled with jars of candy and homemade jellies, pot-bellied stoves, and pleasant employees who let customers take their time.

Together with his friend Tommy Lowe, Evins drew up plans to build his dream restaurant on a parcel of land his family owned on the outskirts of town. On September 19, 1969, Evins opened the first Cracker Barrel Old Country Store, dishing out corn bread made from cornmeal and served with real butter, authentic maple syrup, turnip greens, biscuits and gravy, meatloaf, fried chicken, and mashed potatoes made from scratch daily.

"The goal isn't simply to recreate a time gone by," says a company brochure. "It's to preserve it. Because the way we see it, values of rural America aren't about where you live. They're about how you live."

People took to the idea, and by 1977, Evins had thirteen stores along interstate highways from Tennessee to Georgia. In 1996, there were 260 Cracker Barrels across the United States, and by 2003, there were 463 stores in forty-one states.

STRANGE FACTS

• Originally, Cracker Barrel Old Country Stores also sold gasoline—until the oil embargo in the mid-1970s forced Evins to stop building filling stations.

• In 1981, Cracker Barrel went public with its stock, prompting *Money* magazine to list the company as one of the top ten stocks in the United States.

Do-It-Yourself Recipe

ICE CREAM

WHAT YOU NEED

From the supermarket:

- 1 quart cream
- $3/4$ cup sugar
- $1/8$ teaspoon salt
- $1/2$ teaspoon vanilla extract
- 1 small, clean, empty, coffee can (net weight 13-ounce) with lid
- 1 large, clean, empty coffee can (net weight 39-ounce) with lid
- Rock salt

From the hardware store or drugstore:

- Electrical tape

From the kitchen:

- Mixing bowl
- Measuring cup
- Whisk
- Ice

WHAT TO DO

Heat one cup cream (without boiling) and add sugar and salt, stirring until dissolved. Add the vanilla extract. Chill. Then add three cups cream and mix well with a whisk.

Pour the mixture into the small, clean coffee can. Secure the plastic lid in place and use the electrical tape to make the lid watertight.

Place the small coffee can into the large coffee can. Fill the rest of the large can with ice up to the top of the small can. Fill the rest of the space with rock salt. Secure the plastic lid in place and use the electrical tape to make the lid watertight.

Take the can outside and roll it across the lawn or patio for fifteen minutes. Bring the can back inside, peel the tape from the lid of the large can, pour out the melted ice and salt, and refill with fresh ice and fresh salt. Secure the lid in place again, and roll the can outside for another fifteen minutes.

Bring the can back inside, peel off the tape from the larger can, pour out the melted ice and salt, and wash off the smaller can with tap water from the sink. Dry the can.

Store in the freezer for twelve hours. Peel off the tape from the smaller can, remove the lid, and scoop the contents into bowls.

STRANGE FACTS

• Mixing ice with salt in the compartment around the small can creates freezing temperatures, causing the mixture inside the small can to freeze. Rolling the large can causes the smaller can to roll around in the ice. As the smaller can rolls, air bubbles are whipped into the ice cream, increasing the volume of the mix.

• No one knows when ice cream was first invented or who invented it. In the late 1500s, Europeans used ice, snow, and saltpeter to freeze mixtures of cream, fruit, and spices. (Saltpeter, known to chemists as potassium nitrate, is commonly believed to reduce a man's animalistic urges. It doesn't.)

• Almost all ice cream was made at home until 1851, when Baltimore milk dealer Jacob Fussell established the first ice-cream factory.

• The edible ice-cream cone, invented by Italo Marchiony of Hoboken, New Jersey, was first served at the 1904 World's Fair in St. Louis, Missouri.

• The most popular flavor of ice cream in the United States is vanilla, accounting for approximately one-third of all the ice cream sold in the country. The second most popular flavor is chocolate, followed by strawberry.

• The United States produces more than one billion gallons of ice cream, ice milk, sherbet, and water ice every year.

• Approximate ten percent of all the milk produced in the United States is used to make ice cream and other frozen desserts.

• Americans eat more ice cream than do the people of any other nation in the world.

• The average American eats roughly 14.5 quarts of ice cream in a year.

• On July 24, 1988, Palm Dairies Ltd. of Alberta, Canada, created the world's largest ice-cream sundae—made from 44,689 pounds, 8 ounces of ice cream, 9,688 pounds, 2 ounces of syrup, and 537 pounds, 3 ounces of topping.

Maple Syrup

WHAT YOU NEED

From a maple equipment supplier:
- Standard size spout taps
- Filters (wool or Orlon)

From the kitchen:
- Clean, empty water jugs
- Stainless steel baking pan (approximately 12-by-16-by-3 inches)
- Wooden spoon
- Pot
- Clean empty bottles with screw-on lids

From the workshop:
- Electric drill with a $^7/_{16}$-inch bit
- Hammer

WHAT TO DO

Sap for maple syrup is collected in late winter or early spring when the weather warms and the sap starts flowing. The time to tap maple trees is when the temperature rises above freezing during the day (40 degrees Fahrenheit and sunny is best) and falls below freezing at night.

Identify the tree, making sure it is a sugar maple tree. The leaf of the sugar maple looks like the leaf on the Canadian flag.

Measure the circumference of the tree at 4.5 feet above the ground. A tree with a circumference less than 31 inches should not be tapped. A tree with a circumference between 31 and 63 inches may have no more than one tap. A tree with a circumference from 64 to 79 inches may have up to two taps. A tree with a circumference over 79 inches may have a maximum of three taps. Trees with large crowns extending down towards the ground usually produce the best sap.

On a warm day when the temperature is above freezing, use a $^{7}/_{16}$-inch bit to drill a taphole two inches deep into unblemished bark at a convenient height. If you are using smaller or larger taps, use the appropriate-size bit and drill the tap hole 1.5 inches deep. Drill the taphole at a slightly upward angle to enable the sap to flow freely. Drill more than two feet directly above or below a previous taphole and at least six inches away from the side of a previous taphole. Make sure the drill bit is sharp to avoid clogging the taphole with rough wood, inhibiting the flow of sap and reducing the quality of the sap. Use a hammer to gently tap the spout snuggly into the hole—without splitting the tree. Make certain the tap cannot be pulled out by hand.

Hang a clean, empty water jug on the hook of the spout. Do not leave collected sap in the water jugs, especially in warm weather. Sap will sour like milk if left in the sun. Refrigerate the sap and boil as soon as possible.

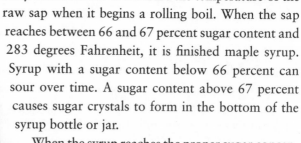

Once you have collected enough sap (2.5 gallons of sap yields one cup of syrup), fill a pan halfway with sap, and boil using a hobby-sized evaporator, an outdoor gas range, an outdoor fireplace, or an indoor wood stove (with a ventilation fan). As the sap boils down, stir frequently with the wooden spoon and add more sap, keeping the level at least 1.5 inches deep in the pan (to avoid burning the syrup). Never leave boiling sap unattended.

Use a syrup hydrometer to measure the sugar content of the syrup, and use a syrup or candy thermometer to measure the temperature of the raw sap when it begins a rolling boil. When the sap reaches between 66 and 67 percent sugar content and 283 degrees Fahrenheit, it is finished maple syrup. Syrup with a sugar content below 66 percent can sour over time. A sugar content above 67 percent causes sugar crystals to form in the bottom of the syrup bottle or jar.

When the syrup reaches the proper sugar concentration and temperature, filter the syrup while still hot through clean wool or Orlon (available from maple equipment dealers) into a pot to remove "sugar sand." If you lack the proper filter, pour the syrup into a jar, and let sit for twenty-four hours, allowing the sediment to settle to the bottom. Pour off the clear syrup (leaving the sediment in the jar), reheat to 180 degrees Fahrenheit, and then pour into sanitized containers for final storage.

Pour the hot syrup into steril-
ized canning jars, leaving very
little air in the jar, and seal.

Store the finished maple syrup
in a cool, dry place, with the jars
turned on their sides to coat the
lids of the jars, sealing the air
space. Refrigerate after opening.
If mold forms on stored syrup, heat the syrup to 190 degrees Fahrenheit, skim off the mold, and store the syrup in a sanitized jar.

Never use soaps or detergents to clean any syrup-making equipment, otherwise the residue will taint the syrup. Clean your equipment with a solution of three-quarters cup chlorine bleach to one gallon water. Scrub with a brush and triple-rinse with hot water. Wash filters with hot water only. Store equipment in a dry place.

STRANGE FACTS

• No one knows who first discovered how to make syrup and sugar from the sap of a maple tree. Native Americans who lived near the Great Lakes and the St. Lawrence River produced maple sugar and syrup long before explorers came to North America. Early French and English explorers wrote of the "sweet water" that the natives drew from trees, collected in buckets made from bark, and heated to make maple products. The Native Americans processed the sap by either freezing it and scooping off the layer of ice which formed on top, or filling the buckets with hot stones that caused the excess water to evaporate.

• Native Americans in the Northeast seasoned virtually all their food with maple syrup and sometimes used cakes of maple sugar as currency.

• Maple sap is generally harvested from early February until mid-April when freezing nights interspersed with warmer days make for ideal weather conditions for collecting sugary sap.

- The average maple tree produces some forty gallons of sap a week.
- The average taphole in a maple tree yields between five and fifteen gallons—depending on the tapping method, tree size, and seasonal variations.
- A single taphole can produce up to eighty gallons of sap in a single year.
- On average, ten gallons of sap yield one quart of syrup.
- Maple trees tend to yield sap with high sugar content in the morning and lower sugar content in the afternoon.
- In the fall, maple trees cease growing and begin storing excess starches throughout the sapwood, primarily in ray cells. Whenever the temperature of the wood nears 40 degrees Fahrenheit, enzymes in the ray cells change the starches to sugars, which then pass into the tree sap.
- When the temperature of the wood rises to roughly 45 degrees Fahrenheit, the enzymes stop functioning, and sugar production ceases. In March and April, the sugar changes back to starch.
- Maple trees grow throughout Europe, but climatic conditions inhibit the trees from producing sweetened sap.
- In medieval times, Europeans pickled maple leaves as a delicacy.
- Maple syrup became more popular among American colonists than imported cane sugar, which was heavily taxed and produced by slave labor.
- Until the turn of the twentieth century, maple syrup was the most popular sweetener in the Northeastern United States.
- Maple trees must be at least thirty-five-years old to produce enough sap to make tapping worthwhile.

Log Cabin Syrup

As demand for maple syrup grew, the liquid gold—produced slowly during a relatively short season in one small corner of the world—became the world's most expensive sweetener. In 1887, to meet the demand and reduce the cost of maple syrup, Minnesota grocer P. J. Towle created Log Cabin Syrup, a hybrid of inexpensive corn syrup flavored with a touch of maple syrup. Sold in a tin canister shaped like President Abraham Lincoln's boyhood home, Log Cabin Syrup became a huge success, paving the way for many similar "maple syrup" products. In 1891, North Dakota alone sold more so-called "Vermont maple syrup" than the state of Vermont produced.

OREO COOKIES

In 1912, following the success of Animal Crackers, Nabisco launched a new variation on the biscuit called "Oreo biscuit," consisting of "two beautifully embossed, chocolate flavored wafers with a rich creme filling." Nabisco eventually renamed the cookie the "Oreo Creme Sandwich," and in 1974, it became the "Oreo Chocolate Sandwich Cookie."

No one at Nabisco knows for certain how Oreo got its name. Some say the name is based on the French word *or*, meaning gold, a color printed on early Oreo packages. Others say that the first chairman of the National Biscuit Company, Adolphus Green, derived the name Oreos from the Greek word *oros*, meaning mountains, because the cookie was originally designed to have a hill-shaped top. Legend also holds that the word Oreo originated by sandwiching the letters *re* from the word *cream* between the two letters O from the word *chocolate*.

Regardless of how the cookie got its name, Oreo immediately became the number-one selling cookie in America. Today, the Oreo is the best-selling cookie in the world.

STRANGE FACTS

• The Oreo measures $1^3/_4$ inches in diameter.
• The original design on the Oreo cookie depicted a thin wreath encircling the word Oreo. Over time, the wreath became more elaborate and a decorative circle surrounded the word Oreo. Today, a ring of posies surrounds the Nabisco logo, which encloses the word Oreo.
• The creme filling used in one year to fill Oreo cookies could ice 4.7 million three-tier wedding cakes.
• If every Oreo cookie ever made (more than 362 billion) were stacked on top of each other, they would reach to the moon and back more than five times.
• Originally the cream filling in Oreo cookies was made with pork lard. Today Oreo cookies are certified kosher and do not contain any animal products.
• Americans eat more than five billion Oreo cookies every year.
• In 1975, Nabisco introduced Double Stuf, an Oreo cookie with twice the amount of creme.
• In 1987, Nabisco launched Fudge Covered Oreo Chocolate Sandwich Cookies and an enormous version of the Oreo called Oreo Big Stuf.

Do-It-Yourself Recipe
HOMEMADE "OREOS"

WHAT YOU NEED

From the supermarket:

- 2$^1/_2$ cups all-purpose flour
- 1 teaspoon baking powder
- $^1/_2$ teaspoon salt
- 3 ounces bittersweet chocolate, melted
- 1$^1/_3$ cups butter
- 1 cup granulated sugar
- 2 eggs
- 1 tablespoon milk
- 1$^1/_2$ teaspoons vanilla extract
- 6 tablespoons cream cheese
- 1$^3/_4$ cups confectioners' sugar
- 1 tablespoon cream

From the tap:

- Water

WHAT TO DO

Mix the flour, baking powder, and salt together in a medium bowl.

Place an inch of water into the bottom section of a double boiler. Heat the water on the stove to a gentle simmer. Do not let the water boil.

With a sharp knife, cut the chocolate into very small pieces or grate it with a grater. Place the chocolate pieces all at once into the top of the double boiler. Stir the chocolate constantly with a spoon until the chocolate melts. Remove the chocolate from the heat the instant it melts (otherwise the chocolate may scorch).

Using an electric mixer on medium speed, beat one cup butter and the granulated sugar for three minutes, or until light and fluffy, then add the melted chocolate. Add the eggs, milk, and

$^1/_2$ teaspoon vanilla extract. Add the flour mixture and blend thoroughly.

Split the dough in half, roll each portion into a log roughly two inches thick and eight inches long. Wrap each log in Saran Wrap and place in the freezer for thirty minutes, or until firm.

Preheat the oven to 375 degrees Fahrenheit. Cut slices from each log $^1/_4$-inch thick. Place the slices two inches apart from each other on ungreased baking sheets. Bake for eight minutes, let cool for two minutes, then place the cookies on a rack to cool completely.

To make the filling, mix the cream cheese, $^1/_3$ cup butter, confectioners' sugar, cream, and one teaspoon vanilla extract thoroughly. Spread the filling on half the cookies, then top with the remaining halves. Makes 25 cookies.

QUAKER OATS

In 1856, Ferdinand Schumacher, a German immigrant running a grocery store in Akron, Ohio, ground up oatmeal in such a way as to reduce cooking time, packing his prepared oatmeal in barrels and convenient glass jars—popularizing oatmeal as a breakfast food. Schumacher founded the German Mills American Oatmeal Company and became known as the "Oatmeal King." His success inspired the launch of dozens of other oatmeal companies, including the Quaker Mill Company, founded in 1877 in Ravena, Ohio, by Henry D. Seymour and William Heston.

Seymour, one of the founders of the American Cereal Company, purportedly originated the name Quaker Oats when he came across an article on the Quakers in an encyclopedia and was struck by the similarity between the religious group's qualities and the image he desired for oatmeal. A second story contends that Seymour's partner, William Heston, a descendant of Quakers, was walking in Cincinnati one day and saw a picture of William Penn, the English Quaker, and was similarly convinced that the name Quaker would denote quality.

At that time, general stores bought oatmeal in nondescript barrels, selling it to customers by scooping it into brown paper bags. In 1880, Henry Crowell, president of the American Cereal Company, purchased the Quaker Mill Company and visualized the advantages of selling packaged products directly to consumers, packaging Quaker brand oatmeal in the now famous cardboard canister and launching an advertising campaign. In 1901, the Quaker Mill Company, the American Cereal Company, and the German Mills American Oatmeal Company merged to form The Quaker Oats Company.

STRANGE FACTS
• The name Quaker Oats inspired several lawsuits. The Quakers themselves unsuccessfully petitioned the United States Congress to bar trademarks with religious connotations.

• Explorer Robert Peary carried Quaker Oats to the North Pole, and explorer Admiral Richard Byrd carried Quaker Oats to the South Pole.

• A gigantic likeness of the Quaker Oats man was placed on the White Cliffs of Dover in England, requiring an act of Parliament to have it removed.

• In 1990, when the Quaker Oats Company used Popeye the Sailor Man in oatmeal ads, the Quakers objected, insisting that Popeye's reliance on physical violence is incompatible with the religion's pacifist principles. The Quaker Oats Company quickly apologized and ended the campaign.

A&P

The Big Boys

In 1859, tea and spice merchants George Huntington Hartford and George Gilman founded the Great American Tea Company as a mail order business. Two years later, the partners opened their first store in New York City, selling teas and coffees at the corner of Broadway and Grand Street.

In 1870, in honor of the completion of the first transcontinental railroad a year earlier, Hartford and Gilman renamed their company the Great Atlantic and Pacific Tea Company. Six years later, A&P had one hundred stores, making the company the nation's first major grocery chain. In the decade that followed, A&P employed peddlers to drive horse-drawn wagons along five thousand routes nationwide.

STRANGE FACTS

• In 1924, A&P sponsored the A&P Radio Hour, America's first national radio program.

• In 1930, A&P introduced private label products at substantial savings to customers over brand-name products.

• In 1937, A&P launched *Woman's Day* magazine. It sold for two cents a copy.

• Over the years, A&P acquired several grocery chains, including Kohl's, Dominion, Waldbaum's, Shopwell-Food Emporium, Farmer Jack, Miracle Food Mart, Ultra Food Mart Stores, and the Barn.

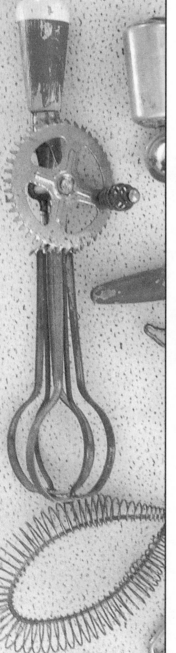

Words of Wisdom

When life seems to get you down,
it might be time to increase your medication.

If a tree falls in the woods,
it's best to move out of its way.

You don't have to go looking for trouble.
Trouble will find you.

If you sleep like a baby,
you don't have one.

Instead of taking wedding vows,
some couples should take vows of silence.

It's difficult to live with yourself
if you have no idea who you are.

The best way to get over amnesia
is to forget about it.

You can't fight fire with marshmallows.

Put your trust in God,
but wear your seat belt just in case.

Winning isn't everything
unless you're playing Russian Roulette.

Early to bed, early to rise
works out exactly the same as
late to bed, late to rise.

Give me the courage to change the things I can,
the wisdom to accept the things I can't,
and the brains to call a plumber if I'm not exactly sure.

If you take the road less traveled,
make sure you have a spare tire and a jack.

It's never too late to say you're sorry,
and it's only five cents a minute
on evenings and weekends.

People who live in glass houses
get an awful lot of advice
considering how few there are.

There's no such thing as a good haircut.

Bank tellers have nothing to tell.

If you borrow from Peter to pay Paul,
make sure Peter has the lowest interest rate.

"New and improved" generally isn't.

No one has ever lost a needle in a haystack.

God helps those who
stop and ask for directions.

A buttered piece of bread
always lands butter-side down.

The pen is mightier than the sword,
unless you're having a duel.

Appearances are deceiving
especially under fluorescent lights.

Be careful what you wish for,
it's sure to be taxable.

I was sad because I had no shoes
until I went to the bowling alley
and saw what kind of shoes they rent.

The people who kick you when you're down and out
always seem to be wearing golf cleats.

Love at first sight saves a lot of time.

Throw yourself into everything you do
—unless you're a grave digger.

You always get a second chance
to make a bad impression.

It's better to have loved and lost
than to be nagged about buying
a damn anniversary gift every year.

Never buy tickets for a Broadway show
advertised on the back of a milk carton.

Happiness is the simple things in life,
like finding the derivative of the function
$f(x)5cx^n$ as its limit approaches 9.

Salisbury Steak is just
a hamburger covered in gravy.

Practice makes perfect
unless you're trying to be spontaneous.

A day without sunshine
is a lot like night.

BON AMI

Around 1886, the Williams Soap Company of Manchester, Connecticut, decided to create a scouring soap to compete against Sapolio, a scouring soap made from finely ground quartz and tallow soap. When mined, quartz was found entwined with feldspar, a softer mineral that was separated from the quartz by handheld "cobbing" hammers and discarded. Realizing that feldspar might be combined with soap to make a less abrasive cleansing product, factory superintendent J. T. Robertson quit his job at the Williams Soap Company and went into business for himself, founding the J. T. Robertson Soap Company of Manchester, Connecticut.

Using an abandoned grist mill on property owned by Gurdon Hicks Childs, Robertson ground feldspar into a fine powder and mixed it with liquid soap in wooden troughs to make cakes of soap embossed with the name Bon Ami (French for "good friend").

In 1890, Child's son, William H. Childs, and his nephew, William Henry Harrison Childs, went into business together as Childs and Childs to serve as the exclusive sales agent for Bon Ami. Wrapped bars of Bon Ami sold for ten cents and featured a depiction of a yellow chick accompanied by the slogan "Hasn't Scratched Yet!" Sales skyrocketed, making Bon Ami one of the most popular cleansers in the United States, but fifty years later, several changes of ownership and management caused sales to plummet. Bon Ami nearly vanished from the marketplace.

In 1971, the Faultless Starch Company bought the Bon Ami product line, and three years later, changed its own name to Faultless Starch/Bon Ami Company.

STRANGE FACTS

• The Bon Ami chick and slogan referred to the fact that a newly hatched chick lives off the nutrients of the yolk for another two or three days before scratching the ground for food. Bon Ami, like a baby chick, "Hasn't Scratched Yet."

• During the first decade of the twentieth century, Bon Ami advertised in leading women's magazines with beautiful full-color, full-page paintings of the

Last Supper Mishaps

• In his mural *The Last Supper* in the church and former Dominican monastery of Santa Maria delle Grazie in Milan, Italy, Leonardo da Vinci depicted a Passover Seder with Jesus and his disciples sitting upright at the table. Jews sit at a Seder table in a reclining position to symbolize their freedom from slavery.

• In his 1480 fresco *Last Supper* in the Church of Ognissanti in Florence, Italy, artist Domenico Ghirlandajo depicted bread rolls on the Passover Seder table. Leavened bread is forbidden during Passover. Jesus and his disciples would have eaten matzah.

• A painting of the *Last Supper* in the cathedral on the northeast side of the Plaza de Armas in Cuzco, Peru, portrays Jesus and his disciples about to dine on an Inca delicacy—roast guinea pig.

chicks by noted Pennsylvania artist Ben Austrian and produced lithographic prints of the original paintings.

• In November 1913, Cornell University suspended the editor of the *Cornell Widow*, the college humor magazine, for publishing the following off-color joke:

> HE: I'll bet you are chicken. Aren't you now?
>
> SHE: Yes, I'm chicken all right, but I'm not scratching for you.

University administrators claimed that the joke contained an antiquated obscenity; the editor insisted that the joke referred to the Bon Ami slogan.

• In 1980, the company ran a national magazine advertising campaign with the headline: "Never Underestimate the Cleaning Power of a 94-Year-Old Chick With a French Name."

• Today, Bon Ami is the third best-selling powdered cleanser in the United States.

• Bon Ami is one of the most environmentally friendly cleaners because it does not contain phosphates, chlorine, bleach, or dyes.

Secret Formula

PEPPERMINT AIR FRESHENER

WHAT YOU NEED

From the supermarket:
- 1 cup distilled white vinegar

From the health food store:
- 25 drops essential oil of peppermint

From the tap:
- $1/2$ cup water, plus a few tablespoons of water

WHAT TO DO

Using a funnel, fill a refillable eight- or sixteen-ounce fine-mist spray bottle with vinegar, add the essential oil of peppermint (or any essential oil you may prefer). Makes eight ounces.

HOW YOU USE IT

Shake well, and spray as necessary to eliminate nasty odors around your house in a jiffy. Vinegar—a timeless classic embraced by homemakers for centuries—magically deodorizes the air, while the hypnotic blend of peppermint delights the senses with an exhilarating blast of homey freshness.

Secret Formula

EUCALYPTUS ALL-PURPOSE CLEANSER

WHAT YOU NEED

From the supermarket:
- 2 tablespoons distilled white vinegar
- 1 tablespoon borax

From the health food store:
- $1/4$ cup Dr. Bronner's Peppermint Oil Soap
- 12 drops essential oil of eucalyptus

From the tap:
- 2 cups hot water

WHAT TO DO

Using a funnel, mix the vinegar and borax in a refillable sixteen-ounce trigger-spray bottle. Fill the rest of the bottle with the hot water. Shake well, making certain the borax is dissolved so it doesn't clog the spray nozzle. Add the liquid soap and essential oil of eucalyptus. Shake well. Makes $2^1/4$ cups.

HOW YOU USE IT

Spray this exhilarating eucalyptus cleanser on counters, walls, tub and tile, or the refrigerator, and wipe clean. It's wholesome, packed with sparkling cleansing power, and fragrant with the delightful old-fashioned aroma of eucalyptus. So why not give the family a clean house they're sure to love!

Secret Formula

PEPPERMINT
ALL-PURPOSE CLEANSER

WHAT YOU NEED
From the supermarket:
- ¹/₄ cup baking soda
- ¹/₄ cup lemon juice
- ¹/₈ cup borax

From the health food store:
- 1 tablespoon Dr. Bronner's Peppermint Oil Soap

From the tap:
- 1 gallon warm water

WHAT TO DO
Mix the ingredients together well in a bucket. Apply with a sponge or mop, then rinse and dry. For stubborn stains, use a nylon scrubber. Or fill a refillable sixteen-ounce trigger-spray bottle. Makes one gallon.

HOW YOU USE IT
Use this zesty cleanser for spot cleaning. It's got the gentle abrasive strength of baking soda and the pure goodness of lemon juice, all fortified with the unfailing power of borax—and topped off with the freshness of peppermint oil.

It all adds up to the cleanest cleanser you ever cleansed clean!

Secret Formula

LEMON ALL-PURPOSE
SCOURING POWDER

WHAT YOU NEED
From the supermarket:
- 1 cup baking soda
- 1 cup salt
- 1 cup borax

From the health food store:
- 20 drops essential oil of lemon

WHAT TO DO
In a large bowl, mix the ingredients well. Fill a plastic flip-top shaker with the mixture. Makes twenty-four ounces.

HOW YOU USE IT
Sprinkle on counters, in the sink, or in the tub, then wipe with a damp sponge. Rinse well.

This remarkable scouring powder—made with three mild abrasives that have stood the test the time—evokes the sweet scent of a lemon grove in the bright morning sun. It's virtually guaranteed to catapult your senses back to that wonderful bygone era best known as yesteryear.

Secret Formula

CARPET CLEANSER

WHAT YOU NEED

From the supermarket or health food store:

- 6 drops Dr. Bronner's Peppermint Oil Soap
- 1 cup club soda

WHAT TO DO

Mix a few drops of Dr. Bronner's Peppermint Oil Soap with club soda in a small bowl to make a foamy cleaner. Makes one cup.

HOW YOU USE IT

Rub this simple yet mighty concoction into the stained area and scrub with a brush. Rinse well with water. Then blot up immediately. Be sure to treat carpet stains the moment they happen. Once they dry into the carpet, they're almost always impossible to clean.

This delightfully effective carpet cleanser is plenty pure and mild, yet strong enough to battle the toughest stains.

Secret Formula

DISHWASHER POWDER

WHAT YOU NEED

From the supermarket:

- 3 cups borax
- 3 cups washing soda (sodium carbonate)

From the drugstore or chemical supply house:

- 1 tablespoon sodium silicate

From the hardware store:

- 3 ounces TSP (trisodium phosphate) (optional)

WHAT TO DO

Mix the borax, sodium carbonate, and sodium silicate in a bowl. (If you need to boost the powder with phosphates, add the TSP.) Remember, phosphates contribute to accelerated eutrophication, causing rapid algae blooms in lakes and ponds that can suffocate aquatic plants and animals. Most commercial automatic dishwasher detergents contain 7.5 percent phosphates; this recipe contains 6.25 percent phosphates.) Blend well. Store in a sealed, airtight container. Keep out of reach of children. Makes nearly $6^1/_2$ cups.

HOW YOU USE IT

Fill the receptacle cup in the dishwasher with this power-packed powder known as a full-fledged menace to dirty dishes. This robust powder will give your dishes a sparkling shine that spells success, inspires poetry, and makes dinner guests marvel at your charms.

The Wife's side...

"I'M THE ONE that's going to use this range—so it's got to be fast! I'm too busy to wait around for the kettle to boil—or the oven to warm up—Yes! I want the instant high heat and the cleanness of Gas—the flexibility of Gas that gives me any degree of heat I need. I want all the wonderful new time-saving and work-saving features I'd get on a modern Gas range—signal simmer burners . . . oven heat control . . . a 'smokeless' broiler . . . lots of storage space . . . automatic lighting . . . Oh! and dozens more! Golly! bet I'd be a better cook, too—if I had a marvelous new Gas range!"

The Husband's side...

"I'M THE ONE that's going to pay the bills for food and fuel—so the economy and efficiency of Gas make sense to me! I want a range that will last for years and won't need costly replacements—that means a Gas range too! And I want one that's as good looking and up-to-the-minute in its way as my new car— One we'll be proud to show our friends—like the beauty I saw in a store window just this morning! Yes! guess it would be smart to take Mary downtown and have her pick one out tomorrow!"

GAS— THE WONDER FUEL FOR COOKING

Show your husband (or wife!) the new Gas ranges at your Gas Appliance Dealer's or Gas Company. The many exclusive advantages of modern Gas service have been made possible by the Gas utilities of America which, through their laboratories and other agencies, are constantly improving their service to you.

AMERICAN GAS ASSOCIATION

ET GAS DO THE BIG JOBS—COOKING • WATER HEATING • REFRIGERATION • HOUSE HEATING

Secret Formula

TEA TREE OIL DISINFECTANT

WHAT YOU NEED
From the supermarket:
- 1 cup distilled white vinegar

From the health food store:
- 30 drops tea tree oil

From the tap:
- 1 cup water

WHAT TO DO
Using a funnel, mix the ingredients in a refillable sixteen-ounce trigger-spray bottle. Makes sixteen ounces.

HOW YOU USE IT
Shake well and spray this unmistakably superb disinfectant to freshen and deodorize the air or as an antiseptic spray to clean counters and faucets with a sponge. You'll love everything about this disinfectant—its natural deodorizing power, its hearty strength, and its keen fresh scent.

Secret Formula

APPLE FLOOR CLEANSER

WHAT YOU NEED
From the supermarket:
- 1 cup distilled white vinegar

From the health food store:
- 20 drops apple fragrance

From the tap:
- 1 cup water

WHAT TO DO
Using a funnel, mix ingredients in a sixteen-ounce trigger-spray bottle. Shake well. Makes sixteen ounces.

HOW YOU USE IT
Most floor cleaners make floors dull because the soap residue left on the floor acts like glue, attracting dirt build-up and compelling you to use noxious ammonia and hot water to remove it. All you really need to keep non-wax floors, polyurethane-finished wood floors, brick floors, ceramic tile floors, or stone floors sparkling clean is to dust mop with this gentle cleanser.

Just spray this simple homemade floor cleaner directly on the floor and wipe clean with a rag or mop, leaving a floor that shines with the exhilarating scent of freshly picked apples. You know what they say about an apple a day!

Secret Formula

FLOOR WAX

WHAT YOU NEED
From a hardware store:
- 1 cup turpentine

From a hobby center or candle supply house:
- 8 ounces carnauba wax shavings
- 8 ounces paraffin shavings

WHAT TO DO
In the top of a double boiler, warm the turpentine, then add the carnauba and paraffin shavings and stir until melted, using caution to make certain this flammable mixture does not overheat or spill on a hot surface. Remove from the heat, pour into a glass jar, and let cool.

If the wax is too hard, soften it in the double boiler and add more turpentine.

Makes two cups.

HOW YOU USE IT
Apply this simple wax to wooden floors with a cloth and buff. In 1886, Samuel Curtis Johnson went into business selling parquet floors out of a hardware store in Racine, Wisconsin.

When customers asked for his help to preserve the wood floors, Johnson mixed up batches of paste wax for sale. By 1898, wax sales had topped the flooring sales, and Johnson suddenly found himself running Johnson Wax, an entirely different business than the one he had started. If a parquet floor salesman can mix up floor wax, obviously you can too.

Secret Formula

ALL-NATURAL LEMON FURNITURE POLISH

WHAT YOU NEED
From the supermarket:
- 2 tablespoons olive oil
- 1/4 cup white distilled vinegar

From the health food store:
- 20 drops essential oil of lemon

From the tap:
- 1 3/4 cups water

WHAT TO DO
Using a funnel, pour the olive oil into a refillable sixteen-ounce trigger-spray bottle. Add the essential oil of lemon, vinegar, and water. Shake well and label. Makes sixteen ounces.

HOW YOU USE IT
Shake well. Spray onto a clean, soft cloth or directly onto furniture, then buff dry.

This powerful all-natural polish gives furniture a fine luster, penetrates deeply, and rejuvenates natural woods, yet it's so gentle you can even use it as zesty salad dressing.

Secret Formula

MOLD AND MILDEW CLEANSER

WHAT YOU NEED

From the supermarket:
- ¹/₂ teaspoon borax
- ¹/₂ teaspoon distilled white vinegar

From the hardware store:
- ¹/₂ teaspoon TSP (trisodium phosphate)

From the health food store:
- ¹/₂ teaspoon Dr. Bronner's Peppermint Oil Soap

From the tap:
- 2 cups warm-to-hot water

WHAT TO DO

Using a funnel, combine the ingredients in a refillable sixteen-ounce trigger-spray bottle and shake well. Makes sixteen ounces.

HOW YOU USE IT

Save time and win happiness by applying this vigorous tile cleanser with a sponge, wearing rubber gloves to protect your delicate hands. Then rinse with clear water. Yes, clean tiles are only a moment away with this easy-to-use, easy-to-make cleanser.

Secret Formula

PINE CLEANSER

WHAT YOU NEED

From the health food store:
- 1 cup Dr. Bronner's Sal Suds
- 10 drops tea tree oil

From the tap:
- 2¹/₂ cups warm water

WHAT TO DO

Using a funnel, mix the ingredients in clean plastic bottle (or empty Pine-Sol bottle), shake well, and label. Makes 22 fluid ounces concentrate (fourteen gallons cleanser).

HOW YOU USE IT

Shake well before using. Add one-quarter cup per gallon warm water in a bucket, then mop or sponge as you would with any pine cleanser. With this homemade cleanser, you get a rejuvenating clean pine scent without an unnecessarily high percentage of pine oil. (Pine-Sol contains 20 percent pine oil. Dr. Bronner's Sal Suds contains less than 1 percent pine needle oil, a much more refined pine oil used primarily as fragrance.)

Secret Formula

OVEN CLEANER

WHAT YOU NEED
From the supermarket:
- 2 teaspoons borax
- $^1/_2$ cup ammonia

From the health food store:
- 1 tablespoon Dr. Bronner's Peppermint Oil Soap

From the kitchen:
- Lemon All-Purpose Scouring Powder (see page 279)

From the tap:
- $1^1/_2$ cups warm water

From the hardware store:
- Rubber gloves
- Respirator
- Protective goggles

WHAT TO DO
Using a funnel, pour the borax, ammonia, soap, and water into a refillable sixteen-ounce trigger-spray bottle. Shake well until all the crystals dissolve to avoid clogging the spray nozzle. Makes two cups.

HOW YOU USE IT
Cover the floor in front of the oven with newspaper.

Open the windows to make certain the area is well ventilated. Wear rubber gloves, respirator, and protective goggles.

Spray the solution onto the oven surface. Wait ten minutes, then sprinkle homemade Lemon All-Purpose Scouring Powder on an area and scrub with a wet steel wool pad. Use more cleanser, water, and scouring powder if necessary. Wipe clean with a sponge and dry.

(Do not use on continuous-clean or self-cleaning ovens. In electric ovens, make sure you don't get any cleaning paste on the heating elements so they don't corrode when heated and short out.)

You'll be awestruck by how easily and effectively this oven cleaner does away with the agony of cleaning the oven.

Secret Formula

ALL-NATURAL TOILET BOWL CLEANER

WHAT YOU NEED
From the supermarket:
- 2 cups baking soda
- 2 tablespoons distilled white vinegar

From the health food store:
- 1/2 cup Dr. Bronner's Peppermint Oil Soap
- 1/2 teaspoon (50 drops) tea tree oil

From the tap:
- 1/4 cup water

WHAT TO DO
Using a funnel, mix the soap, baking soda, and water together in a twenty-two-ounce plastic squirt bottle (or clean, empty dishwashing liquid bottle). Shake well, then add the vinegar and tea tree oil. Makes twenty-two ounces.

HOW YOU USE IT
Shake well, then squirt the toilet bowl cleaner into the bowl and under the rim. Brush and flush. This cleanser is also gentle enough to use with a sponge on the toilet seat and rim. Rinse well. This powerful, nontoxic toilet bowl cleaner lets you plunge into cleaning your toilet with wild abandon. At last, a homemade cleaner that really does belong in the toilet!

Secret Formula

WINDOW CLEANSER

WHAT YOU NEED
From the supermarket:
- 1 cup white vinegar
- 5 drops blue food coloring

From the tap:
- 1 cup water

WHAT TO DO
Fill a refillable sixteen-ounce trigger-spray-bottle with the vinegar, water, and the food coloring (optional). Shake well and label. Makes sixteen ounces.

HOW YOU USE IT
A mixture of wholesome vinegar and regular water is all it takes to get your windows sparkling clean.

If you've been brainwashed by fast-talking Madison Avenue advertising execs that only a solution colored blue has the power and strength necessary to clean your windows, add a few drops of blue food coloring to this mixture to allay your fears.

Spray and wipe clean with a soft, lint-free cloth or a balled up sheet of newspaper.

This simple homemade recipe does a fantastic job cleaning windows for a fraction of the cost.

Secret Formula
WHOLE MILK SILVER POLISH

WHAT YOU NEED
From the supermarket:
- 1 cup whole milk
- 2 teaspoons cream of tartar (or 1 tablespoon white vinegar)

From the tap:
- Cold water

WHAT TO DO
Mix the milk and cream of tartar (or vinegar) in a shallow pan.

HOW YOU USE IT
Place the silverware in the milky mixture. Let stand, then rinse clean, and dry thoroughly. After a night luxuriating in this cool milk bath, your silver should shine like it did when Aunt Violet gave it to you for your wedding! Isn't it time you sent her a thank you card?

Secret Formula
MIRACLE SILVER POLISH

WHAT YOU NEED
From the supermarket:
- Reynolds Wrap aluminum foil
- Arm & Hammer Baking Soda

From the kitchen:
- A metal cake pan
- Measuring spoons
- Cooking thermometer

From the tap:
- 1 quart water

WHAT TO DO
Line the bottom of the metal cake pan with a sheet of Reynolds Wrap and fill with enough water to cover the silverware (roughly two inches). Add two tablespoons baking soda per quart of water.

HOW YOU USE IT
Using the cooking thermometer, heat the water above 150 degrees Fahrenheit. Place the tarnished silverware in the pan so it rests on the aluminum foil. Do not let the water boil. Let the silverware soak over the heat for ten minutes, then turn off the heat and let the water cool before removing the silverware.

The silver comes out sparkling clean—without any scrubbing. And Grandma will be bursting with pride! You can bet on it!

If It's Open 24 Hours, Why Is It Called 7-Eleven?

The Big Boys

The name 7-Eleven originated in 1946 when the stores were open from 7 A.M. to 11 P.M. Today, nearly 95 percent of all 7-Eleven stores in the United States and Canada are open twenty-four hours a day, making the store name a misnomer.

In 1927, Claude Dawley, son of an ice company pioneer, formed the Southland Ice Company in Dallas to buy four other Texas ice plant operations. Dawley put Joe Thompson, an employee at one of his newly acquired ice plants, in charge of the company's ice operations.

Thompson had demonstrated his business savvy by selling chilled watermelons from the truck docks, increasing profits

for the company. When an ice dock manager in Dallas showed Thompson how he stocked a few food items to sell to customers, Thompson instituted the convenience stores at all company locations. He called them U-Tote'm Stores, put up Alaska-made totem poles by the docks to promote them, and began building gas stations at some of the ice plants.

In 1930, Chicago utility magnate Martin Insull, who had financed Claude Dawley's initial bid to buy the four ice plants, bought out Dawley and made Thompson president. By 1946, the company had bought other Texas ice-retail operations, changed its name to the Southland Corporation, and renamed its stores 7-Eleven.

After Joe Thompson died in 1961, his eldest son, John, became president, opened new 7-Eleven stores in other states, and began buying other grocery

Sunbeam
BREAD WITH A BONUS
More Energy
More Nutrition
More Flavor

STRANGE FACTS

• Silver gradually darkens because silver chemically reacts with sulfur-containing substances in the air to form silver sulfide, which is black. With this secret formula, a chemical reaction converts the silver sulfide back into silver—without removing any of the silver. Like silver, aluminum forms compounds with sulfur—but with a greater affinity than silver. With this formula, sulfur atoms are

chains. Southland franchised the 7-Eleven format in the United Kingdom in 1971 and in Japan in 1973.

In 1988, Thompson and his two brothers borrowed heavily to buy 70 percent of Southland's stock in a leveraged buyout. Two years later, they defaulted on 1.8 billion dollars in loans and filed for bankruptcy, clearing the way for Southland's Japanese partner, Ito-Yokado, to buy 70 percent of the company for 430 million dollars.

7-Eleven stores are geared toward people who need to buy a quart of milk, a bottle of aspirin, a cup of coffee, or a lottery ticket in a hurry. Each store carries a selection of up to three thousand different products and services tailored to meet the needs and preferences of local customers. Today, 7-Eleven is best known for its Slurpee, Big Gulp, and Slim Jims.

STRANGE FACTS

• 7-Eleven sells more lottery tickets and prepaid phone cards than any other retailer in the United States.

• 7-Eleven stores in North America serve approximately six million customers every day.

• 7-Eleven has filed for bankruptcy twice: first, during the Depression, and again in 1990 after President John Thompson and his two brothers could not pay back 1.8 billion dollars in loans.

• There are at least one thousand more 7-Eleven stores in Japan than in the United States.

• There are more 7-Eleven stores in Hong Kong than in New York, New Jersey, and West Virginia combined.

• Armed robbers hit 7-Eleven stores more often than any other chain in the United States.

transferred from silver to aluminum, freeing the silver metal and forming aluminum sulfide. The warm baking soda solution carries the sulfur from the silver to the aluminum, creating aluminum sulfide, which adheres to the aluminum foil or forms tiny yellow flakes in the bottom of the pan.

• The silver and aluminum must be in contact with each other for this secret formula to work because a small electric current flows between them during the reaction.

• Polishing silverware with an abrasive cleanser removes the silver sulfide and some of the silver from the surface. Other chemical tarnish removers dissolve the silver sulfide, but also remove some of the silver.

8

APPAREL & FOOTWEAR

Keeping Your Pants Up and Your Feet Warm

In small town America, most people made their own clothes from woven fabrics, using an invention developed by Elias Howe and Isaac Singer—the sewing machine. In the mid-1800s, manufacturers began making inexpensive "ready-made" clothing. Still, most Americans continued making clothes by hand, aided by the paper dress pattern, invented and patented in 1864 by Ebenezer Butterick of Sterling, Massachusetts. As improved manufacturing methods helped lower the cost of "ready-made" clothing, people began wearing mass-produced clothes. The country store carried a wide variety of corsets, suspenders, boots and shoes, mittens and gloves, hats, long underwear, and modest lingerie—not to mention a wide variety of soaps and gadgets needed to keep them clean and pressed.

FAULTLESS STARCH

In 1886 in Kansas City, Missouri, Major Thomas G. Beaham bought into Smith & Moffit, a company that sold coffee, tea, and spices. Soon renamed Beaham & Moffit, the company acquired the formula for Faultless Starch from Bosworth Manufacturing Company. In 1891, the company renamed itself Faultless Starch Company.

Homemakers quickly accepted the dry white starch for clothes because the product was simple to use and did not require lengthy boiling. Homemakers soon discovered that Faultless Starch also added an elegant finish to embroidery and lace, and could be used as a baby powder and a bath powder.

In the 1890s, salesman John Nesbitt brought wagonloads of books, designed as a supplement or substitute for school texts and primers, to Texas and attached them to boxes of Faultless Starch with rubber bands, popularizing Faultless Starch in the Lone State.

The company sold only dry laundry starch until 1960, when the company developed an aerosol starch. The introduction of permanent press and synthetic fabrics in the 1970s caused a drop in starch sales—until the use of cotton increased again, due to the rising price of synthetic, petroleum-derived fabrics and the return to more conservative and stylish fashions. The company is still run by the Beaham family with Gordon T. Beaham, III, the great-grandson of Major Thomas G. Beaham, serving as president and chairman of the board.

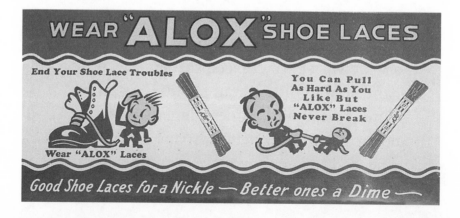

IRON

In the fourth century B.C.E., ancient Greeks used a heated cylinder called a "goffering iron" like a rolling pin to smooth wrinkled linen robes and create pleats. Two hundred years later, Roman slaves used a flat metal mallet called a "mangle" to hammer out creases and press wrinkled garments.

In the tenth century, Norse Vikings used an iron shaped like an upside-down mushroom to press wrinkles out of garments. Pleats in clothing distinguished the upper class from lower class because they could be achieved solely through time-consuming work, requiring slaves or servants. Five hundred years later, upper class Europeans owned irons with compartments that held heated coals. The lower classes used flat irons heated over a fire.

In the nineteenth century, inventors created gas-heated irons, but the devices, connected to gas lines, frequently leaked, exploded, and ignited fires. In 1882, Henry W. Weely invented the first electric iron. When plugged into its stand, the iron heated up. While being used, the iron cooled down rapidly, requiring the user to continually reheat the iron.

At the turn of the twentieth century, manufacturers produced a variety of electric irons—all weighing more than ten pounds. Unfortunately, most consumers could use this laborsaving device only at night because until 1905, most electric companies only ran their generators between

Now! Two Irons In One!

The G-E ALURON
(FOR "ALL YOU IRON")

New! Revolutionary! This amazing General Electric Double-Purpose Iron is the greatest contribution to easier, better ironing since the invention of the electric iron itself!

1. STEAM IRONS every kind of fabric from velvet to organdy. You can dial the steam for rayon, silk, woolens etc. No pressing cloth needed.

2. DRY IRONS cottons and linens. You can switch to "regular ironing" in one second! Gives you all the speed and light-gliding ease of America's Favorite Iron.

HERE'S a Double-Purpose iron that does all your ordinary ironing, and irons all these things you never dared touch with an iron before!
For steam ironing, the G-E Aluron gives you for the first time, controlled steam. Ready in 2 minutes! You can "dial" the steam as well as the fabric!
For dry ironing, this light,

streamlined beauty brings you the famous G-E "Dial-the-Fabric" and all the other improvements that make the G-E America's Favorite Iron.
So if you want to save time, work—plus money on pressing and cleaning bills—see the G-E Aluron today at your dealer's. Two irons in one. Only $16.95, taxes included!

All Prices and Specifications Subject to Change Without Notice. See Your Dealer.

GENERAL ELECTRIC

J.C. Penney and The Golden Rule

In 1902, twenty-six-year-old James Cash Penney, son of a Baptist minister, borrowed fifteen hundred dollars to team up with two former employers to open a dry goods store, The Golden Rule, in the small mining town of Kemmerer, Wyoming. Penney bought out his partners in 1907, giving him three stores, and he began opening more Penney's Golden Rule stores. Basing his customer service policy on his Baptist heritage, Penney insisted that his employees (called "associates") adhere to the Golden Rule, namely to treat customers as you would like to be treated.

Penney offered his store managers, usually former sales clerks, one-third partnerships in new stores, propelling the company's rapid expansion. The company incorporated in Utah in 1913 as the J. C. Penney Company, then moved its headquarters to New York City the following year. Between 1917 and 1929, the number of stores grew from 175 with fourteen million dollars in annual sales to 1,395 stores with 209 million dollars in sales. The company went public in 1929 and, with its reputation for high quality goods at low prices, continued expanding during the Depression. By the 1930s, Penney had a store in practically every town with more than five thousand people. Sales surpassed one billion dollars in 1951, four billion dollars in 1970, and sixteen billion dollars in 1990.

STRANGE FACTS

- JCPenney has more merchandizing space than any other department store in the United States—more than 114 million square feet. That's equal to 3,653 football fields.
- In 1995, the JCPenney Bridal Catalog sold more bridal apparel and accessories than any other store in the industry.
- The JCPenney Catalog is the number-one catalog in sales in the United States.
- As of 1995, JCPenney employed over 205,000 "associates." That's nearly half the population of Wyoming, the state where JCPenney began.
- The JCPenney Museum is located in the JCPenney Home Office in Plano, Texas.

The Big Boys

sunset and sunrise. Meanwhile in Ontario, California, Earl Richardson, a meter reader for an electric company, devised a homemade lightweight iron, and persuaded the power company to generate electricity all day on Tuesdays, the day most homemakers on his route ironed clothes. As housewives used more electricity, the power plant began generating electricity for longer hours.

In 1906, Richardson began manufacturing irons, which he named "Hot Point," after the fact that his original irons distributed the heat unevenly along the iron's flat plate, concentrating most of the heat at one spot.

By the time the first electric steam irons were introduced in 1926, Americans were buying more than three million electric irons a year. Steam irons did not catch on until twenty years later when clothing makers introduced synthetic fabrics that scorched easily under a hot iron. To sell more irons, steam iron manufacturers began increasing the number of steam holes as a competitive marketing gimmick. The number of holes in the bottom of a steam iron slowly escalated from eight large holes to seventy small holes—in what industry insiders called a "holy war."

I heard her say—
Maytag washes **everything**!

► CALM YOUR FEARS, Angus—you're safe. So, too, is *all* the family laundry that's washed in the spacious Maytag square tub. Even silks and heirloom linens are safe from strain and wear as they wash spic and span clean in Maytag's gentle gyrafoam water action. They're safe as they lose their suds and water in the selfadjusting damp-drier. And it's a safe bet that you'll exclaim over the speed and the lack of work that's connected with washing the Maytag way. Visit your Maytag dealer— try this new Maytag . . . and see for yourself.

THE NEW *Maytag*
COMMANDER

MRS. STEWART'S LIQUID BLUING

Color experts have distinguished approximately three hundreds shades of white—from pink-white to gray-white. The brightest whites have a slight blue hue. In its original state, white cotton fabric and white raw wool is yellowish. Most synthetic fibers are a grayish off-white. All these fabrics are

bleached, usually by a chemical treatment, to remove the yellow color. Manufacturers then "blue" them, making them look snow white. Eventually the bleach and the bluing agent wash out—returning the white fabrics to their original color. Adding a little diluted bluing to the rinse cycle gives white fabrics this blue hue again.

In the early and middle 1900s, Americans who wanted white wash used bluing, which could be found in virtually all laundries. When washing was done by hand or in wringer washers, the second rinse tub was the bluing rinse. To capitalize on this trend, manufacturers began coloring their detergents and other additives blue. Many claimed that their products contained bluing.

Mrs. Stewart's Liquid Bluing, a very fine blue iron powder suspended in water, optically whitens white fabric. It does not remove stains or clean, but merely adds a microscopic blue particle to white fabric that makes it appear whiter. Mrs. Stewart's Liquid Bluing is non-toxic, biodegradable, non-hazardous, and environmentally friendly.

In the late 1870s, Alan Stewart, a traveling salesman for a Chicago whole-sale grocer, acquired the right to the formula for this bluing product, began making it at home, and decided to rename it after his wife. When she refused to let him use her photograph on the bottles, Stewart used a photograph of his mother-in-law. While seeking someone to manufacture the bluing, Stewart met Luther Ford, the owner of a store called the Five and Ten Cent Bazaar in Minneapolis, who also ran a wholesale business, selling notions, toys, and fireworks. An accidental fireworks explosion in the Five and Ten Cent Bazaar prompted Ford to seek a less dangerous business. He bought the rights from Alan Stewart to manufacture Mrs. Stewart's Bluing, and sold the first bottle of the bluing on July 30, 1883.

STRANGE FACTS

• Both a brand new white shirt and a white shirt that has been laundered for a year appear white. But when the two shirts are placed next to each other, the blue hue in the new shirt becomes evident.

• When two pieces of white fabric are placed under a spectrograph, the one with blue added will reflect more light, making the fabric appear its whitest.

• To use Mrs. Stewart's Liquid Bluing in the wash cycle for your laundry, mix one-quarter teaspoon of Mrs. Stewart's Liquid Bluing into an empty, gallon plastic container, fill with cold water, shake well, then pour into the machine with clothes present. To use in the rinse cycle, mix less than one-eighth teaspoon of Mrs. Stewart's Liquid Bluing into an empty, gallon plastic container, fill with cold water, shake well, and then pour into the machine with clothes present.

• If you accidentally spill Mrs. Stewart's Liquid Bluing on fabric or use more bluing in your wash than directed and the clothes turn blue, put the clothing in a five-gallon bucket with a tight lid (or a plastic bag with a twist tie). Add a solution of two cups ammonia to one gallon cold water. Seal tightly to keep the fumes in. Let soak for 24 hours. Then run the clothing through a regular wash cycle with detergent only. Do not use bleach. Bleach will cause the bluing to set in permanently.

• Some pool manufacturers and dealers who use Mrs. Stewart's Liquid Bluing in their display pools claim it helps close a sale.

• Because blue-white is the most intense white, most artists when portraying a snow scene will use blue color to intensify the whiteness.

• Some pet owners use Mrs. Stewart's Bluing to whiten white pet fur.

• Freshly cut carnations placed in a vase with a high content of Mrs. Stewart's Bluing in the water will by osmosis carry the blue color into the tips of the petals quickly.

297

Do-It-Yourself Recipe

MAGIC CRYSTAL GARDEN

WHAT YOU NEED

From the supermarket:
- Five charcoal briquettes
- 1 tablespoon ammonia
- 6 tablespoons salt
- 6 tablespoons of Mrs. Stewart's Liquid Bluing
- Food coloring

From the kitchen:
- 2-quart glass bowl
- Clean, empty glass jar

From the workshop:
- Hammer

From the tap:
- 2 tablespoons water

WHAT TO DO

Break up the charcoal briquettes into 1-inch chunks with the hammer, and

place the pieces in the bottom of the bowl. In the jar, mix the ammonia, salt, bluing, and water. Mix well.

Pour the mixture over the charcoal in the bowl. Sprinkle a few drops of food coloring over each piece of charcoal. Let the bowl sit undisturbed in a safe place for seventy-two hours.

WHAT HAPPENS

Fluffy, fragile crystals form on top of the charcoal, and some climb up the sides of the bowl. To keep the crystals growing, add another batch of ammonia, salt, bluing, and water.

STRANGE FACTS

• As the ammonia speeds up the evaporation of the water, the blue ion particles in the bluing and the salt get carried up into the porous charcoal, where the salt crystallizes around the blue particles as nuclei. These crystals are porous, like a sponge, and the liquid below continues to move into the openings and evaporate, leaving layers of crystals.

• All solids have an orderly pattern of atoms, which is repeated again and again. This orderly pattern, called crystallinity, can be seen in simple crystals because their shapes reveal their particular atomic structure to the naked eye.

• Some New Age enthusiasts believe that wearing a crystal—usually an amethyst, rose quartz, or clear quartz—around the neck attracts good vibrations and can be used to better arrange a person's spiritual and physical energies. There is no scientific evidence to support this superstition.

• Crystals grow by attracting the atoms of similar compounds, which join together in an orderly pattern. Impure atoms can invade the atomic structure of the crystal and create mixed crystals of dazzling hues.

• In the fifteenth century, amethyst was believed to cure drunkenness.

• Some scientists theorize that birds have a tiny magnetic crystal in their brain, enabling them to navigate during migration by detecting the earth's magnetic field.

• Crystal gardens became popular during the Depression and are still known to some as a "Depression flower" or "coal garden."

• The word crystal is derived from the Greek word kyros, meaning "icy cold." Rock crystal, a colorless quartz, was believed to be ice that had frozen so cold it would never melt.

• In 1921, Henry Ford, eager to find a use for the growing piles of wood scraps from the production of his Model Ts, learned of a process for turning the wood scraps into charcoal briquettes. One of his relatives, E. G. Kingsford, helped select the site for Ford's charcoal plant. In 1951, Ford Charcoal was renamed Kingsford Charcoal.

OXYDOL

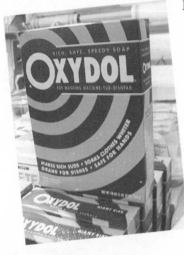

In 1914, William Waltke developed a new laundry detergent in St. Louis, Missouri, and named his product Oxydol. In 1927, Procter & Gamble purchased the William Waltke Soap Company and the rights to Oxydol. Procter & Gamble marketed Oxydol, its first laundry detergent, by sponsoring "Ma Perkins," a radio show first heard in Cincinnati in 1933. The program, described as a romantic drama, was subsequently heard on the NBC and

CBS radio networks. Oxydol's sponsorship helped give birth to the phrase "soap opera," and "Ma Perkins" became one of the nation's first and longest-running soap operas.

Procter & Gamble created new marketing techniques to sell Oxydol, including door-to-door sampling, metal "coin" coupons (later replaced with paper coupons), and "slice of life" magazine cartoon advertisements.

When Procter & Gamble introduced Tide laundry detergent in 1946, sales of Oxydol began to wane. By 1999, Tide generated $1.4 billion in annual sales. Oxydol produced $6.6 million in annual sales. In 2000, Procter & Gamble decided to discontinue the 86-year-old soap brand, but two Procter & Gamble executives, Richard Owen and Todd Wichmann, secured private financing, created a new company, Redox Brands Inc., and acquired the rights to Oxydol.

SEWING MACHINE

In Lyon, France, in 1830, tailor Barthélemy Thimmonier invented a machine to sew chain stitches. The French army purchased eighty of his sewing machines. Thimmonier's fellow tailors, afraid of being put out of business, raided his shop, destroyed all the machines, and forced him to flee for his life. By 1834, New York inventor Walter Hunt devised a machine that sewed a locked stitch into fabric, but possibly afraid of putting seamstresses out of business, decided against filing for a patent. In 1846, Boston inventor Elias Howe received a patent for his lock-stitching machine, but failed to find a market for his invention. When another Boston machinist, Isaac Singer, introduced his vastly improved sewing machine in 1851 (creating the same locking stitch patented by Howe), Howe sued for patent infringement, winning a royalty for every Singer sewing machine sold. Singer energetically promoted his sewing machine, making it a universal household appliance.

What Makes OshKosh B'Gosh the Genuine Article?

The Big Boys

Grove Manufacturing was founded in 1895 at 112 Otter Avenue in Oshkosh, Wisconsin, to make one product: rugged work overalls for Midwestern farmers and railroad workers. A year later, J. H. Jenkins and J. G. Clark bought the company and changed its name to Oshkosh Clothing Manufacturing Company. In 1910, the company began making child-sized overalls as a novelty item. After hearing "OshKosh B'Gosh" in a New York vaudeville skit, general manager William Pollock adopted OshKosh B'Gosh as the company's garment brand name. In 1934, Earl W. Wyman and his associates bought controlling interest from the retiring Pollock, changing the company's name to OshKosh B'Gosh in 1937. OshKosh B'Gosh has been a family-run company ever since.

In 1968, OshKosh B'Gosh entered the children's clothing market by accident when Miles Kimball, an Oshkosh-based mail order firm, featured OshKosh B'Gosh children's overalls in its national Christmas catalog. OshKosh B'Gosh was inundated with nearly fifteen thousand orders. In 1972, Chairman Charles "Fritz" Hyde launched a direct-mail campaign to specialty children's stores across the United States, and in 1975, at the request of Hyde's son Douglas, OshKosh B'Gosh started producing the children's overalls in bright colors and stripes. Three years later, Bloomingdale's, Macy's, Lord & Taylor, and Saks Fifth Avenue started stocking the colorful children's clothing. In 1981, OshKosh B'Gosh opened it first outlet store in West Bend, Wisconsin. In 1994, children's wear sales, which represented 5 percent of the company's sales twenty years earlier, accounted for 94 percent. Sales had grown from forty million dollars in 1980 to 365 million dollars in 1994.

STRANGE FACTS

• During the 1930s, OshKosh B'Gosh ran a series of testimonial ads quoting people who had been "saved" by wearing sturdy OshKosh B'Gosh clothing. Railroad worker Jesse Gilbert of Champaign, Illinois, claimed: "I had gone out on the pilot to throw the switch to head in. As I jumped, my jacket slipped over the flagstaff. With a terrific jerk I stopped in mid-air, neither hands nor feet touching anything. Had the coat ripped, no telling where I would have fallen, but I escaped unhurt!"

• For a 1937 promotional campaign, OshKosh B'Gosh created a pair of bib overalls that stood two stories tall.

• OshKosh B'Gosh presented pairs of bib overalls to President Dwight D. Eisenhower, President John F. Kennedy, and Senator Eugene McCarthy.

• On The Tonight Show, Johnny Carson once modeled a pair of OshKosh B'Gosh overalls made from gold lamé.

THE AMERICAN SHIRT FRONT: *Bridge Party*

Common Shirt Faults   *Arrow's Remedies*

1. The tight collar.   { All Arrow Shirts are guaranteed to fit *permanently.* They're Sanforized-Shrunk, fabric shrinkage less than 1%!

2. The messy collar.   { Arrow has made collars since 1861 and no one makes them better. Try Arrow Hitt, Dart, or Dale—all have non-wilt collars.

3. The bunchy midriff.   { Arrow Shirts have the exclusive "Mitoga" figure-fit: sloped shoulders, curved waist, tapered sleeves.

4. *Arrow Shirts* have an unbeatable combination of virtues: perfect styling, tailoring, and fit. See them at your Arrow Dealer's today. $2, $2.25, $2.50, $3.50, and $5.

ARROW SHIRTS
Made by Cluett, Peabody & Co., Inc., Troy, New York

TIDE

Before Tide, people simply used soap flakes to clean clothes. In 1933, Procter & Gamble scientists invented Tide, the best-selling heavy-duty laundry detergent in the United States today. A decade earlier, scientists at Procter & Gamble discovered synthetic surfactants that suspended dirt and grease from clothes until it could be washed away. A decade later, Procter & Gamble scientists discovered special chemical compounds called "builders" that help surfactants penetrate clothes fibers more deeply, allegedly "making them more effective than soap flakes, even on tough greasy stains." Procter & Gamble introduced Tide in 1946 as the "New Washday Miracle." *Consumer Reports* claims, "No laundry detergent will completely remove all common stains," and reports very little difference in performance between major name brand powdered detergents.

Secret Formula
LAUNDRY DETERGENT

WHAT YOU NEED
From the supermarket:
- ¹/₂ cup borax
- ¹/₄ cup baking soda

From the health food store:
- ¹/₄ cup Dr. Bronner's Sal Suds

WHAT TO DO
Add Dr. Bronner's Sal Suds, borax, and baking soda to a full load of laundry. Makes one cup.

HOW YOU USE IT
Use this miraculous mixture as you would any other detergent.

This nontoxic, homemade concoction uses Dr. Bronner's Sal Suds, a biodegradable detergent, as the main ingredient, boosted by the wholesome goodness of borax and baking soda, to help you turn the tide on laundry detergents and make all your clothes washday fresh.

IMAGINE! Besides <u>washing</u> clothes, a <u>BENDIX</u> saves you <u>ten</u> other <u>washday jobs!</u>

NOTHING SIMPLER! JUST PUT DRY CLOTHES IN THE BENDIX, TURN A DIAL, ADD SOAP...

GO OR STAY, AS YOU PLEASE! THE BENDIX DOES ALL THE WORK, THEN SHUTS ITSELF OFF!

AND THEN... A MIRACLE! THE BENDIX HAS WASHED, RINSED, DAMP-DRIED THE CLOTHES! THEY'RE SUPER CLEAN, AND READY FOR THE LINE!

LOOK! A BENDIX DOES ALL THESE ELEVEN JOBS!

1. Fills itself with water
2. Controls water temperatures for different fabrics
3. Washes clothes
4. Changes water for each rinse
5. Rinses clothes
6. Rinses clothes *again*
7. Rinses clothes *third* time
8. Damp-dries clothes
9. Cleans itself
10. Drains itself
11. Shuts itself off

. . . AND ONCE YOU'VE TURNED THE STARTING DIAL YOU DON'T EVEN <u>TOUCH</u> THE BENDIX!

Holds more clothes by half than the average washer! You just put the dry clothes in the Bendix Home Laundry, and . . .

No water touches your hands! You set two controls —one takes care of water temperature, one starts the Bendix. Add soap and . . . that's *all!* You're *through!* The rest of the work is done by the Bendix, *all by itself!* Right away, it . . .

Washes clothes thoroughly, immaculately! They're lifted and tumbled through suds, hundreds and hundreds of times—gently, carefully—without the wear and tear of an agitator! Then . . .

Three rinses in three changes of water! The dirty water is drained away, and the Bendix tumbles the

clothes through *three separate rinses!* Each and every rinse equals hundreds of tiresome dousings by hand! And *yet* . . .

The Bendix uses less water and less soap than you'd use with the average washer!

No wringer! No danger! Isn't that *grand?* The water is *whirled* out of the clothes as the Bendix spins them

BENDIX
AUTOMATIC HOME LAUNDRY

'round and 'round! They're damp-dried, fluffy, and ready for the line! And now . . .

No set-tubs or floors to clean! Think of it! And no machine to scrub, either! The Bendix has sprayed and cleaned itself—then automatically shut itself off!

Look! It's easy to own a Bendix! Liberal allowance for your old washing machine on a new, modern Bendix Home Laundry! Easy payments made still *easier* by savings on water, soap, and clothing wear! Automatic washing, originated by Bendix, has brought thrilling washday freedom to more than a quarter of a million homes all over the country! For full information on what the Bendix Home Laundry can do for *your* home, mail the coupon today!

Delighted Users Speak For More Than A Quarter Million Bendix Owners

"Washing baby clothes would be a full-time job for me if it weren't for my Bendix. But it does all the washing so I have plenty of time for baby and for my regular housework."
Mrs. Adeline Davidson, Denver, Colorado

"My maid hated washing clothes as much as I did. No fear of her leaving me now, though. Not with a Bendix in the house. She's never behind in her work now!"
Mrs. Pauline Gugenberger, Williimansett, Mass.

"Washday doesn't put me to bed, too tired and worn out to move. I go out and enjoy myself on washday now, because, you see, my Bendix takes care of everything."
Mrs. Morris Verson, St. Paul, Minn.

"I have a new dress I wasn't counting on this year. All because of my new Bendix too . . . it's so economical to use!"
Mrs. H. B. Driver, Oklahoma City, Okla.

Copyright 1941, Bendix Home Appliances, Inc.

BENDIX HOME APPLIANCES, INC.
3385 Sample Street, South Bend, Indiana
Please send me your booklet, telling the whole story of the Bendix, inside and out . . . with illustrations and descriptions of all models. No obligation to me.

Name . . . .

Address . . . .

City . . . .

County . . . . State . . . .

Just paste this coupon on a penny postcard.

Secret Formula

FABRIC SOFTENER

WHAT YOU NEED
From the supermarket:
- 1 gallon white distilled vinegar

From the health food store:
- 20 drops apple fragrance

WHAT TO DO
Simply add 20 drops of apple fragrance to the gallon jug of vinegar, and label. Makes one gallon.

HOW YOU USE IT
Add $^1/_2$ cup of this simple solution to your rinse cycle to soften clothes and eliminate static cling, giving clothes the fluffy gentleness you and your family so richly deserve. And here's a delightful bonus! During the rinse cycle, the vinegar helps dissolve lingering detergent residue. Who could ask for anything more?

Secret Formula

WOOL CLEANER

WHAT YOU NEED
From the supermarket:
- $^1/_2$ cup borax
- 2 tablespoons liquid laundry detergent

From the tap:
- 1 gallon warm water

From the workshop:
- Bucket

WHAT TO DO
Mix ingredients together in a bucket and stir to dissolve the borax. Let cool. Makes roughly one gallon.

HOW YOU USE IT
Soak your woolens in this simple yet potent solution for twenty minutes. Squeeze suds through gently, then rinse thoroughly in cool water. Without wringing, press out as much water as possible, then spread woolens out to dry on towels. You'll be amazed at how effective this magical mixture really is!

Clothes Make the Movie

- In the 1933 film *The Invisible Man*, Claude Rains becomes invisible, except for his clothes. At the end of the film, he strips naked to escape from the police, but the cops follow after his footprints in the snow—footprints made by shoes that the invisible man was not wearing.

- In the 1935 movie *The Crusades*, directed by Cecil B. DeMille and taking place between 1189 and 1199, King Richard the Lion-Hearted flips back his cloak to check his watch. Watches were not invented until at least the 1400s, and wristwatches did not become popular for men until the 1900s.

- In the 1941 movie *The Maltese Falcon*, when Humphrey Bogart slaps Peter Lorre in the face, Lorre is wearing a polka-dot tie. When Lorre turns back, his tie suddenly has stripes.

- In the Cecil B. DeMille's 1956 movie *The Ten Commandments*, which takes place sometime around 1200 B.C.E., a blind man is seen wearing a wristwatch.

- In the 1957 movie *Jailhouse Rock*, Elvis Presley wears a prison uniform numbered 6239. Later in the film he wears number 6240.

- In the 1960 movie *Spartacus*, a fictional account of an actual slave revolt against the Roman Empire, some of the Roman soldiers wear wristwatches.

T-Back Design

Finally, A T-Back Bra For The Fuller Figure

Our full-figure T-back bra lends extra support and the straps are closer to the neck so they won't slip off your shoulder. The soft cups and cushioned straps are lined with breathable, absorbent cotton and stretchy mesh inserts under the cups let air circulate. 5-hook front closure. Color is white. Polyester, nylon, spandex, cotton. Machine wash, line dry. Imported.
SIZES: 34-46 even, B, C, D cups.
No.39262 Full-Figure T-Back Bra $12.95

Pour Yourself *a pair of* **Stockings**

And let MINER'S LIQUID MAKE-UP give your bare legs the same velvety attractiveness it does to face, neck and arms

Try the new *Hawaiian* or any of the 4 other shades of

MINER'S *Liquid* MAKE-UP

25¢ & 59¢ at cosmetic counters; trial size at 10¢ stores

FREE Generous Sample
Send coupon and 3¢ stamp

| HAWAIIAN .... □ |
| SUNTAN ...... □ |
| PEACH .... □ |
| RACHELLE .... □ |
| BRUNETTE .... □ |

MINER'S 12 E. 12th St Dept M-80, New York, N Y
I enclose 3¢ stamp to cover mailing cost. Send me generous sample of Miner's Liquid Make-up FREE!
Name........
Address........

" Wish we knew which way to jump!"

ARE YOU ON THE FENCE — hesitating between percale and Service Weight muslin sheets? Well, look around and see what's what. Then jump, ladies, jump! . . . You won't pick wrong, either way, if you just remember this:

The percale side of the fence offers you luxurious sleeping comfort . . . sheets to flatter your guests and make you feel like a pampered princess . . . Expensive? No, not at all, if you choose percale with the Lady Pepperell label. The lightness of Lady Pepperell percale, too, means cheaper laundry bills at pound rates.

Now, over on the other side, there's another famous Lady Pepperell sheet . . . called Lady Pepperell Service Weight. This fine sheet isn't at all like ordinary light-weight muslin. It has a smooth, sturdy texture and is generally considered the most serviceable, longest-wearing sheet that can be bought, regardless of price.

Perhaps you will prefer luxurious percale. Perhaps your household needs long-wearing Service Weight muslin. Or you may, like many women, choose both — percales for "best" and Service Weights for "everyday." But however

you choose, remember that the Lady Pepperell label means real value for your shopping dollars — on sheets . . . as on towels and blankets.

FREE BOOKLET — to help you buy Right!
▶ Pepperell's "Sheet Shopping Guide" is crammed with thrifty information! If you want to know the difference in detail between percales and Service Weight muslins . . . to know which is right for you . . . send for the "Sheet Shopping Guide." It also contains stories of both sheets. Write Pepperell Manufacturing Company, 165 State Street, Boston, Mass.

LADY PEPPERELL
Percale and Service Weight

SHEETS
ALSO . . .
BLANKETS AND TOWELS

Secret Formula

SPRAY STARCH

WHAT YOU NEED
From the supermarket:
- 1 to 3 tablespoons cornstarch

From the tap:
- 2 cups cold water

WHAT TO DO
Using a funnel, mix the ingredients in a refillable sixteen-ounce fine mist trigger-spray bottle. For a light starch, use 1 tablespoon cornstarch. For a heavier starch, use 3 tablespoons. Shake well to dissolve cornstarch completely. Keep out of reach of children. Makes two cups.

HOW YOU USE IT
Shake this fantastic formula well, spray the garment to be starched, and iron immediately for clothes that are pressed to perfection. Say goodbye to unsightly wrinkles and hello to precise pleats that are sure to make you the talk of the town.

Secret Formula

STAIN REMOVER

WHAT YOU NEED
From the supermarket:
- 1/4 cup clear liquid detergent (Ivory or Palmolive)

From the drugstore:
- 1/4 cup glycerin

From the tap:
- 1 1/2 cups of water

WHAT TO DO
Using a funnel, combine the liquid detergent, glycerin, and water in a refillable dishwashing liquid squirt bottle or a refillable sixteen-ounce trigger-spray bottle. Shake well. Makes two cups.

HOW YOU USE IT
Wet the stain, squirt this modest mixture over the affected area, let sit for thirty minutes, then launder as usual—keeping your clothes stain-free, fresh, and looking like new.

Secret Formula

SADDLE SOAP

WHAT YOU NEED

From the supermarket:
- 2 bars Ivory Soap
- Pam Cooking Spray

From the hobby center or craft store:
- $1/2$ cup beeswax

From the shoe store or sporting goods store:
- $1/4$ cup neat's-foot oil

From the tap:
- $3^1/2$ cups water

WHAT TO DO

Spray the grater with a thin coat of cooking spray (to make cleanup afterwards easier). Grate the bars of soap into flakes. Bring water to a boil in a large pot, then lower to simmer. Slowly add $3/4$ cup soap flakes and stir slowly. In the top of a double boiler, heat the neat's-foot oil and beeswax until the beeswax melts, then stir to mix well. Slowly pour the oil and wax solution into the soap mixture, and stir until the blend thickens. Pour into containers, such as old shoe polish tins or margarine canisters, and let cool. Makes five cups.

HOW YOU USE IT

Your leather will love this treatment! Apply this creamy mixture to leather with a damp sponge, then buff dry with a soft cloth to waterproof and soften boots, shoes, and saddles.

(Test this saddle soap on an inconspicuous spot first. Neat's-foot oil can darken some leathers and may prevent a fine polish).

Fleece Ear Pops Keep Your Ears Warm Without A Hat

If you don't like to wear a hat or earmuffs but want warm ears, try Ear Pops. These little acrylic fleece muffs slip over your ears without bands or wires to protect your ears even on the coldest days. Very comfortable and easy to keep in your pocket. Made in USA.
COLORS: Hunter Green (GRN), Navy (NAV), Gray (GRY), Black (BLK), Beige (BGE).

Measure from top to bottom of your ear:
S(1½"-2¼"), **M**(2¼"-2¾"), **L**(2¾"-3")

SIZES: S, M, L.
No.20164 Ear Pops $8.95
Special: 2 or More Pairs $8.00 each

Our Pretty Lace Bra Has Two Hidden Pockets for Valuables

Need a safe place to stash away a little mad money on your next outing or vacation? Keep it in the two pockets concealed within the top of the cotton-lined cups of this lacy bra. Pockets are large enough to hold an ID, credit card, key, or some cash, and close securely with Velcro®. Finished with adjustable satin straps and a two-hook back closure with four adjustment positions. Polyester, cotton, nylon, spandex. Hand wash, line dry. Made in USA or imported.
SIZES: 36-42, B, C, D cups.
(Not available in 42B, 42C.)
No.41799 Hidden Pocket Bra $32.95

Perspiration is Acid
Actually ROTS Stockings!

But NEW IVORY SNOW care guards against this danger . . . even chiffon stockings last up to 1/5 longer!

● Perspiration has now been revealed as a common and neglected cause of serious damage to stockings. It is normally distinctly *acid*. It rots stockings!

Runs, weakened fibres, that "old" look—all these are vastly increased by acid perspiration.

To help *your* stockings give the longer wear that is today *so* important —turn to this daily Ivory Snow care. Ivory Snow is the new improvement on "fine fabrics" soaps. Ivory-pure. Made in "snowdrop" form, to give rich suds in 3 seconds, even in *cool* water.

Carelessness about washing stockings costs money. Tests show that daily Ivory Snow care brings up to 1/5 longer wear—it's just like getting a new pair of stockings *free* every 2 months!

Undies, too, look and last better under this gentle, safe care.

"Try my easy daily care You'll get longer stocking wear!" —*Miss Ivory Snow*

THE DANGER OF ACID PERSPIRATION:
Every day, in all seasons, the normal human body gives off at least a pint of *acid perspiration*—much of it unseen, unfelt. This perspiration quickly starts to weaken fibres of stockings and undies.

ONLY IVORY SNOW COMBINES BOTH THESE ADVANTAGES

1 Pure soap in quick-dissolving tiny "snowdrop" form . . .

2 Bursts into pure, rich suds in 3 seconds . . . even in *cool* water.

Ivory Snow acts quickly, surely, safely against dangerous acid perspiration . . . to help stockings last far longer.

TRADEMARK REG. U. S. PAT. OFF. © PROCTER & GAMBLE

IVORY SNOW

NEW!

Safer for silks and woolens

WANT LOVELIER HANDS IN 12 DAYS? THEN CHANGE FROM ANY ONE OF THE 5 LEADING PACKAGED SOAPS THAT MAY BE ROUGHENING YOUR HANDS — WASH DISHES REGULARLY WITH **IVORY SNOW.** CUTS GREASE AS FAST AS THE STRONGEST LAUNDRY SOAP!

99 44/100% PURE

RICH, SAFE SUDS IN 3 SECONDS — EVEN IN COOL WATER

Just What Is Victoria's Secret?

In 1982, Victoria's Secret was a chain of four money-losing stores in Ohio and a catalog specializing in women's lingerie with seven million dollars in annual sales. That same year, The Limited—a chain of clothing stores founded in 1963 by then 26-year-old Leslie Wexner with five thousand dollars borrowed from his aunt—bought Victoria's Secret.

Wexler changed Victoria's Secret from a business aimed at making men comfortable buying lingerie to a company run, according to *Forbes* magazine, "almost exclusively by women for women who are mainly buying to please themselves." Wexler remodeled the stores to be more graceful and indulgent, rather than sexy, and changed the catalog from steamy shots of men and women grappling each other to elegant photographs of cultured women pampering themselves. Wexler also added a line of sportswear and eveningwear. Annual sales soon exceeded more than 100 million dollars.

In 1995, The Limited spun off Intimate Brands, Inc., comprised of its personal-care and lingerie stores, including Victoria's Secret and Bath & Body Works, which accounted for about half of The Limited's profits.

"Our very first lingerie shop was inspired by the belief that luxury should be a part of every day," explains the Victoria's Secret catalog. "We continue that tradition by inviting you to indulge in the world's finest lingerie, and most importantly, to discover the simple pleasure of treating yourself glamorously."

STRANGE FACTS

• Victoria's Secret was named after prudish British Queen Victoria to suggest that

in private she indulged in not-so-Victorian fantasies.

• The typical Victoria's Secret customer buys eight to ten bras a year. The typical American woman buys two.

• In 1995 alone, Victoria's Secret mailed out 324 million catalogs. That's more than all the magazines sold that year by *Playboy, Sports Illustrated,* and *People Weekly* combined.

• In his best-selling book *Couplehood,* comedian Paul Reiser (star of television's *Mad About You*) explains that the Victoria's Secret catalog is actually a novella about a group of insecure woman who don't know what to wear to a slumber party at a hunting lodge. The women, says Reiser, bring several outfits and then try them on for each other, hoping to gain each other's approval. Toward the end of the catalog, the women begin putting on sweaters, coats, and carrying luggage, explains Reiser, because they're getting ready to leave the slumber party. The reader, however, can expect to see the same women back in the next month's catalog because they have yet to reveal which one of them is Victoria or what her secret is.

• In 1995, Victoria's Secret sold 1.28 billion dollars worth of lingerie and intimate apparel. That's equal to selling a black lace teddy to four out of five married women in the United States.

• In 1995, Victoria's Secret catalog sales exceeded 661 million dollars. That's equal to selling a black lace teddy to the remaining married women and all the single women in the United States.

IN HER SPENCER she lost ugly BULGES!

(Above) In ordinary corset and brassiere, note the lack of support to abdomen and breasts which permitted sagging lines and unlovely bulges. *(Above, at right)* In her Spencer Corset and Brassiere figure lines are lifted into beauty, her posture is improved and all bulges have disappeared. Her Spencer is guaranteed never to lose these lovely lines. *(At right)* Note how lovely her gown looks over her Spencer.

Why don't you get rid of your bulges? You know they are unlovely—and uncomfortable. Your family and friends may not mention it, but they notice that your figure is less lovely than it could be.

How to lose your bulges

Your Spencer corset and brassiere will effectively correct any figure fault because every line is designed, every section cut and made to solve your figure problem, and yours only. It will relieve backache and nervous fatigue when caused by faulty posture.

Spencers are light and flexible, yet every Spencer is *guaranteed* to keep its lovely lines as long as it is worn! No other corset, to our knowledge, has this guarantee. Prices are moderate—depending on materials. Stop experimenting with corsets that lose their shape after only a few weeks' wear!

Have a figure analysis—free

At any convenient time, a Spencer Corsetiere, trained in the Spencer designer's method of figure analysis, will call at your home. A most interesting study of your figure will cost you nothing.

See your future beauty lines in fascinating free booklet

Send us the coupon below, or look in your telephone book under "Spencer Corsetiere" and call your nearest Corsetiere for interesting illustrated booklet, "Your Figure Problem." This will not obligate you in any way.

Write Anne Spencer Sept. 19, 1941
Please send me your helpful booklet. I have checked my figure faults at right.

Do You Want to Make Money?
Ambitious women may find business openings as corsetieres in every state. We train you. If interested, check here. ☐

Bulging hips
Bulging abdomen
Lordosic
backbone

Anne Spencer, Spencer Corset Co., Inc., 155 Derby Avenue, New Haven, Conn.

Name
Address

Also made in Canada and England at Rock Island, Quebec, and 33 Old Bond, London, W. 1.

SPENCER *INDIVIDUALLY DESIGNED* Corsets and Brassieres

9

SOURCES

Where to Get Everything

INGREDIENTS

You can find most of these items in your local supermarket, drugstore, health food store, craft store, or hardware store.

• **BAKING SODA** (Supermarkets). The best known brand is Arm & Hammer Baking Soda, followed by generic brands. It's all 100 percent bicarbonate soda.

• **BEESWAX** (Craft stores and some hardware stores). Beeswax, a commercial wax obtained by processing and purifying the crude wax secreted by honeybees to construct honeycombs, is typically used to make candles, crayons, and polishes.

• **BENZOIN** (Drugstores). Benzoin, the balsamic resin of certain tropical Asian trees, is commonly used to make perfumes and medicines.

• **BORAX** (Supermarkets and health food stores). The best known borax is 20 Mule Team Borax. An excellent disinfectant, borax has antifungal and antiseptic qualities.

• **BORIC ACID** (Drugstores). Boric acid, an antiseptic and preservative, is a powder used in fireproofing compounds, cosmetics, cements, and enamels.

• **CAMPHOR** (Drugstores). Camphor, obtained naturally from the wood or leaves of the camphor tree, is commonly used as an insect repellent and to make mild pain relievers and itch relievers.

- **DISTILLED WHITE VINEGAR** (Supermarkets). The best-known brand is Heinz.
- **DR. BRONNER'S PEPPERMINT OIL SOAP** (Health food stores, camping stores, and some supermarkets and drugstores). This biodegradable liquid soap made from plants is an excellent alternative to detergents and other harsh cleansers.
- **DR. BRONNER'S SAL SUDS** (Health food stores and some supermarkets and drugstores). This pine-scented all-purpose cleaner comes in a quart bottle and should be diluted one tablespoon per gallon of water.
- **ESSENTIAL OILS** (Health food stores and some drugstores). Distilled from a single plant or herb oil, essential oils, available in a variety of aromas—including lemon, peppermint, lavender, tree tea—add fragrance to these secret formulas without any synthetic chemicals. If you discover that you have an allergy to one essential oil, substitute another. When buying essential oils, be sure that the label specifies that the oil is naturally derived and contains no synthetic fragrance. Also available by mail order.
- **GLYCERIN** (Drugstores). Glycerin, obtained from fats and oils as a byproduct of saponification, is used as a solvent, an antifreeze, a plasticizer, and a sweetener and in the manufacture of dynamite, cosmetics, liquid soaps, inks, and lubricants.
- **ISOPROPYL ALCOHOL** (Drugstores and supermarkets). Isopropyl alcohol comes in 70 percent, 91 percent, and 99 percent—in order of escalating price.
- **LANOLIN** (Drugstores). Lanolin is a grease derived from the wool of sheep. The sheep are shaved and the lanolin is taken from the wool.
- **LEMON JUICE** (Supermarkets and health food stores). Lemon juice, available in bottles or by squeezing the fresh fruit yourself, is an excellent cleanser.
- **SODIUM PERBORATE** (Health food stores). Sodium perborate is an alternative to sodium hypochlorite bleach.
- **TRISODIUM PHOSPHATE (TSP)** (Hardware stores). An excellent substitute for products containing ammonia and lye, TSP is the least toxic cleanser in this class. Not all products labeled TSP contain trisodium phosphate, so read the label carefully before you buy.
- **WASHING SODA** (Supermarkets and health food stores). This strong cleaner is also known as soda ash, sal soda, and sodium carbonate. You can find it alongside the laundry powders in the supermarket.
- **WITCH HAZEL** (Drugstores or supermarkets). Witch hazel, a mild astringent discovered by Native Americans, is an alcoholic solution that contains an extract of the bark and leaves of the witch hazel plant.

COMPANIES

The following companies carry products related to formulas in this book. Simply look under a topic of interest, and you'll find the sources you need.

BEER MAKING SUPPLIES

Anderson's Orchards & Vineyards
430 East US Highway 6
Valparaiso, IN 46383
phone (219) 464-4936
www.andersonsvineyards.com

Beer and Wine Hobby
180 New Boston Street
Woburn, MA 01801
phone (800) 523-5423
www.beer-wine.com/index.html

Beer, Beer & More Beer
P.O. Box 4538
Walnut Creek, CA 94596
phone (800) 600-0033
www.morebeer.com

Bierhaus International Inc.
3723 West 12th Street
Erie, PA 16505
phone (888) 273-9386
http://frontpage.erie.net/bierhaus

Brew & Grow
1824 North Besly Court
Chicago, IL 60622
phone (773) 395-1500

Brew City Supplies
14835 West Lisbon Rd
Brookfield, WI 53005
phone (262) 783-5233
www.brewcitysupplies.com

Brew4Less
843 West San Marcos Boulevard
San Marcos, California 92069-4112
phone (800) 296-9991
www.brew4less.com

Brew House
5674 Timuquana Road
Jacksonville, FL 32210
phone (800) 780-7837

The Cellar Homebrew
14411 Greenwood Avenue North
Seattle, WA 98133
phone (800) 342-1871
www.cellar-homebrew.com

Defalco's Home Brew
8715 Stella Link
Houston, Texas 77025
phone (800) 216-2739
www.defalcos.com

HopTech
6398 Dougherty Road Suite 7
Dublin, CA 94568
phone (800) 379-4677
www.hoptech.com/index2.html

Karp's Homebrew Shop
2 Larkfield Road
East Northport, NY 11731
phone (631) 261-1235
www.homebrewshop.com

E. C. Kraus
P.O. Box 7850
733 S. Northern Boulevard
Independence, MO 64053
phone (816) 254-0242

Lake Superior Brewing Company
7206 Rix Street
Ada, MI 49301
phone (800) 745-CORK

Niagara Tradition
7703 Niagara Falls Boulevard
Niagara Falls, NY 14304
phone (800) 283-4418

Northern Brewer Ltd.
1150 Grand Avenue
St. Paul, MN 55105
phone (800) 681-BREW
www.northernbrewer.com

Oak Barrel Winecraft
1443 San Pablo Avenue
Berkeley, CA 94702
phone (510) 849-0400
www.oakbarrel.com

James Page Brewing Company
1306 Quincy Street Northeast
Minneapolis, MN 55413
phone (800) 234-0685
www.pagebrewing.com

SABCO Industries
4511 South Avenue
Toledo, OH 43615
phone (419) 531-5347
www.kegs.com

Semplex
P.O. Box 11476
4171 Lyndale Avenue North
Minneapolis, MN 55412
phone (888) 255-7997
www.semplexofusa.com

U-Brew
5674 Timuquana Road
Jacksonville, FL 32210
phone (866) 904-2739
www.ubrewit.com

William's Brewing Company
2594 Nicholson Street
San Leandro, CA 94577
phone (800) 759-6025
www.williamsbrewing.com

Wine Art Indy
5890 North Keystone Avenue
Indianapolis, IN 46220
phone (800) 255-5090
www.wineartindy.com

CANDLE MAKING SUPPLIES

American Candle Classics
19 East Martin Street
Allentown, PA 18103
phone (610) 791-7768
www.americancandleclassics.com

B & B Honey Farm
5917 Hop Hollow Road
Houston MN 55943
phone (507) 896-3955

The Candle Factory
4411 South Interstate Highway 35
Georgetown, TX 78626
phone (512) 863-6025
www.thecandlefactory.com

Cierra Candles
4750 Longley Lane #103
Reno, NV 89502
phone (800) 281-4337
www.cierracandles.com

Glorybee Candlemaking Supplies
120 North Seneca
P.O. Box 2744
Eugene, OR 97402
phone (800) 456-7923
www.glorybeefoods.com

Mann Lake Supply
County Road 40 & 1st Street
Hackensack, MN 56452
phone (800) 233-6663

Mid-Continent Agrimarketing Inc.
8833 Quivira Road
Overland Park, KS 66214
phone (800) 547-1392

MoonAcre IronWorks
62 Chambersburg Street
Gettysburg, PA 17325
phone (717) 337-9200
www.moonacre.com

Nasco
901 Janesville Avenue
Fort Atkinson, WI 53538
phone (800) 558-9595

North Country Crafts
912 4th Street
Marinette, WI 54143
phone (715) 735-3030

NW Candle Making, Inc.
P.O. Box 515
Vashon, Washington 98070
phone (866) 205-6376
www.nwcandlemaking.com

Pourette Candle Making Supplies
P.O. Box 70469
Seattle, Washington 98107-3737
phone (800) 888-9425
www.pourette.com

The Wax House
15009 Held Circle
Cold Spring, MN 56320
phone (320) 363-0411
www.waxhouse.com

CANDY MAKING SUPPLIES

Albert Uster Imports Inc.
9211 Gaither Road
Gaithersburg, MD 20877
phone (800) 231-8154
www.auiswiss.com

Assouline & Ting Inc.
2050A Richmond Street
Philadelphia, PA 19125
phone (800) 521-4491

Kitchen Krafts
P.O. Box 442
Waukon, IA 52172
phone (800) 776-0575
www.kitchenkrafts.com

Lorann Oils
4518 Aurelius Road
Lansing, MI 48909
phone (888) 4LORANN
www.lorannoils.com

Meadow's Chocolate & Cake Supplies
110-16 Liberty Avenue
Richmond Hill, NY 11418
phone (718) 835-3600

COUNTRY STORES

Cracker Barrel Old Country Store
P.O. Box 787
Lebanon, TN 37087
phone (800) 333-9566
www.crackerbarrel.com

Lehman's
One Lehman Circle
P.O. Box 321
Kidron, OH 44636
phone (877) 438-5346
www.lehmans.com

Vermont Country Store
Route 100
Weston, VT 05161
phone (802) 362-8460
www.vermontcountrystore.com

DOLLHOUSE KIT MAKERS

Bauder-Pine Limited
P.O. Box 518
Langhorne, PA 19047
phone (215) 757-5566

Celerity Miniature Homes
700 North 6th Avenue
Birmingham, AL 35203
phone (800) 444-3961
www.celerityminiaturehomes.com

Creative Concepts in Wood Inc.
64 Hay Avenue
Nutley, NJ 07110
phone (973) 667-0656
members.aol.com/ccwmfg/
roombox.htm

Corona Concepts
436 Lake Road
Schenevus, NY 12155
phone (800) 253-7150
www.corona-concepts.com

Dura-Craft Inc.
P.O. Box 459
Newberg, OR 97132
phone (503) 538-3100
www.dura-craft.com

Earth & Tree Miniatures and Dollhouses
276 Route 101, Unit 1
Amherst, NH 03031
phone (877) 801-8707
www.dollhouse-miniatures.com/
index.html

G.E.L. Products
19 Grove Street
Vernon, CT 06066
phone (860) 872-6539
www.toydirectory.com/GELProducts

Greenleaf Steel Rule Die Corp.
436 Lake Road
Schenevus, NY 12155
phone (607) 638-5000
www.greenleafsrd.com

The Lawbre Company
888 Tower Road
Mundelein, IL 60060
phone (800) 253-0491

The Moonbeam Dollhouse Company
102 Spruce Street
Tillsonburg, Ontario
Canada N4G 5V3
phone (519) 688-3522

Real Good Toys
10 Quarry Hill
Barre, VT 05641
phone (802) 479-2217
www.realgoodtoys.com

Walmer Dollhouses
4307 Wheeler Avenue
Alexandria, VA 22304
phone (703) 461-9330

ESSENTIAL OILS

Aroma Vera
5310 Beethoven Street
Los Angeles, CA 90066
phone (800) 669-9514
www.aromavera.com

Aveda
509 Madison Avenue
New York, NY 10022
phone (866) 823-1425
www.aveda.com

Caswell-Massey Company
97 Commerce Way
Dover, DE 19904
phone (800) 326-0500
www.caswellmassey.com

Frontier Natural Products Co-op
P.O. Box 299
3021 78th Street
Norway, IA 52318
phone (800) 669-3275
www.frontiercoop.com

A Garden Eastward
Ludowici, GA 31316
phone (912) 545-8896
http://addy.com/brinkley/supplies.html

Hové Parfumeur
824 Royal Street
New Orleans, LA 70116
phone (504) 525-7827
www.hoveparfumeur.com

Mint Meadow Country Oils
112 Schreier Drive
Camp Douglas, WI 54618
phone (608) 427-3561
www.mintmeadow.com

My Sweet Victoria
P.O. Box 212
Mechanicsville, PA 18934
phone (215) 258-0805
www.fragrancesupplies.com

MAPLE SYRUP TAPPING SUPPLIES

Danforth's Sugarhouse
U.S. Route 2 East, Box 284B
Montpelier, VT 05651
phone (802) 229-9536

G. H. Grimm
P.O. Box 130
2 Pine Street
Rutland, VT 05701
phone (802) 775-5411

KITE MAKING SUPPLIES

Coastal Kites
P.O. Box 14144
San Luis Obispo, CA 93106
phone (877) 544-KITE

Into the Wind
1408 Pearl Street
Boulder, CO 80302
phone (303) 449-5356
www.intothewind.com

Kite Studio
5555 Hamilton Boulevard
Wescoville, PA 18106
phone (800) KITE-991
www.kitebuilder.com

MARBLES

Land of Marbles
www.landofmarbles.com

Moon Marble Company
600 East Front Street
Bonner Springs, KS 66012
phone (913) 441-1432
www.moonmarble.com

Sirius Sunlight Glass Studio
218 High Street
Mineral Point, WI 53565
phone (608) 987-2716
www.siriusmarbles.com

POTPOURRI SUPPLIES

Caswell-Massey Company Ltd.
Catalog Division
100 Enterprise Place
Dover, DE 19901
phone (800) 326-0500

The Essential Oil Company
8225 SE 7th Avenue
Portland, OR 97207
phone (800) 729-5912
www.essentialoil.com

Gathered Blossoms Flower Shop & Gifts
P.O. Box 147
Otisville, MI 48463
phone (810) 631-6572

The Herb Lady
P.O. Box 2129
Shepherdstown, WV 25443
phone (800) 537-1846
www.theherbladyco.com

San Francisco Herb Company
250 14th Street
San Francisco, CA 94103
phone (800) 227-4530
www.sfherb.com

Tom Thumb Workshops
59 Market Street
Onancock, VA 23417
phone (800) 526-6502
www.tomthumbworkshops.com.com

Well-Sweep Herb Farm
205 Mount Bethel Road
Port Murray, NJ 07865
phone (908) 852-5390
www.nj.gov/travel/virtual/gardens/
    wellsweep.html

SOAP MAKING SUPPLIES

The Essential Oil Company
P.O. Box 206
Lake Oswego, OR 97034
phone (800) 729-5912

Pourette Manufacturing
P.O. Box 70469
Seattle, WA 98107-3737
phone (800) 888-9425
www.pourette.com

Summers Past Farm
15602 Old Highway 80
Flinn Springs, CA 92021
phone (800) 390-9969
www.summerspastfarms.com

SunFeather
Handcrafted Herbal Soap Company
1551 State Highway 72
Potsdam, NY 13676
phone (800) 771-7627
www.sunsoap.com

Willow Way LLC
5697 East 300 North
Greenfield, IN 46140
phone (317) 467-8645
http://soapequipment.com

Ye Olde Soap Shoppe
15602 Old Highway 80
Flinn Springs, CA 92021
phone (619) 390-3525
www.soapmaking.com

WOODEN AND COLLECTIBLE TOYS

Back to Basics Toys
4315 Walney Road
Chantilly, VA 22021
phone (800) 356-5360

Brandine Woodcraft Company
JMC Sales and Marketing
908 Douglas St
Joliet, IL 60435
phone (800) 487-1666

Damhorst Toys Ltd
3A Danuser Drive
Hermann, MO 65041
phone (800) 458-3960
www.damhorsttoys.com

Gordy's
P.O. Box 201
Sharon Center, OH 44274
phone (330) 239-1657

Mountain Craft Shop
American Ridge Road
New Martinsville, WV 26155
phone (304) 455-3570

Whippoorwill Crafts
1 Fanueil Hall Marketplace
Boston, MA 02109
phone (800) 497-5937

Wisconsin Wagon Company
507 Laurel Avenue
Janesville, WI 53545
phone (608) 754-002 0026
www.wisconsinwagon.com

COUNTRY STORE MUSEUMS

The following country store museums are all worth a visit if you'd like to find yourself inside an authentic country store.

Arrowheads/Aerospace Museums
24 Campground Road
Manchester, TN 37355
phone (931) 723-1323

The Brick Store Museum
117 Main Street
Kennebunk, ME 04043
phone (207) 985-4802

Chester County Historical Society
225 North High Street
West Chester, PA 19380
phone (610) 692-4800
www.chestercohistorical.org

Doon Heritage Crossroads
10 Huron Road at Homer Watson
    Boulevard
Kitchener, Ontario
Canada N2P 2R7
phone (519) 748-1914

Harold Warp's Pioneer Village
138 East Highway 6
P.O. Box 68
Minden, NE 68959
phone (800) 445-4447
www.pioneervillage.org

The Henry Sheldon Museum of
    Vermont History
1 Park Street
Middlebury, VT 05753
phone (802) 388-2117
www.henrysheldonmuseum.org

Kready's Country Store Museum
55 North Water Street
Lititz, PA 17543
phone (717) 626-5684
www.lititzjunction.com/KreadysMuseum/
    KreadysMuseumHomePage.asp

Lincoln's New Salem State Park
Route 97
Petersburg, IL 62675
phone (217) 632-4000
www.petersburgil.com/p_newsalem
    .html

Martha Barker Country Store Museum
3815 North Custer Road
Monroe, MI 48162
phone (734) 240-7780

Northampton County Museum
203 West Jefferson Street
P.O. Box 664
Jackson, NC 27845
phone (252) 534-2911

Old Sturbridge Village
1 Old Sturbridge Village Road
Sturbridge, MA 01566
phone (508) 347-3362
www.osv.org

Patterson's Mill Country Store
5109 Farrington Road
Chapel Hill, NC 27514
phone (919) 493-8149

Shelburne Museum
U.S. Route 7
P.O. Box 10
Shelburne, VT 05482
phone (802) 985-3346
www.shelburnemuseum.org

The Southampton Historical Museum
17 Meeting House Lane
Southampton, NY 11968
phone (631) 283-2494

St. Augustine's Oldest Store Museum
4 Artillery Lane
St. Augustine, FL 32084
phone (904) 829-9729

Storrowton Village Museum
1305 Memorial Avenue
West Springfield, MA 01089
phone (413) 205-5051

ACKNOWLEDGMENTS

At Rodale, I am grateful to my editor, Ellen Phillips, for championing my cause, sharing my enthusiasm, and making this book a labor of love. I am also deeply indebted to Tami Booth, Stephanie Tade, Karen Bolesta, my brilliant copy editor Jennifer Bright Reich, Linda Hager, Shannon Ray, Donna Bucchin, Emily Dufton, Andy Carpenter, and layout designer Keith Biery. Endless thanks to the astounding talents of Mary Lengle, Heidi Krupp, Jennifer Heeseler, and Kim-from-LA.

My heartfelt thanks also go out to all the wonderful people at The Vermont Country Store, most notably Lyman Orton and Andrea Diehl, for all their help and kindness. I am also indebted to Debbie Green for her outstanding research work; Jeremy Wolff for his beer-making prowess and maple syrup tapping skills; Arthur and Anne Weissman for sharing their remarkable collection of kitchen tools and appliances; Alan Corcoran for collaborating on "Words of Wisdom;" Jill Holtzman Leichter for her tin can collection; Andy and Désirée Steinberg for sharing their collection of toys, Bakelite, and kitchenware; Richard Steinberg for his erector toy; my father, Robert Green, for his incredible model railroad and his collection of Lionel trains; my mother, Barbara Green, for her photographs of several country stores; and my mother-in-law, Elaine White, for joining me on my journey to Vermont. A very special thank you to my agent Jeremy Solomon, my manager Barb North, and my website partner Michael Teitelbaum.

I am also indebted to Bill Whyte at W. S. Badger Company (owner of Badger products), Barbara Norris Allen at Dairy Association Co. (owner of Bag Balm), Roxanne Quimby at Burt's Bees (owner of Burt's Bees products), Bob Murray, Susanna Boutillier, and Scott Thompson at Colgate-Palmolive (owner of Cashmere Bouquet, Colgate, Octagon, and Palmolive), Sherry Boyd at Procter & Gamble (owner of Crest and Ivory Snow), Anne Robinson at Caswell-Massey (owner of Dr. Hunter's and Caswell-Massey), Gwen Calvier at Living Nail (owner of Living Nail), Kathy Wright of B & P Company (owner of Frownies), Wendy House at Hanford Pharmaceuticals (owner of Hanford's Balsam of Myrrh), Kaki Hinton at Pfizer (owner of Listerine), Jim Ames at Dumont Company (owner of No-Crack Hand Cream), Reese Killion at Percy Medicine (owner of Percy Medicine), Jeanine Sortisio at the Mentholatum Co. (owner of Fletcher's Castoria), Ron Lee at Lee Pharmaceuticals (owner of Sloan's Liniment), David Barnett at F & F Foods (owner of Smith Brothers), Vivian Smith Clipp at Rosebud Perfume Co. (owner of

Smith's Rosebud Salve), Karen Clarke at Thayers Natural Pharmaceuticals (own of Thayer's products), Marty Lum at Prince of Peace Enterprises (representative of Tiger Balm), Robert J. Stuber at Watkins (owner of Watkins products), Doris Johnson at the Z-M-O Company (owner of ZMO Oil), Ava Baffoni at Nestlé (owner of Baby Ruth, Bit-O-Honey, and Carnation), Elizabeth Stewart Bradley at Cadbury Adams (owner of Chiclets), Ellen Gordon at Tootsie Roll Industries (owner of Dots, Junior Mints, Sugar Daddy, Sugar Babies, Tootsie Rolls, and Tootsie Pops), Tara Grecco and Shannon Cooke at Concord Confections (owner of Dubble Bubble), Pierre Redmond at Quality Candy Company (owner of Gilliam candies), Mitchell Goetze at Goetze's Candy Co. (owner of Goetze's Caramel Creams), Lois Duquette at Hershey Foods (owner of Good & Plenty, Hershey's, Hershey Kisses, Milk Duds, and Mr. Goodbar), Michelle Graber and Steven Luitjens at Farley's & Slathers Candy Co. (owner of JuJyFruits), Joe Davis, Jr., at McKee Foods Corporation (owner of Little Debbie), Bertille Glass at M&M Mars (owner of M&M's), Dawne Marshall at New England Confectionary Company (owner of Necco Wafers), Eric McCormick at Good Humor-Breyers Ice Cream (owner of Popsicle), John Doninger at Dart Industries (owner of Tupperware), Ann Marie Gondek at Ferrara Pan Candy Company (owner of Red Hots and Lemonhead), Alson Smith at Paul K. Guillow (owner of Guillow's Balsa Wood Airplanes), Dianna Sparrow at Binney & Smith (owner of Crayola), Russet Morrow, Helen Van Tassle, and Kathy Carpano at Hasbro (owner of Lincoln Logs, Monopoly, Mr. Potato Head, Play-Doh, Fun Factory, Raggedy Ann and Raggedy Andy, and Scrabble), Meredith Carlo at Morgan Lewis (representing the Gruelle Family), Cara Orchard at Lionel (owner of Lionel), Ray Dallavecchia at James Industries (owner of Slinky), Robert Pasin as Radio Flyer Inc. (owner of Radio Flyer), Scott Cavagnaro at Smethport Specialty Company (owner of Wooly Willy), Olivier LeCocq at DaimlerChrysler (owner of Plymouth), Judy Schuster at 3M (owner of Scotch Tape), Lynn Nowicki at Fox Run Craftsmen (owner of Stick-Um), Karen Baker at Rock City (owner of Rock City), Gary Austin at SallyeAnder (owner of SallyeAnder), Rich Oliver at Grandpa Brands Company (owner of Grandpa and Grandma products), Jim Liggett at J. R. Liggett Ltd. (owner of J.R. Liggett products), Eric McCormick at Unilever (owner of Lifebuoy and Lux), Ken Hathi at Kirk's Natural Products (owner of Kirk's), Frank Shofner at Col. Ichabod Conk Products (owner of Col Ichabod Conk's Moustache Wax), Zvi Ryzman at American International Industries (owner of Pinaud, Clubman, and Lilac Vegetal), Brooks O'Kane at Sunpoint Products (owner of Red Cross Nurse), Thomas Moloney III at Royall Lyme (owner of Royall products), Billy Ennis at the Pictsweet Company (owner of Pictsweet), Bette Steele at Campbell Soup Company (owner of Campbell's products), Tom Payne at Hulman & Company (owner of Clabber Girl), Becky Jennings at Cracker Barrel Old Country Store, Lisa Farrell at Canandaigua Wine (owner of Paul Garrett and Virginia Dare), Gordon Beaham III at Faultless Starch Company (owner of Bon Ami and Faultless Starch), Kate Watson at American Gas Association (owner of American Gas Association), Lisa Castaldo at PepsiCo (owner of Pepsi-Cola), Pat Doyle at Malco Products (owner of Twinkle), Norm Trapp at Quality Bakers of America (owner of Sunbeam), Gary Sheffer at General Electric (owner of Aluron), Bruce Watson at Maytag (owner of Maytag), Brad Norman at Luther Ford & Company (owner of Mrs. Stewart's), Jacqui Barnett at the Columbus Washboard Company (owner of Sunnyland Washboards), Rich Owen at Redox Brands (owner of Oxydol), Elina Smith at Cluett, Peabody, & Co. (owner of Arrow Shirts), and Toni Cauble at Westpoint Stevens (owner of Lady Pepperell Sheets).

Above all, all my love to Debbie, Ashley, and Julia for enduring my senseless journey down memory lane.

BIBLIOGRAPHY

- *Advertising in America: The First 200 Years* by Charles Goodrum and Helen Dalrymple (New York: Harry N. Abrams, 1990)
- *America's Stupidest Business Decisions: 101 Blunders, Flops, and Screwups* by Bill Adler Jr. and Julie Houghton (New York: Quill, 1997)
- *The American Woman's Cook Book* edited and revised by Ruth Berolzeimer (New York: Doubleday, 1972)
- *Aromatics: Potpourris, Oils, and Scented Delights to Enhance Your Home and Heal Your Spirits* by Angela Flanders (New York: Clarkson Potter, 1995)
- *Backyard Sugarin'* by Rink Mann (Woodstock, Vermont: Countryman Press, 1976)
- *Baking Soda Bonanza* by Peter A. Ciullo (New York: HarperPerennial, 1995)
- *The Blunder Book: Colossal Errors, Minor Mistakes, and Surprising Slipups That Have Changed the Course of History* by M. Hirsh Goldberg (New York: Quill, 1984)
- *The Book of Lists* by David Wallechinsky, Irving Wallace, and Amy Wallace (New York: William Morrow, 1977)
- *The Book of Lists, No. 2* by Irving Wallace, David Wallechinsky, Amy Wallace, and Sylvia Wallace (New York: William Morrow, 1983)
- *The Book of Potpourri: Fragrant Flower Mixes for Scenting and Decorating the Home* by Penny Black (New York: Simon & Schuster, 1989)
- *Brewing* by Michael J. Lewis and Tom W. Young (New York: Kluwer, 2000)
- *The Children's Room* by Collins & Brown Limited (New York: Watson-Guptill, 1998)
- *Chocolate Fads, Folklore and Fantasies: 1,001 Chunks of Chocolate Information* by Linda K. Fuller, Ph.D. (Binghamton, New York: Harrington Park Press, 1994)
- *Clean and Green: The Complete Guide to Non-Toxic and Environmentally Safe Housekeeping* by Annie Berthold-Bond (Woodstock, New York: Ceres Press, 1994)
- *Clean House, Clean Planet: Clean Your House for Pennies a Day, the Safe, Nontoxic Way* by Karen Logan (New York: Pocket Books, 1997)
- *The Comics: An Illustrated History of Comic Strip Art* by Jerry Robinson (New York: G. P. Putnam's Sons, 1974)

- *The Cone with the Curl on Top: The "Dairy Queen" Story* by Caroline H. Otis (Minneapolis: Dairy Queen, 1990)
- *Confessions of a Sneaky Organic Cook* by Jane Kinderlehrer (Emmaus, Pennsylvania: Rodale, 1971)
- *Cookies, Brownies, Muffins, and More* by Anne Egan (Emmaus, Pennsylvania: Rodale, 2000)
- "Crazy for Crackers" by Victoria Doudera in *The Old Farmer's Almanac 2001* (Dublin, New Hampshire: Yankee Publishing, 2001)
- *Dave Miller's Homebrewing Guide: Everything You Need to Know to Make Great-Tasting Beer* by Dave Miller (North Adams, Massachusetts: Storey Publishing, 1995)
- *Designing Great Beers: The Ultimate Guide to Brewing Classic Beer Styles* by Ray Daniels (Boulder, Colorado: Brewers Publications, 1997)
- *Dictionary of Trade Name Origins by Adrian Room* (London: Routledge & Kegan Paul Books Ltd., 1982)
- *Do It Yourself and Save Money!* by the editors of *Consumer Guide* (New York: Harper & Row, 1980)
- *The Doctors Book of Home Remedies: Thousands of Tips and Techniques Anyone Can Use to Heal Everyday Health Problems* by the editors of *Prevention* magazine health books (New York: Bantam, 1991)
- "Doing What Comes Naturally" by Phyllis Austin, *Maine Times,* 2000
- *Easy-to-Make Candles* by Gary V. Guy (New York: Dover, 1979)
- *The Encyclopedia of Candle Making Techniques: A Step-By-Step Visual Guide* by Sandie Lea (Philadelphia: Running Press, 1999)
- *Everybody's Business: A Field Guide to the 400 Leading Companies in America* by Milton Moskowitz, Robert Levering, and Michael Katz (New York: Doubleday, 1990)
- *Exploring Cuzco* by Peter Frost (Bucks, England: Bradt Enterprises, 1984)
- *Fabulous Fragrances: How to Select Your Perfume Wardrobe—The Women's Guide to Prestige Perfumes* by Jan Moran (Beverly Hills: Crescent House, 1994)
- *The Film Encyclopedia* by Ephraim Katz (New York: Perigee, 1979)
- *Folk Art: Style & Design* by Stewart and Sally Walton (New York: Sterling, 1993)
- "Good Things Come in Small Batches at Waco Company," *TABC Today* (Texas Alcoholic Beverage Commission), 2000
- "The Happy Storekeeper of the Green Mountains," by Edward Shenton, *The Saturday Evening Post,* March 15, 1952

- *Healthy Favorites from America's Community Cookbooks* edited by Jean Rogers and the food editors of *Prevention* magazine (Emmaus, Pennsylvania: Rodale, 1996)
- *A History of American Foreign Policy, 2nd edition,* by Alexander DeConde (New York: Charles Scribner's Sons, 1971)
- *Homebrew Favorites: A Coast-To-Coast Collection of over 240 Beer and Ale Recipes* by Karl F. Lutzen and Mark Stevens (North Adams, Massachusetts: Storey Books, 1994)
- *Hoover's Handbook of American Business 1995* (Austin: Reference Press, 1995)
- *How to Clean Practically Anything* by the editors of Consumer Reports Books with Edward Kippel (Yonkers, New York: Consumer Reports Books, 1996)
- *How to Do Just About Everything* by Courtney Rosen and the eHow Editors (New York: Simon & Schuster, 2000)
- *Inventions and Discoveries 1993* by Valérie-Anne Giscard d'Estaing and Mark Young (New York: Facts on File, 1993)
- "Inventors," http://inventors.about.com/library/inventors
- "It's Balms Away at W.S. Badger" by Michael McCord, *New Hampshire Business Review,* Friday, June 28, 2002
- *The Joy of Cooking* by Irma S. Rombauer and Marion Rombauer Becker (New York: Bobbs-Merrill Company, 1975)
- *Kiteworks: Explorations in Kite Building and Flying* by Maxwell Eden (New York: Sterling, 1989)
- "Liquid Gold" by Jim Coleman with Candace Hagan, *Restaurant Report,* 1996
- *Lionel: A Century of Timeless Toy Trains* by Dan Ponzol (New York: Friedman/Fairfax, 2000)
- *The Look of the Century* by Michael Tambini (New York: DK Publishing, 1996)
- *Made in America* by Sam Walton with John Huey (New York: Doubleday, 1992)
- *Make It Yourself: A Consumer's Guide to Cutting Household Costs* by Dolores Riccio and Joan Bingham (Radnor, Pennsylvania: Chilton/Haynes, 1978)
- *The Maple Sugar Book* by Helen and Scott Nearing (New York: Schocken Books, 1970)
- *Maple Syrup Production for the Beginner* by Anni L. Davenport and Lewis J. Staats (Ithaca, New York: Cornell Cooperative Extension, 1998)

- *Medical Blunders* by Robert M. Youngson and Ian Schott (New York: New York University Press, 1996)
- *Military Intelligence Blunders* by John Hughes-Wilson (New York: Carroll & Graf, 1999)
- *The Natural Formula Book for Home and Yard* edited by Dan Wallace (Emmaus, Pennsylvania: Rodale, 1982)
- *Nontoxic, Natural and Earthwise: How to Protect Yourself and Your Family from Harmful Products and Live in Harmony With the Earth* by Debra Lynn Dadd (Los Angeles: J. P. Tarcher, 1990)
- *The Nontoxic Home and Office* by Debra Lynn Dadd (Los Angeles: J. P. Tarcher, 1990)
- *North American Maple Syrup Producers Manual,* edited by Melvin R. Koelling and Randall B. Heiligmann (Ohio: Ohio State University Extension, 1996)
- *Now It Can Be Told: The Story of the Manhattan Project* by General Leslie Groves (New York: Harper & Row, 1962)
- *The Old Country Store* by Gerald Carson (New York: Oxford University Press, 1954)
- *100 Years of American Newspaper Comics: An Illustrated Encyclopedia* by Maurice Horn (New York: Gramercy, 1996)
- "107 Years Later, a Family Still Stops to Sell the Rosebud" by Martha M. Hamilton, *The Washington Post,* June 28, 1999
- *Oops! A Stupefying Survey of Goofs, Blunders & Botches, Great & Small* by Paul Kirchner (Los Angeles, General Publishing Books, 1996)
- "Oops! A Horribly Regrettable Mix-up," *Time,* March 31, 1980
- *The Origins of Everyday Things* by the editors of *Reader's Digest* (London: Reader's Digest, 1999)
- *Over the Counter and on the Shelf: Country Storekeeping in America, 1620–1920* by Laurence A. Johnson (Rutland, Vermont: Charles E. Tuttle Company, 1961)
- *The Oxford Companion to English Literature, Fourth Edition,* edited by Sir Paul Harvey (Oxford: Claredon Press, 1973)
- *Panati's Extraordinary Origins of Everyday Things* by Charles Panati (New York: Harper & Row, 1987)
- *The People's Almanac Presents the Twentieth Century: The Definitive Compendium of Astonishing Events, Amazing People, and Strange-But-True Facts* by David Wallechinsky (New York: Little, Brown, 1995)
- *Perfumes, Splashes & Colognes* by Nancy M. Booth (Pownal, Vermont: Storey Books, 1997)

- *Practical Problem Solver* by *Reader's Digest* (Pleasantville, New York: Reader's Digest Association, 1991)
- *Prevention's the Healthy Cook* by the food editors of *Prevention* magazine (Emmaus, Pennsylvania: Rodale, 1997)
- *Reader's Digest Book of Facts* (Pleasantville, New York: Reader's Digest, 1987)
- "The Rexall Rx: Dropping out of retailing to be a distributor," *Business Week*, March 1, 1982
- *Rodale's Book of Practical Formulas* edited by Paula Dreifus Bakule (Emmaus, Pennsylvania: Rodale, 1991)
- *The Safe Shopper's Bible: A Consumer's Guide to Nontoxic Household Products, Cosmetics, and Food* by David Steinman and Samuel S. Epstein (New York: Macmillan, 1995)
- *Scientific Blunders: A Brief History of How Wrong Scientists Can Sometimes Be . . .* by Robert Youngson (New York: Carroll & Graf, 1998)
- *Sears: Yesterday and Today* (Chicago, Illinois: Sears, Roebuck & Co., 1994)
- *Starring John Wayne as Genghis Khan: Hollywood's All-Time Worst Casting Blunders* by Damien Bona (Secaucus, New Jersey: Citadel Press, 1996)
- *A Story of Sweet Success* (Minneapolis: Dairy Queen, 1991)
- *Strange Stories, Amazing Facts: Stories That Are Bizarre, Unusual, Odd, Astonishing and Often Incredible* (Pleasantville, New York: Reader's Digest, 1976)
- *Super Formulas, Arts & Crafts: How to Make 360 Useful Products that Contain Honey and Beeswax* by Elaine C. White (Starkville, Mississippi: Valley Hills Press, 1993)
- *Sweet Maple: Life, Lore & Recipes from the Sugarbush* by James M. Lawrence and Rux Martin (Shelburne, Vermont: Chapters, 1993)
- *Teddy Bears Past and Present: A Collector's Identification Guide* by Linda Mullins (Cumberland, Maryland: Hobby House Press, 1986)
- *Time Almanac Reference Edition 1994,* (Washington, D.C.: Compact Publishing, 1994)
- *25 Kites That Fly* by Leslie L. Hunt (New York: Dover, 1971)
- *The U.S. Candy and Gum Market* by Marigny Research Group, Inc. (New Orleans, Louisianna: Packaged Facts, 2000)
- *Victorian Tea Party Style* by the editors of *Organic Gardening* magazine (Emmaus, Pennsylvania: Rodale, 2000)
- *The Well-Fed Backpacker* by June Fleming (New York: Vintage, 1986)
- *Why Did They Name It . . . ?* by Hannah Campbell (New York: Fleet, 1964)

- *Wooden Toys* by Gene and Katie Hamilton (New York: Sedgewood Press, 1987)
- *The World Almanac and Book of Facts 1993* (Mahwah, New Jersey: World Almanac Books, 1993)
- *The World Almanac and Book of Facts 1996* (New York: Scripps Howard, 1996)
- *The World Almanac and Book of Facts 1998* (Mahwah, New Jersey: World Almanac Books, 1998)
- *The World Almanac and Book of Facts 2000* (Mahwah, New Jersey: World Almanac Books, 2000)
- *The World Book Encyclopedia* (Chicago: World Book, 1985)
- *World's Worst Aircraft* by James Gilbert (New York: St. Martin's Press, 1979)
- *Yankee Church Supper Cookbook* by the editors of *Yankee Magazine* (Emmaus, Pennsylvania: Rodale, 1991)

TRADEMARK INFORMATION

Photographs of The Vermont Country Store and clips from its mail order catalog used with permission of The Vermont Country Store. "The Vermont Country Store" is a registered trademark of The Vermont Country Store. Used with permission.

1 Apothecary

"Badger" is a registered trademark of WS Badger Company Inc. Used with permission.

"Bag Balm" is a registered trademark of the Dairy Association Co, Inc. Used with permission.

"Burt's Bees" is a registered trademark of Burt's Bees, Inc. Used with permission.

"Castoria," the script "Chas H Fletcher," and "Fletcher's," are registered trademarks of The Mentholatum Company, Inc. Historical advertisement reproduced with permission.

"Colgate" is a registered trademark of the Colgate-Palmolive Company. Used with permission.

"Crest" and "Look, Mom, no cavities" are registered trademarks of Procter & Gamble. Used with permission.

"Dr. Hunter's Foot Crème" is a registered trademark of Caswell-Massey Co. Ltd. Used with permission.

"Frownies" is a registered trademark of B & P Company, Inc. Used with permission.

"Hanford's Balsam of Myrrh" is a registered trademark of Hanford Pharmaceuticals. Used with permission.

"Listerine" is a registered trademark of Pfizer, Inc. Used with permission.

"Living Nail" is a registered trademark of Living Nail. Used with permission.

"No-Crack" is a registered trademark of Dumont Company. Used with permission.

"Percy Medicine" is a registered trademark of Merrick Medicine Co., Inc. Used with permission.

"Sloan's Liniment" is a registered trademark of Lee Pharmaceuticals, Inc. Used with permission.

"Smith Brothers" is a registered trademark of F & F Foods, Inc. Used with permission.

"Smith's Rosebud Salve" is a registered trademark of Rosebud Perfume Co. Used with permission.

"Thayers" is a registered trademark of Thayers Natural Pharmaceuticals. Used with permission.

"Tiger Balm" is a registered trademark of Haw Par Corporation Limited. Used with permission.

"Watkins" is registered trademark of Watkins Incorporated. Used with permission.

"ZMO Oil" is a registered trademark of The Z-M-O Company. Used with permission.

2 The Candy Counter

"Baby Ruth" and "Bit-O-Honey" are registered trademarks of Nestlé. Used with permission.

"Chiclets" is a registered trademark of Cadbury Adams, USA LLC. Used with permission.

"Dots," "Junior Mints," "Sugar Babies," "Sugar Daddy," "Tootsie Pops," and "Tootsie Rolls" are registered trademarks of Tootsie Roll Industries, Inc. Used with permission.

"Dubble Bubble" is a registered trademark of Concord Confections Inc. Used with permission.

"Ferrara Pan," "Red Hots," and "Lemonhead" are registered trademarks of Ferrara Pan Candy Company, Forest Park, Illinois. Used with permission.

"Gilliam" is a registered trademark of Quality Candy Company. Used with permission.

"Goetze's" is a registered trademark of Goetze's Candy Co., Inc. Used with permission.

"Good & Plenty," "Hershey's," "Kisses," the "Kisses" wrapped conical configuration, the "Kisses" plume device, "Milk Duds," and "Mr. Goodbar" are registered trademarks used with permission.

"JuJyFruits" is a registered trademark of Farley's & Sathers Candy Company, Inc. Used with permission.

"Little Debbie" is a registered trademark of McKee Foods Kingman, Inc. Used with permission.

"M&M's," "Snickers," "Milky Way," and "The Chocolate Melts in Your Mouth—Not in Your Hand" are registered trademarks of Mars, Incorporated and its affiliates. Used with permission. Mars, Incorporated is not associated with Rodale, Inc., or Joey Green. © Mars, Incorporated 2004.

"Necco" is a registered trademark of New England Confectionery Co. Used with permission.

"Popsicle" is a registered trademark of Good Humor - Breyers Ice Cream. Used with permission.

"Tupperware" is a registered trademark of Dart Industries, Inc., and is used with the permission of Tupperware Corporation.

3 Toys

"Crayola" is a registered trademark of Binney & Smith Inc. Used with permission.

"Guillow's" is a registered trademark of Paul K. Guillow, Inc. Used with permission.

"Hasbro" and its logo, "Playskool" and its logo, "Lincoln Logs," "Tinkertoy," "Mr. Potato Head," "Play-Doh," "Fun Factory," "Raggedy Ann," and "Raggedy Andy" are trademarks of Hasbro and are used with permission. The "Monopoly" name and logo, the distinctive design of the game board, the four corner squares, the "Mr. Monopoly" name and character, as well as each of the distinctive elements of the board and playing pieces are trademarks of Hasbro for its property trading game and game equipment. "Scrabble" is a trademark of Hasbro in the US and Canada and is used with permission. © 2004 Hasbro. All rights reserved. "Raggedy Ann" and "Raggedy Andy" were created by Johnny Gruelle.

"Lionel" is a registered trademark of Lionel LLC. Used with permission.

"Radio Flyer" is a registered trademark of Radio Flyer, Inc. Used with permission.

"Slinky" is a registered trademark of James Industries. Used with permission.

"Wooly Willy" is a registered trademark of Smethport Specialty Company. Used with permission.

4 Gadgets

"Plymouth" is a registered trademark of DaimlerChrysler. Used with permission.

"Scotch" and "3M" are registered trademarks of 3M. Used with permission.

5 Home and Hearth

"See Rock City" is a registered trademark of Rock City. Used with permission.

"Stick-Um" is a registered trademark of Fox Run Craftsmen. Used with permission.

6 Barber Shop

"Cashmere Bouquet" and "Octagon" are registered trademarks of the Colgate-Palmolive Company. Used with permission.

"Caswell-Massey" is a registered trademark of Caswell-Massey Co. Ltd. Used with permission.

"Clubman," "Lilac Vegetal," and "Pinaud" are registered trademarks of American International Industries. Used with permission.

"Col. Ichabod Conk" is a registered trademark of Col. Ichabod Conk Products, Inc. Used with permission.

"Grandpa's" is a registered trademark of Grandpa Brands Company. Used with permission.

"J.R. Liggett's" is a registered trademark of J.R. Liggett, Ltd. Used with permission.

"Kirk's" is a registered trademark of Kirk's Natural Products Corp. Used with permission.

"Lifebuoy" and "Lux" are registered trademarks of Unilever. Used with permission.

"Palmolive" is a registered trademark of the Colgate-Palmolive Company. Used with permission.

"Red Cross Nurse" is a registered trademark of Sunpoint Products, Inc. Used with permission.

"Royall," "Royall BayRhum," "Royall Lyme," "Royall Muske," and "Royall Spyce" are registered trademarks of Royall Lyme Ltd. Used with permission.

"SallyeAnder" is a registered trademark of SallyeAnder. Used with permission.

7 Kitchen

"American Gas Association" is a registered trademark of American Gas Association. Used with permission.

"Bon Ami" and "Faultless" are registered trademarks of Faultless Starch Company. Used with permission.

"Campbell's" is a registered trademark of Campbell Soup Company. Used with permission.

"Carnation" is a regsitered trademark of Nestlé. Used with permission.

"Clabber Girl" is a registered trademark of Clabber Girl Corporation. Used with permission.

"Cracker Barrel Old Country Store" is a registered trademark of CBOCS General Partnership. Used with permission.

"Garrett's" and "Virginia Dare" are registered trademarks of Canandaigua Wine. Used with permission.

"Pepsi" is a registered trademark of PepsiCo. Used with permission.

"Pictsweet" is a registered trademark of The Pictsweet Company. Used with permission.

"Sunbeam" is a registered trademark of Quality Bakers of America, Inc. Used with permission.

"Twinkle" is a registered trademark of Malco Products, Inc. Used with permission.

8 Apparel

"Aluron" and "General Electric" are registered trademarks of General Electric. Used with permission.

"Arrow" is a registered trademark of Cluett, Peabody & Co, Inc. Used with permission.

"Ivory Snow" is a registered trademark of Procter & Gamble. Used with permission.

"Lady Pepperell" is a registered trademark of Westpoint Stevens. Used with permission.

"Maytag" is a registered trademark of Maytag Corporation. Used with permission.

"Mrs. Stewart's Bluing" is a registered trademark of Luther Ford & Company. Used with permission.

"Oxydol" is a registered trademark of Redox Brands, Inc. Used with permission.

"Sunnyland" is a registered trademark of the Columbus Washboard Company. Used with permission. Visit them on the Internet at www.columbuswashboard.com.

_I_ NDEX

Boldface page references indicate photographs.
Underscored references indicate boxed text.

ABOUT THE AUTHOR

Joey Green—author of *Polish Your Furniture with Panty Hose, Paint Your House with Powdered Milk, Wash Your Hair with Whipped Cream,* and *Clean Your Clothes with Cheez Wiz*—got Jay Leno to shave with Jif peanut butter on *The Tonight Show,* Rosie O'Donnell to mousse her hair with Jell-O on *The Rosie O'Donnell Show,* and Katie Couric to drop her diamond engagement ring in a glass of Efferdent on *Today.* He gave Meredith Vieira a facial with Elmer's Glue-All on *The View,* conditioned Conan O'Brien's hair  with Miller High Life beer on *Late Night with Conan O'Brien,* and rubbed French's Mustard on Wayne Brady's chest on *The Wayne Brady Show.* He has been seen polishing furniture with Spam on *Dateline NBC,* cleaning a toilet with Coca-Cola in *The New York Times,* and washing his hair with Reddi-wip in *People.*

Green, a former contributing editor to *National Lampoon* and a former advertising copywriter at J. Walter Thompson, is the author of more than twenty-five books, including *The Zen of Oz: Ten Spiritual Lessons from Over the Rainbow, You Know You've Reached Middle Age If . . . ,* and *The Mad Scientist Handbook.* A native of Miami, Florida, and a graduate of Cornell University, he wrote television commercials for Burger King and Walt Disney World, and won a Clio Award for a print ad he created for Eastman Kodak. He backpacked around the world for two years on his honeymoon, and lives in Los Angeles with his wife, Debbie, and their two daughters, Ashley and Julia.

Visit Joey Green on the Internet at:

www.wackyuses.com